PLATE XV

STRENGTH OF H.Q SECTION IS:—

MEDITERRANEAN SAFARI

*"There was dust on the road to Tunis*
*in our eyes and in our hair.*
*There was dust on the road to Tunis*
*but we got there, yes we got there."*

4th Division Concert Party Song.

Dedicated to the Officers and Men of Five Nine Field Company who fought in North Africa and Italy in 1943 and 1944

*The Canal Monumemt at Gebel Maryam, Ishmalia. 25 January 1944*

# MEDITERRANEAN SAFARI

March 1943 – October 1944

50

Five Nine Field Company, Royal Engineers

*With an introduction by the Chief Royal Engineer*
*General Sir George Cooper, G.C.B., M.C.*

A. P. de T. (Tony) Daniell, O.B.E., M.C., T.D.

Buckland Publications
125 High Holborn, London WC1V 6QA

ISBN 0 7212 0816 9

Printed and bound in Great Britain by
Buckland Press Ltd., Dover, Kent.

## CONTENTS

| | | page |
|---|---|---|
| Introduction | | 9 |
| Foreword | | 11 |
| ***1.*** | Departure and Arrival | 15 |
| ***2.*** | Beja – Tunisia | 29 |
| ***3..*** | Medjez-El-Bab – Tunisia | 41 |
| ***4.*** | The Battle for Tunis | 47 |
| ***5.*** | Tunisia – Cap Bon | 57 |
| ***6.*** | Algeria – Bougie | 71 |
| ***7.*** | Italy – Operation "Pitchfork" | 89 |
| ***8.*** | Towards Cassino | 95 |
| ***9.*** | Cassino – Planning... | 103 |
| ***10*** | Cassino – The Final Battle | 111 |
| ***11*** | Palombara and beyond | 125 |
| ***12.*** | Orvieto to Florence | 137 |
| ***13.*** | Across to Rimini | 149 |
| Epilogue | | 163 |

Appendix

| | | |
|---|---|---|
| I | German Order for Operation on Medjez El Bab | 165 |
| II | Army Commander's Message for Operation "Honker" | 167 |
| III | List of Bailey Bridges built | 169 |
| IV | "Amazon Bridge Epic" *Eighth Army News* | 171 |
| V | Daimler "Dingo" Scout car | 173 |

# MAPS


| | | page |
|---|---|---|
| Map 1 | Algiers – Kelibia – Bougie – Algiers ... ... ... ... ... ... | 14 |
| Map 2 | "Hunt's Gap", Beja ... ... ... ... ... ... ... ... ... | 28 |
| Map 3 | German attack on 20/21 April ... ... ... ... ... ... ... | 40 |
| Map 4 | Initial attack and breakthrough, 6 May ... ... ... ... ... ... | 46 |
| Map 5 | Surrender in North Africa ... ... ... ... ... ... ... ... | 56 |
| Map 6 | The "Gustav" Line at the time of Cassino ... ... ... ... ... | 70 |
| Map 7 | The Garigliano Mule Tracks ... ... ... ... ... ... ... | 88 |
| Map 8 | The "Inferno" track ... ... ... ... ... ... ... ... ... | 94 |
| Map 9 | Plans for "Blackwater" bridge ... ... ... ... ... ... ... | 102 |
| Map 10 | "Amazon" bridge ... ... ... ... ... ... ... ... ... | 110 |
| Map 11 | The road to Palombara ... ... ... ... ... ... ... ... | 124 |
| Map 12 | The final push to Florence ... ... ... ... ... ... ... ... | 136 |
| Map 13 | Assault crossing of River Marano ... ... ... ... ... ... | 148 |
| Map 14 | Progress north through Italy ... ... ... ... ... ... ... | 162 |


All the maps have been redrawn by the author from original campaign maps

# ILLUSTRATIONS


| | | page |
|---|---|---|
| Strength of H.Q. Section 59 Fd. Coy. | | Front Endpaper |
| Canal Monument | | Frontispiece |
| 1 | 'By jove! What a perfectly *excellent* tobacco!' Author Tony Daniell* ... | 16 |
| 2 | Peter Boston. Self Portrait* ... | 20 |
| 3 | 'What's all this bloody stuff in my IN tray' R. M. Hamilton* ... | 24 |
| 4 | German *Tellermine* ... | 31 |
| 5 | Kelibia* ... | 59 |
| 6 | The *'Kelibia'* ... | 66 |
| 7 | Ben Chubb and Robert Hutchinson* ... | 72 |
| 8 | Anse des Aiguades, Bougie* ... | 73 |
| 9 | John Notley* ... | 74 |
| 10 | View of the Officers' Mess Bath House, Bougie* ... | 77 |
| 11 | 4 Div. R.E. Concert* ... | 78 |
| 12 | Keep it under hat. Malcolm Drummond* ... | 80 |
| 13 | Lieut. The Hon. Ed Humdrum. Eddie Meldrum* ... | 81 |
| 14 | Siesta in the desert* ... | 83 |
| 15 | A much contemplated scene, Bougie* ... | 86 |
| 16 | Before the rains came* ... | 90 |
| 17 | Desert cinema ... | 91 |
| 18 | My Company Forward HQ ... | 97 |
| 19 | Our kit on the way up to Harrogate Dump* ... | 98 |
| 20 | Monastery Hill, Cassino from Cox's corner* ... | 104 |
| 21 | Evening smoke shells falling on Cassino ... | 115 |
| 22 | Terence Cuneo's picture of Amazon Bridge ... | 119 |
| 23 | The O.C. in his new hat* ... | 126 |
| 24 | The house of Paulo Mancini ... | 139 |
| 25 | Breakfast time on the Arno* ... | 147 |
| 26 | Demolished viaduct Pergola ... | 152 |
| 27 | German *"Schu"* mine ... | 155 |
| 28 | Daimeler "Dingo" Scout car ... | 173 |
| Strength of No. 3 Section 59 Fd. Coy. ... | | Back Endpaper |


*Note all illustrations marked with an asterisk are by Peter Boston, M.C. as are the chapter title illustrations. The others are by the author. The book jacket illustration of Amazon Bridge by Terence Cuneo is by kind permission of the officers of the Corps of Royal Engineers.

# INTRODUCTION

by

General Sir George Cooper, G.C.B., M.C.

Chief Royal Engineer

In the dark days of 1941, few people, other than the British, could have envisaged the return of their forces to the mainland of Europe. Yet, little over a year later, The British, with the help of her American allies, were landing in North Africa, an essential preliminary to attacking the soft under-belly of Europe. By May 1943, the last of the Axis Powers had been expelled and the Allied plans for the first invasion of Europe began to take shape.

While the Allies could count on being able to cross the Channel in force in 1944, it was essential that, meanwhile, they should maintain the pressure on Germany and endeavour to dissipate her forces. It was also important to knock Italy out of the war as soon as possible and thus free the Mediterranean for the passage of convoys to the Middle and Far East. Sicily was chosen as the next objective, the first large-scale amphibious operation since Gallipoli, to be followed swiftly by the invasion of Italy. It is often forgotten that the re-conquest of Europe started in the Mediterranean and it is the cause of no little satisfaction to those who were there that the first surrender of the German Armies in Europe took place in Northern Italy, rather than in North-West Europe.

Tony Daniell's story starts at Kirkcudbright in 1942/43. He commanded the same unit, 59 Field Company, Royal Engineers, right through to 1944. He kept a diary, no doubt forbidden, so there is an authoritative air about everything he says and he tells of the remarkable comradeship that existed between all ranks, between the peculiar mix of civilian officers and regular soldiers that comprised his famous Company, a unit that boasted of a VC in World War I and is now an Independent Commando Squadron, Royal Engineers.

The title, *"Mediterranean Safari"*, may conjure up a picture of 'Sunny Italy' but, to those who took part, it is probably best remembered as a land of pouring rain, biting cold and sticky mud, interspersed in summer by glorious warm days, marred by the all-pervasive dust thrown up by the hundreds of vehicles moving along inadequate roads and tracks. The book is an exceedingly modest account of their activities – Tony Daniell does not even mention how he won his Military Cross – and gives a very good picture of what life was like in a field unit in the United Kingdom in the early days of the war, and then in North Africa and Italy. Tony Daniell is a natural story-teller, and also a talented artist, which together with Peter Boston's sketches combine to bring it all to life. There is little about strategy and tactics, and this is not surprising – at unit level in war, one knows little or nothing of outside events; one just gets on with the task in hand, and there was certainly plenty to do.

The tempo of events and everyday activities are well brought out and it is heartening that one of their greatest exploits, the building of the Amazon Bridge over the River Rapido, has been immortalised in Terence Cuneo's picture that hangs in the Royal Engineers Headquarters Mess in Chatham and is further portrayed in the memorial plaque to Sir Donald Bailey which was unveiled at Christchurch in September 1989.

# FOREWORD

My aim in putting together this account is to record as accurately as possible the adventures and activities of Five Nine Field Company Royal Engineers from March 1943 to October 1944.

At the outbreak of World War II I was already in the T.A. and later on went to France, only to return shortly via Dunkirk. After some time of moving about in the U.K. I was very lucky to be appointed as a major to the command of Five Nine Field Company, Royal Engineers, in July 1942, and remained in this job for two and a quarter years, until October 1944. I had previously been Second-in-Command of the Company for six months.

The Company was at that time in Scotland training with 4th (British) Division. In March 1943 the Company, as an integral unit of the Division, left Scotland for North Africa to join 1st Army in Algeria.

The book traces the fortunes of Five Nine Company through the final battles in Tunisia, when the Germans were pushed out of North Africa, and throughout the Italian Campaign. This included the key battle of Cassino, which was a turning point in the Italian Campaign, and tells the story of chasing the Germans up the leg of Italy, finally to get bogged down in the mud of the Lombardy Plain.

Throughout this period of nineteen months, the Company, as a unit of 4th Division, played a prominent role in all the major battles of this campaign and served throughout with distinction. This I attribute to good training, physical fitness, and above all to high morale and close comradeship.

The purpose of this book is to relate both the day-to-day events as well as the highlights of this period, and if I have omitted any significant events or persons, my sincere apologies.

I have been persuaded to write up this account as a record of just one small unit of the Allied Armies' advance into Europe from the Mediterranean.

I also owe it to the men of Five Nine Company to record their endeavours in this crucial period.

We were a very happy company of men and we had a remarkably successful "safari" in the Mediterranean area.

"The Fighting Fifty-Ninth" was the nickname the Company earned for itself in the 1914-18 War, originating during a withdrawal when the Company was ordered to dig trenches for the 6th Battalion of the Black Watch Regiment to fall back to – but it was the Company itself who had to fight as infantry from those very trenches, and the "line" was held. In World War II the Company found itself fighting in North Africa, where it adopted the fairly general motto of First Army as the Company war cry for all occasions – "Bash on regardless".

My grateful thanks to my wife for her encouragement and help, to Allan Weedon who helped me compile the diary upon which this account is based, to Alun Fon Jones who persuaded me to write it, to Helen McPhail who so painstakingly typed it, to Peter Boston for his delightful illustrations and many anecdotes, to Joan Tate for her help and advice, and to John Thorpe, my publisher, for taking it on.

Tony Daniell,
Frodesley Shropshire.

MAP 1

# ALGIERS - KELIBIA - BOUGIE - ALGIERS

OUT 26—31 MARCH 1943 • BACK 30 JUNE—4 JULY 1943

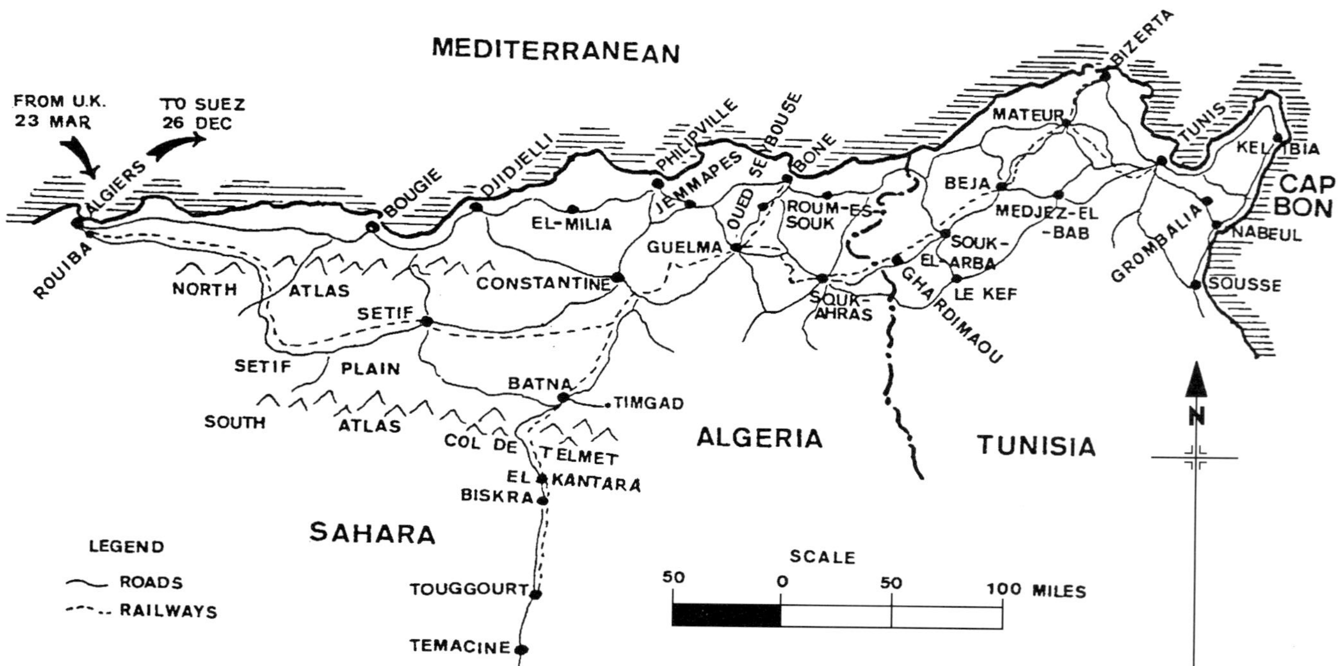

# CHAPTER I

## Departure and Arrival

The Company spent eleven months in the small west coast town of Kirkcudbright. As a Unit of 4th (British) Division, with headquarters at Dumfries and units billeted all over Galloway, our object had been to get well trained and really fit and to get to know the Division as a prelude to going into battle. It had been on the whole a very happy time.

Most of the men came from Kent and East London, and the Company's peace-time base had been Canterbury. The majority were Cockneys and over the next two years I was to get to know and appreciate the sterling qualities of East Enders.

All the senior NCOs and the majority of the men were regular soldiers, but by this stage of the war all the officers except John Barnikel (Barney) were civilians in uniform. Barney was at Sandhurst at the outbreak of war, training to be a regular Sapper officer. All the original regular officers had by now moved on or up, as the case might be. Barney was second in command of the Company and a captain. I was a Territorial Army officer, a civil engineer by trade, and had been called up at the outbreak of hostilities on 3 September 1939. I had been to France and back, via Dunkirk. R. M. Hamilton (Ham), a Scot, was training to be a land agent; like so many Scots he was meticulous over detail and intensely loyal, both to his men and to me. Ham, a lieutenant, was in charge of 1 Section.

Freddie Leadbeter, the oldest but still young at just over 30, was a local authority highways surveyor, a charming and kindly man, albeit unmilitary, but loved by his men. Freddie was also a lieutenant, in charge of 3 Section. Peter Boston was an architect just beginning his career, very artistic and with a mind of his own. He probably showed more initiative than anyone else in the company and was endowed with a splendid sense of humour. He too was a lieutenant, in charge of 2 Section. Lastly, Robert Hutchinson was by trade a salesman and very active, at the same time intensely loyal. At the start of the North African campaign Robert, a second lieutenant, was in charge of the headquarters section of the Company, with the title of Reconnaissance Officer. He was also first reserve in case one of the other officers fell out, as indeed Freddie Leadbeter did in our first battle to come.

I believe, looking back, that the mixture of officers with a wide variety of backgrounds but with a common motivation to lead their men in battle, and regular senior NCOs and men, was an excellent one, particularly for the Sappers, whose role in battle is to support the infantry and tanks to give them freedom of movement. Added to this, we had all trained and worked together as a team in Scotland for the best part of a year: it was a good team.

Almost the most important member of the Unit is the Company Sergeant Major – CSM for short. In Five Nine Company CSM Tutton was a regular soldier with up to twenty years' service. He was stocky and strong and by his upright stance demanded respect which he gave in return. The CSM is responsible for discipline, good order, and strict compliance with Company Orders. In some respects he is a lonely man. He has considerable power and is often much feared. However I don't think CSM Tutton was feared in the Company, but he certainly was respected.

He was a martinet for good order, always smartly turned out, and by the sheer force of his own personality and appearance earned the genuine respect of every man in the Company. Towards the officers he was respectful but firm, for he knew so much more about army discipline and the management of men than they. He was always helpful with advice but seldom gave it, to the officers, gratuitously. On the other hand, with NCOs he did not hesitate with "advice" which he gave with forthright and picturesque language.

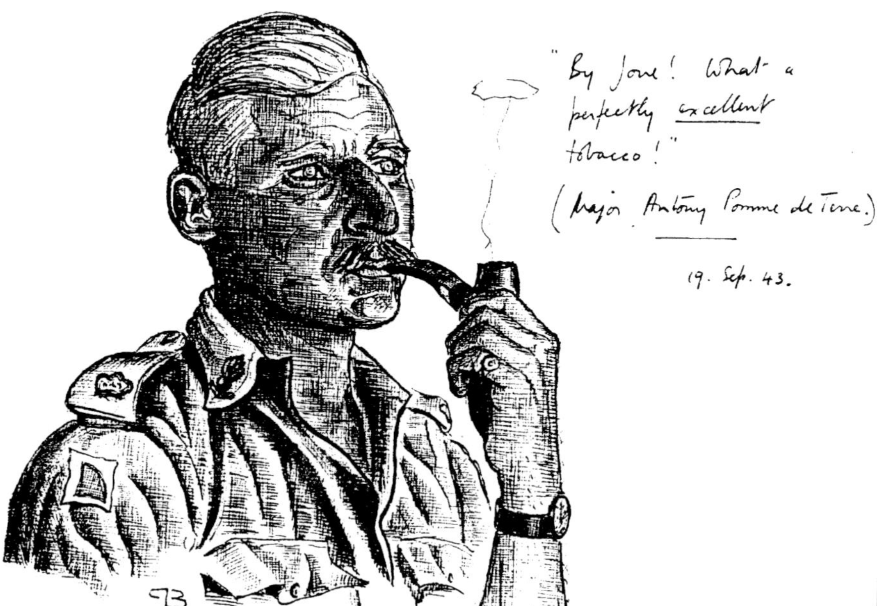


*'By Jove! What perfectly* excellent *tobacco! Author Tony Daniell*

He and I had complete understanding. I always took and valued his advice and understanding of a situation. He always carried out my requests at once. I never gave him an order, that would have hurt his dignity. Although full responsibility for the Company's actions must always rest with the OC, we always tried in the Company to adopt a climate of consensus rather than of direct orders. There were of course the "daily orders" but in times of stress and battle, action was often the result of agreement rather than diktat; and this seemed to work reasonably well because the Company undoubtedly did have a good record.

As a result we had remarkable cohesion within the Company and very little indiscipline. The performance of a unit in war depends very largely upon the influence of the CSM although he is seldom present working with the men. He stands between the officers and the other ranks. Such is the role of the warrant officer rank. The really good ones are few and far between. CSM Tutton was one of the best. Once when a piece of shrapnel blew into the office truck, narrowly missing him, his immediate reaction was "Who the hell do these Germans think they are"!

Before we left Kirkcudbright CSM Tutton took charge every Saturday afternoon of the "Company Run". This was nine miles cross country in a big loop up to nearly 1,000ft. and down to sea level again, and nearly impossible to cheat. He and I devised it together for all officers, NCOs and men, including cooks and batmen. There were no exceptions. The CSM was in his element. He would course up and down the Company encouraging and cajoling all equally with Chaucerian language. It stood us in very good stead later on.

Kirkcudbright is a small estuary town at the end of a branch line, very much off the beaten track and with a strong feeling of independence. The Kirkcudbrians had taken the Sappers into their homes and into their hearts; we had no competition from any other unit and, as Sappers are also fairly independent-minded, we fitted in well. During the eleven months of our stay five of the unit had married local girls.

Because our main object had been to get fit and trained, our area of activity had been much larger than the town of Kirkcudbright itself. We had made many friends amongst the farmers and landowners across whose lands we had squelched through bogs, often stumbling in total darkness, falling over sleeping sheep, getting lost, slithering into ditches, and being rescued in time for a farmhouse breakfast.

During this period the officers quartered the Lowlands fairly extensively on various interesting missions, such as inspecting all the road bridges to confirm their load-bearing classifications, as well as carrying out various odd jobs of an engineering nature for the various infantry battalions, who were mainly billeted in large country mansions in the Dumfries/Hawick area. One of these missions provided an interesting and unforgettable day for Peter Boston (in charge of 2 section) which can best be told in his own words.

"I was informed that 2 DCI (Duke of Cornwall's Light Infantry) required us to demolish a large tree stump at their battalion headquarters. It sounded a fairly simple operation, so I collected a small quantity of explosives, a Danarm saw, and an auger and set off in my pick-up truck with Sgt. Hellen and a reliable sapper.

I had not previously visited this Bn. HQ but as we drove up the long narrow drive which wound through beech woods I was at once entranced with the place. The woods parted, and we turned a corner to come face to face with an impressive sandstone mansion standing amid generous lawns which fell away to a lake. It struck me that there must be people (still alive) whose minds are full of childhood memories of this place in happier times – leisurely teas on the lawn, the feel of the solid internal joinery, midnight swimming in the lake, etc.

Over the centre of the house was a large glazed structure giving light to the first floor landing and I was duly ushered up the stairs beneath this to report to the CO, a tough and cheerful character by the name of Colonel Pengelly, whom I had previously met and instantly liked. He gave me carte blanche to do what I thought necessary and dispatched his 2 I/C to show me the problem.

This turned out to be the stump of a large beech tree which had been cut down to about two feet above ground level. The remaining stump was about 4 feet in diameter, with massive roots firmly embedded in the ground and thus inaccessible to saws. The stump was almost touching the end of the Sergeant's Mess – a precast concrete structure which it was proposed to extend. The immediate surroundings consisted of a beech wood in which every available piece of ground between the trees was covered by Nissen huts and vehicles. It was obvious that only the most modest and carefully-controlled use of explosives could be contemplated in such a crowded situation, since otherwise unthinkable damage could result. However, I was aware from study of the RE Pocket Book of a formula for shaking tree stumps in such a way as to loosen the earth from the roots without actually dislodging the stump from the ground, so I decided to adopt this method.

Following the formula, I calculated the approximate volume and weight of the stump and my calculations revealed (if I recall correctly) that I should drill three holes, 1" in diameter, into the stump round the bottom perimeter, each approximately 8" deep and place one gun cotton primer in each hole. With the aid of the augers this was achieved in half an hour or so and I instructed Sgt. Hellen to start assembling the detonators and fuses while I made a calm scrutiny of the work done so far. I had never tackled a "real" demolition job before, and realised the need for circumspection.

Now, I have always believed that formulae are no substitute for common sense and it was obvious to my inexperienced eye that the small charges we had inserted were woefully inadequate to the task involved. I therefore doubled the dose. (I had thought of trebling it.) We inserted the detonators, linked up the fuses and carefully tamped the holes in the stump with mud. I then arranged for sentries to be posted in each direction along the drive to stop any vehicle which might approach and arranged for one of the DCLI sergeants to instruct all personnel to stay in their huts in case there should be any flying gravel. I then lit the fuse, giving us ten seconds' delay, and we walked round to the far end of the Sergeants' Mess hut, where we stood with our fingers in our ears, confident of a simple job expertly done.

In due course the earth shook and, after the anticipated few seconds of falling gravel and thudding clods of earth, we walked round to examine our handiwork. The tree stump had entirely disappeared! I stood, like stout Cortez, gazing "in a wild surmise" into an empty crater. I could only deduce that our charge had totally disintegrated the stump. Sgt. Hellen, however, was more perceptive; *"Christ!"* he shouted. Something in his tone prompted me to turn and look at him. He was gazing heavenwards, where a huge object, that reminded me of a grand piano, was slowly rotating in the sky.

My first impression was that this was about to descend on to the centre of the big house, crashing through the glass dome – or even on to Colonel Pengelly himself. I had a sharp vision of the mansion in ruins and my own military career in the same state. As we watched, in horrified suspense, the Thing began to increase rapidly in size and I became aware of a whistling screech as it hurtled earthwards. It was now obviously falling much nearer than the big house, but this prospect was not reassuring as I thought of the tightly packed DCLI huts and vehicles all around us.

I had hardly time to formulate these thoughts before the stump crashed down into a small clearing about forty yards away from us, just short of a wooden hut, out of which an agitated figure had run after hearing the blast. On emerging from his door he had seen an apparent meteorite hurtling towards him and had hurled himself to the ground about five yards from where it fell. He staggered up, looked round wildly, and came towards us like an offended bull at an unsteady but determined run. As he approached I could see that his hands and battle dress were spattered with mud. He had forgotten his hat in his agitation but the crowns on his shoulders told me that Trouble was on the way. He was almost incoherent with rage and shock, but there was no mistaking the gist of his observations; which were to the effect that I was an incompetent little idiot, playing around with materials I did not know how to handle; that it was a miracle I had not killed dozens of people; and in particular, was I not aware that it was forbidden to use explosives without permission from the Garrison Engineer – whom I eventually understood him to be. "How dare you – HOW DARE YOU indulge in this sort of madness without my authority? I am going straight back to report this to the Corps Commander. I shall tell him you're a disgrace to your Regiment and make sure you never get another opportunity of behaving in this way."

I had never given serious thought, prior to the last 20 seconds or so, to the possibility of being cashiered and this was rather a blow. This was also the first time that I had ever encountered a Garrison Engineer. I had a dim recollection of garrisons in the context of Caesar's Conquest of Gaul, and the word had also cropped up in prep. school history books; but in my innocence I had never connected the word "garrison" with contemporary life; nor could I recall that the existence of Garrison Engineers had ever been mentioned in my military training, so that this sudden appearance of an irate and formidable adversary out of the unknown was a little disconcerting.

While I was adjusting my thoughts to this situation another figure came running towards us and I recognised Colonel Pengelly. "O God," I thought, "this is the end!", and braced myself for the final humiliation. Nevertheless there was something in his eye which gave me courage. "Boston," he said, panting somewhat after his sprint, "I really don't know how you chaps do it! I saw the whole thing from my window. The way you managed to bring that thing down in the only clear space in a quarter mile radius was an absolute delight to watch. I just had to come down and tell you how impressed I am! And look – the end of the Sgts' Mess isn't even scratched!

I was beginning to feel that all might not yet be lost and thanked him calmly in such terms as allowed him to believe that everything had gone exactly according to plan. "What's more," he added, "I shall be seeing the Chief Engineer on Tuesday and shall tell him you're a bloody miracle!

Courage returning, I endeavoured to meet the Garrison Engineer's eye at this point, but he appeared to be lost in mental redrafting of his report to higher authority and was looking absently into the distance. Whatever report he submitted, I heard no more of the matter. (Nor, for that matter, did I ever consult – or even find – a Garrison Engineer before carrying out any subsequent demolition task.)

Over the years I have occasionally gone cold at the realisation of the height to which the stump must have risen. The time required for us to shelter until gravel stopped falling, to travel the length of the Sgts' Mess, and to look stupidly into the hole cannot have amounted to less than about 12-15 seconds, and even then our missile must have been all of 200 feet above us. Only Colonel Pengelly had seen the complete trajectory, and I felt that to question him would spoil the effect.

I drove thoughtfully back to Kirkcudbright, exaltation at the satisfactory outcome being overlain by guilt at the contemplation of the disaster which might so easily have occurred: above all, with a heightened respect for the RE Pocket Book (which I still keep by me and find indispensable, professionally, 46 years later!)"

*Peter Boston. Self Portrait*

One particular friend, Andrew Brown, the local Fiscal (the Scottish equivalent of the local magistrate) became our guide and mentor in all matters secular. The two Ministers, Episcopal and Wee Free, together with the Catholic priest, competed to provide better and better "welfare for the troops". Kirkcudbright had wholeheartedly adopted Five Nine Field Company, and therefore the shock to the town can be imagined when on the morning of 10 March 1943 it became known that the Company would be leaving by train at 2100 hours that very evening en route for Glasgow, to embark for service overseas.

The Company's equipment had been quietly packed into the transport during the last few days, but this was a common occurrence for exercises and nobody had noticed the special labelling. I had taken my labrador home to Anglesey a few nights before. At noon on 10 March, the Company transport left in a convoy, under command of John Barnikel and Robert Hutchinson, for embarkation on the Clyde. We did not see them again until 31 March.

In the town arrangements were quickly put in hand for a suitable send-off. Large quantities of beer and whisky were made available; both Protestant churches and the Catholics mustered their ladies to arrange tea, coffee, and buns on the platform, and the shops closed early to give extra time for the preparations.

During this afternoon I received by hand the following rather nice letter from the Chief Constable. This came as a direct result of the influence upon the Company of Sergeant Major Tutton:

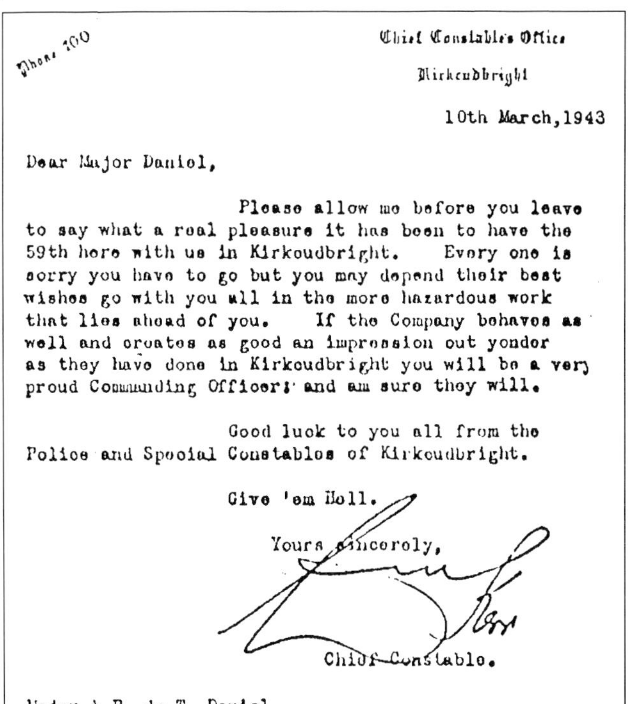

Phone 100

Chief Constable's Office
Kirkcudbright

10th March, 1943

Dear Major Daniel,

Please allow me before you leave to say what a real pleasure it has been to have the 59th here with us in Kirkcudbright. Every one is sorry you have to go but you may depend their best wishes go with you all in the more hazardous work that lies ahead of you. If the Company behaves as well and creates as good an impression out yonder as they have done in Kirkcudbright you will be a very proud Commanding Officer; and am sure they will.

Good luck to you all from the Police and Special Constables of Kirkcudbright.

Give 'em Hell.

Yours sincerely,

Chief Constable.

Major A.P. de T. Daniel,

Meanwhile, I had called a meeting of the officers – Lieut. Hamilton, 1 Section, Peter Boston, 2 Section, Freddie Leadbeter, 3 Section, and Company Sergeant Major Tutton – to impress upon them that we at least must remain sober. I felt sure that trouble was brewing. Those men not on special duties were allowed into the town to say goodbye to their sweethearts and friends, but had to be back at the Drill Hall for supper and parade at 1800 hours By the time the Company marched on to the platform the Kirkcudbrians outnumbered the Sappers by about five to one or more. Andrew Brown and the local policeman were discreetly there, but in fact no trouble ensued.

The train consisted of non-corridor carriages, allowing eight men to a compartment; but as fast as we got them into their carriage they tumbled out of the door behind, and there were as many locals in the carriages as there were Sappers. Picnic parties started spontaneously on the platform – only with spirits rather than tea, for after all we were in Scotland. Searches started for missing Sappers, and there was a state of almost total chaos as officers, sergeants, and the harassed Station Master did their best to restore order.

Time marched on, and at 2230 hours the engine driver very apologetically confessed that he no longer had sufficient water to get up the hill to the junction at Castle Douglas. There was no water tower at Kirkcudbright station, so we had to resort to filling his saddle tank with a galvanised bath filled from a stand-pipe on the platform. The entire Company looked on, voicing practical advice. The colourful language of our East Enders somewhat shocked the local Ministers. We finally moved off at about 2300 hours in spite of the assembled population's efforts to hold back the train by holding on to the door handles. There really was no hurry, after all, for we only had to get to Glasgow and we had all night before us.

A holy calm settled on our train as it chugged away into the night up to Castle Douglas and on to Glasgow.

Next day, Wednesday 11 March, Five Nine Field Company was the first unit to board the S.S. *Orion*, the flagship of the Orient Line, in the King George V dock in Glasgow, followed during the day by the whole of 10th Infantry Brigade group and Divisional Headquarters. The next four days were spent in settling in, boat drills, physical training, and taking on more troops, including the absconders who had missed the train. By Sunday, our complement was complete at 5,560 all ranks. On Monday 15 March we sailed, a total of 26 liners and merchantmen with six accompanying destroyers: a very imposing convoy. We now knew that we were bound for North Africa. The voyage was uneventful as far as enemy action was concerned and rather cold.

During the day, the rest of the convoy made an impressive sight – ships all sailing in formation, a quarter to half a mile apart, extending nearly to the horizon in all directions. We began to recognise the other ships by their silhouettes – sometimes broadside on, sometimes from directly ahead or astern, depending on the direction of the convoy at the time. Each ship had a character of its own and we speculated on the mystery of their individual private lives.

One ship in particular had a sombre fascination for Peter, to which later events were to add piquancy. It had ancient low-lying lines with a large old-fashioned counter at the stern and evidently suffered from boiler trouble since, alone among all the others, it laid down a long trail of oily black smoke which hung over the water for miles astern and must have put the convoy at severe risk if spotted by an enemy plane or U boat. Peter discovered from conversations with the crew that it was the S.S. *Banfora*. It reminded him of an old cockroach and he used to refer to it as the "hell-ship".

On 17 March I arranged for Peter to give a lecture to all the Gunner officers (and others) on board, on the subject of German mines and booby traps. Unfortunately he was not a good sailor, and I subsequently learned that he had, on one occasion, been sick on a cross-channel ferry at Dover while it was still moored in the harbour! He had hardly begun his lecture to about 300 expectant faces when he was overcome by nausea and could not be sure whether, when he opened his mouth, words or matter would emerge. He announced his regrets, apologised for his rapid departure, and went to gather up his papers in preparation for a headlong dash to the nearest basin.

He had expected everyone to stand up with a certain amount of laughter and shrugging of shoulders, but nobody moved a muscle or made a sound. This presented a challenge which he felt he could not duck, so he started again and somehow or other managed to complete an hour's talk with reasonable fluency before escaping at the double and just reaching sanctuary with less than a second to spare. I am glad to report that after this triumph of mind over matter his sea-sickness left him and he was able to revel in the rough weather. Much the same story could be told of all of us including myself.

There was nothing much to do beyond the usual boat drills, a few lectures, physical training and kit inspections. It was a time to take stock, particularly for the officers. Apart from myself the next most senior was Captain John Barnikel; "Barney", as he was known to all, had the driest of humour. When, later on, he became Adjutant of the Divisional Engineers the first thing he did was to put up a large notice over his desk saying "Haven't you heard, it's all been changed", which usually applied to the current operation orders.

We were never short of rations and never short of company orders. As a Captain he was in many respects the mentor of the junior officers. If I asked anyone a question about their work, the reply would invariably be "because Barney said so". We got on together extremely well. I never had to worry – much – about administration, and of course he and CSM Tutton saw completely eye to eye both metaphorically and physically.

Next in seniority was Lieut. R.M. Hamilton, "Ham" as he was always known, who was a Scot and a natural staff officer. When we went overseas he was in charge of 1 Section, which gave him most valuable experience of the work of the Sappers on the ground. But he really came into his own later on when Barney left the Company to become Adjutant and he was promoted Captain and Second-in-Command of the Company.

Then came Peter Boston, in charge of 2 Section. He was a strikingly different character to most, tall, dark, good-looking, and highly intelligent. He was, later on, to display considerable qualities of leadership and inventiveness. He was also a good

*'What's all this bloody stuff in my IN tray' R. M. Hamilton*

draughtsman artist and produced excellent maps. I include in this book a number of his pen and ink sketches. He had done some gliding before the war and as a result was extremely observant of the weather and topography. I doubt if he could ever be lost, and this also endeared him to his Sappers.

3 Section was commanded by Freddie Leadbeter. He was in some respects a father figure to the Company, being the oldest. He was a very gentle, quiet person with a soft, quiet voice, and often with a rather distant look. He was very much loved by 3 Section, and for a while he was greatly missed by his men when he was wounded and left the Company in the forthcoming "Hunts Gap" battle.

Our reserve officer was Robert Hutchinson who before being called up was a salesman, he was resourceful and tremendously energetic.

It was not until the following Sunday, 21 March, that our special convoy of eight ships turned eastwards and passed through the Strait of Gibraltar into the Mediterranean. Next night, our little convoy was attacked and the SS *Windsor Castle* sunk by an airborne torpedo, the survivors being picked up by our accompanying destroyer. This was rather frightening as our ship, the SS *Orion*, was a much bigger target. However, we were not attacked.

Next day, Tuesday, 23 March, we docked at Algiers. Peter Boston with the drivers re-embarked on another ship to go on to the port of Bone, to link up with our transport. To Peter's horror the ship to which he was now directed was his "hell-ship",

SS *Banfora*. He embarked with a feeling of foreboding. He told me later that it was full of Gothic panelling, with dark, narrow passages and innumerable dead ends, and the thought of having to escape from it in an emergency was not one that he relished. On the move, the ship proceeded with a sinuous, jerky motion like that of a dog swimming. I hasten to add that, in spite of Peter's premonitions and the smoke trail, they reached Bone safely.

The rest of the Company marched a few miles out of Algiers to a brick factory at Le Hamiz, which was to be our home for a few days only. Just as well, as it was exceedingly uncomfortable, hot by day and difficult to sleep in at night on account of the incredible noise of bull-frogs in the clay-pit behind the factory.

We were visited at Le Hamiz by the CRE (Commander Royal Engineers), Lieut.Col. Pat Foley and his reconnaissance officer, Brian Roberts, who arrived unexpectedly in an ancient taxi – all our transport had gone on to Bone on another ship. Brian reminded me recently of the ludicrous conditions in the brick factory; it was endeavouring to continue production of bricks with just one or two Arabs and with a company of Sappers living amidst the machinery.

There was a slow-moving continuous cable with trays hanging from it, which wound in and out of the sheds carrying bricks from one place to another. We eventually got quite good at avoiding being hit on the head by a passing tray. There was much consternation and embarrassment on the first morning when unsuspecting Sappers woke up to find the brick conveyor had started up early and had moved some of their clothes around the factory, causing a frantic search for shirts and trousers. Sergeant-Major Tutton placed a marked brick on a tray which he swore was still perambulating round the works when we left.

On Saturday 26 March, we received orders to pack up and march to Rouiba station a few miles east of Algiers for another rail journey to Souk-el-Arba, just inside Tunisia. This was a very different journey from our last one, from Kirkcudbright to Glasgow. Although there was to be a Gunner Unit on the train, as we were the first arrivals on the train and we had already set up our cook-house in the middle for everyone under CSM Tutton, I was able to persuade Major Hutt, RA to leave it all to the Sappers. The Gunners being senior to the Sappers would normally take over command of the train. We were joined on the train by 22 Field Regiment RA. The train consisted entirely of cattle trucks except for one third class carriage behind the engine for Officers, Warrant Officers and Senior NCOs. The engine was a huge French steam locomotive, driven by a cheery English Sapper driver and Sapper fireman. We left again on Sunday and proceeded quite slowly eastwards across the Algerian plain towards Tunisia. (See Map 1 on page14.)

The journey was pleasant enough, through cork oak forests up on to the high Setif plain. In the forests we had our first glimpse of the colourful pink and brown hoopoes flitting amongst the trees, but saw no Barbary apes. On the plain a poor wheat crop was ripening; away to the south were the High Atlas mountains, some still with snow on them, and to the north the Mediterranean.

From time to time there would be air raid alarms, when the engine gave a long whistle, the train came to a stop, and everyone leapt out. This was followed by a frantic rounding up of all the troops when the engine gave the all-clear with a series of pip-pips on the whistle. It was generally an excuse to open the cook-house for an issue of tea, which tended to delay restarting. We stopped for two nights in sidings to sleep, cook supper and breakfast, and generally stretch our legs. The total distance was about 600 miles.

The high point of this journey came on Tuesday morning, when we arrived at Guelma junction. Guelma is on a high, bare, windy plain with no redeeming features, a small white station building, a signal box and water tower, and a few shacks. It was hot and dusty with no shade or cover had we been attacked from the air. Our line joined the line from Biskra in the south to Bone in the north, and as all the lines were single track there was a loop at Guelma station to allow trains to pass each other; but because our train was much too long for the loop, our engine went as far as it could and there we stopped, allowing all the troops to leave the train.

After a while there was great excitement in the station, with shouts of "Attention, attention, la grande vitesse arrive tout de suite!" In the distance, coming from the south, there appeared an engine and two coaches which slowly drew up in the station, thus allowing our train to move forward to clear its rear.

The new arrival from Biskra was headed by a positively huge locomotive with a vast water tank behind the cab, which had an additional set of driving wheels beneath it as well as those under the boiler. From out of the cab in the middle no less than five drivers and firemen emerged, all wearing long black coats and black berets. Meanwhile the troops from our train, fascinated by this huge engine and only two coaches, crowded round to inspect it. More shouts of "Attention, attention!" of which no one took the slightest notice; whereupon the drivers opened the large soot door in the front of the boiler and proceeded to blow through the boiler tubes with steam, emitting clouds of soot over the admiring soldiers. That done, the five drivers and firemen climbed aboard and with much whistle-blowing moved off north to Bone.

CSM Tutton was appalled at this behaviour on the part of the engine crew and swore at them in his most picturesque vocabulary, to the delight of the Sappers. The Gunners looked on with rather haughty indifference.

Apparently this was a regular occurrence at Guelma, where there was usually nobody at all. As all the locomotives were wood burning they had, from time to time, to blow out the soot. However it was not popular with our men there being no water for washing.

During the afternoon we stopped briefly at Souk-Ahras, which is quite a big town on a high plateau, and our first sight of a truly African town, with narrow streets crammed full of Arabs, goats, sheep and camels. The houses were built of mud with apparently no windows but courtyards with a few tall palm trees. However we soon moved on to Ghardimaou, our destination, where we left the train and our friends the Gunners, who went on a few miles to their own destination of Souk-el-Arba, which was then the end of the line. The date was 31 March 1943. (See map 1 on page 14.)

The next day Peter Boston arrived from Bone with six of our trucks and some equipment, followed soon after by Barney and Robert Hutchinson with our full complement of transport and equipment. Once again the Company was complete with everyone present.

Ghardimaou turned out to be rather a squalid little village with no amenities whatsoever. We arrived quite late, setting up our bivouacs in some olive groves, where we spent a thoroughly uncomfortable night. However, we all felt that this was the beginning of active service and was after all what we had been training for over the past year. We did not realise that night how soon we would be active participants in the North African battle against the Germans.

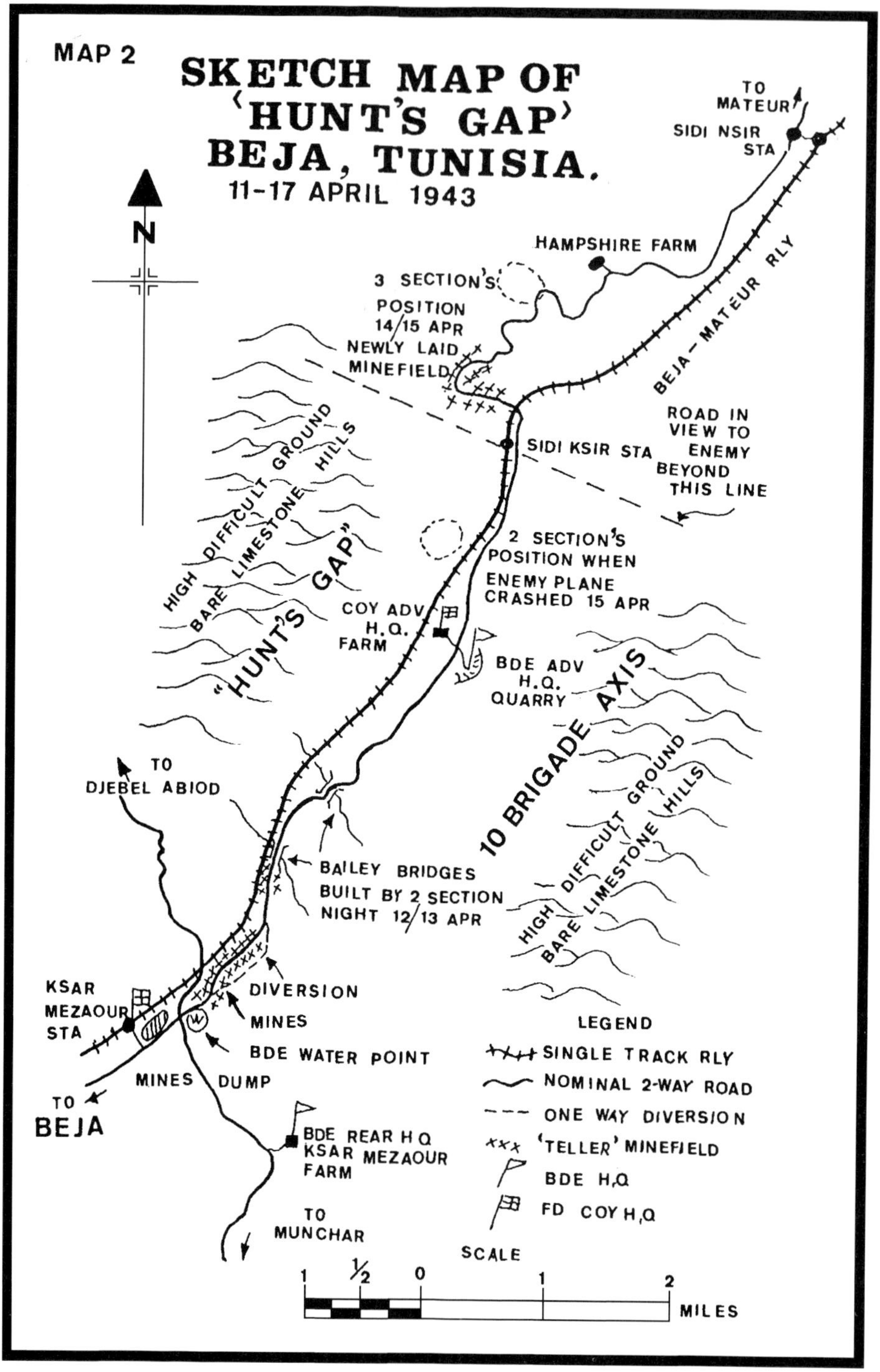

MAP 2
SKETCH MAP OF 'HUNT'S GAP' BEJA, TUNISIA.
11-17 APRIL 1943
N
TO MATEUR
SIDI NSIR STA
HAMPSHIRE FARM
3 SECTION'S POSITION 14/15 APR
NEWLY LAID MINEFIELD
BEJA - MATEUR RLY
SIDI KSIR STA
ROAD IN VIEW TO ENEMY BEYOND THIS LINE
HIGH DIFFICULT GROUND
BARE LIMESTONE HILLS
"HUNT'S GAP"
2 SECTION'S POSITION WHEN ENEMY PLANE CRASHED 15 APR
COY ADV H.Q. FARM
BDE ADV H.Q. QUARRY
10 BRIGADE AXIS
TO DJEBEL ABIOD
BAILEY BRIDGES BUILT BY 2 SECTION NIGHT 12/13 APR
HIGH DIFFICULT GROUND
BARE LIMESTONE HILLS
KSAR MEZAOUR STA
DIVERSION
MINES
BDE WATER POINT
MINES
DUMP
TO BEJA
BDE REAR H Q KSAR MEZAOUR FARM
TO MUNCHAR
LEGEND
SINGLE TRACK RLY
NOMINAL 2-WAY ROAD
ONE WAY DIVERSION
'TELLER' MINEFIELD
BDE H.Q
FD COY H.Q
SCALE
1 ½ 0 1 2
MILES

# CHAPTER II

## Beja, Tunisia

The Company moved next day, 1 April, from Ghardimaou to the pleasant little country town of Beja, where we were able to get everyone billeted in houses or buildings of some sort, and for a week we spent the time getting to know where other units of 10th Infantry Brigade were, as we were affiliated to this Brigade. Our Sapper senior officer was Lieut.Colonel Pat Foley, the Divisional Commander Royal Engineers (CRE), who also established his H.Q. at Beja. It soon became apparent that an attack on the Germans in this area was being planned.

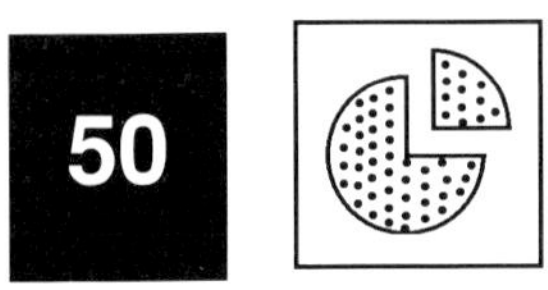


The Company's number,in the division, 50, was shown in white figures on a blue background and the 4th Division sign was a red quadrant detached from a red disc. These two signs were painted on all our vehicles and equipment. All ranks in the Division wore the red quadrant on their left shoulder, for visual identification.

The battle started on Saturday 10 April and lasted a week. It gave the Company its first period of active service and for every man in the Company it was his initiation into battle. This subsequently proved of very great value in the much bigger struggle at Medjez-el-Bab in giving us all that extra confidence which only battle experience can provide.

At this point I should perhaps explain the organisation of the Company and its relationship to other units within the Brigade and Division. At this period of the war in North Africa, Divisions were organised on the three-part principle, I think on the general idea of two up and one in reserve. 4th (British) Division – so called to differentiate it from 4th (Indian) Division – was slightly different specifically for the

North African campaign, in that it had only two infantry Brigades, Nos. 10 and 12 (11 Brigade having left the Division before we left England) and 21st tank Brigade. Each of the two infantry Brigades had three Battalions of infantry and the tank Brigade had three tank Regiments, the theory being that the infantry Brigades would create the opportunity for the tanks to break through; this is in fact what happened in the final battle for Tunis.

In the Division there were three Field Companies of Royal Engineers – numbers 7, 59 and 225 – each affiliated to a Brigade. There was one Field Park Company – No. 18 – which held bridging equipment and bulldozers which could be called up by any of the three Field Companies. Each Field Company had three working Sections of four Sub-sections each, the Section being commanded by a Subaltern and the Sub-section by a sergeant or a corporal. Each Section was accustomed to work with the same Battalion unless the whole Field Company was concentrated on a particular Sapper job. The Field Company had a Headquarter Section with the second in command, a Captain, and one Subaltern. The Field Company was commanded by a Major. An illustrated detail of a Field Company is shown on the front and back endpapers.

Thus it came about that 59 Field Company was affiliated to 10 Brigade in 4th Division and its three working Sections were normally attached – 1 Section (Lieut. Hamilton) to 2nd Battalion Bedfordshire & Hertfordshire (2 Beds & Herts) Regiment, 2 Section (Lieut. Peter Boston) to 2nd Battalion Duke of Cornwall's Light Infantry (2 D.C.L.I.), and 3 Section (Lieut. Freddie Leadbeter) to 1st/6th Battalion East Surreys (1/6 Surreys). The 2 i/c of the Company (Captain Barnikel) normally commanded the H.Q. Section with a reconnaissance officer (Lieut. Robert Hutchinson). The OC, myself, had the roving job of holding it all together and keeping close to Brigade Headquarters in order to anticipate the sort of jobs which would be required of the Sappers, whose official motto is "Ubique", meaning literally "everywhere". Generally this set-up worked very well.

Now to return to the operation being planned at Beja. It was given the code name "Hunt's Gap", and was designed to push the enemy, the Germans, back along the Mateur road towards Tunis and the sea. The plan was to advance about 12 miles along this road, as far as Sidi Nsir station. Other Divisions of 1st Army would be advancing and attacking on our flanks. (See map 2 on page 28.)

This stretch of road, code-named "Hunt's Gap", consisted of a single track road flanked by a railway track which switched from side to side, often on spectacular masonry viaducts, although it was of course disused. The road was fairly level but twisted between high and bare rocky hillsides parallel to it on the north and south, very difficult ground, easy for the Germans to hold. The road itself had a water-bound macadam surface which quickly became covered with mud when it rained, and was already severely pot-holed, resulting in a very bad surface; it was barely wide enough for two way traffic. Luckily the weather was fine and dry and we prayed that it would remain so.

10 Brigade under Brigadier J.H.Hogshaw, MC, was to advance with 2 Beds & Herts on the right and 1/6 Surreys on the left, with Brigade HQ, Gunners and 59 Field

Company, together with 2 DCLI in reserve, following along the road, which was the axis of advance. It was thought that there might be thick minefields guarding the entrance to this defile and probably all the way: this proved correct.

59 Field Company's role was to clear mines and generally assist the Brigade in its advance. We had done this many times on exercises in Scotland – now it was for real. A Subsection of 1 Section was attached to 2 Beds & Herts and a Subsection of 3 Section to 1/6 Surreys. The remainder of 1 Section – Lieut. Hamilton – was given the task of clearing mines from the road itself, and the remainder of 3 Section – Lieut. Freddie Leadbeter – to clear the verges. 2 Section – Lieut. Peter Boston – (who normally worked with 2 DCLI) remained with Company HQ in reserve and kept close to Brigade HQ following along the cleared road in a series of leaps and bounds.

Our method of checking and clearing mines at this time was quite simple and involved Sappers working in pairs. One carried the mine detector with its battery, which he swung from side to side as close to the ground as possible, like a scythe; when it passed over a mine or other lump of steel there would be a sharp whistle in his earphones. At this point his mate would mark the spot with a cardboard cap or something similar, and start to uncover the mine very carefully with a trowel, at the same time using a spike to probe the soil in order to locate the mine itself. If the minefield was very dense other Sappers or Pioneers working with the Infantry would uncover the mines as they were marked.

Once uncovered, the brass fuse on the top of the mine casing would be turned from "Scharf" to "Sicher" to make it safe to handle, which could be done with a coin. Then a cord was looped round the fuse or tied to the handle of the mine and the mine would be yanked out of the ground from a distance, in case it had been booby-trapped. Meanwhile the Sapper party, while they were sweeping, finding and clearing mines, would be covered by Infantry patrols on either side and ahead against a surprise attack.

*German "Teller' mine fuse in brass    sicher - safe    Scharf - set*

The German Tellermine was about 12" in diameter by 4" thick, and weighed about 20lbs, containing 10lbs of high explosive. The fuse, fixed to the lid, operated when pressure was exerted upon it. The load to fire it was about 100lbs. Any vehicle was at risk including a running man but not usually at a walking pace. In the flat country of

North Africa the Tellermines were the principal defence used by the Germans, and they were used in great numbers. Sometimes the minefields were marked for their own information, but more often were unmarked.

The "Hunt's Gap" operation started at 0200 a.m. on the morning of Sunday 11 April. Initial advance was rapid as no enemy resistance was encountered and was determined only by the rate at which the small party of Sappers could check and clear a safe path for their battalion's Bren gun carriers, at the same time marking the cleared track with white tape. In fact for two days these two Sapper parties were virtually lost, as they were continually asked by Gunners and others as well as the Infantry to check their positions for mines. They worked continuously, except for about two hours at night between 0200 and 0400 when it was too dark to see.

Meanwhile the remainder of 1 Section under Lieut. Hamilton moved along the road, sweeping continuously with their mine detectors, and in the first mile or so lifted a large number of German Tellermines, as well as many of our own British Mark V mines which were being relaid by the Germans. Because there were so many, progress was slow, and some impatience was expressed, for by the afternoon of Sunday 11 April the flanking Battalions were well ahead of the Brigade supply column.

Although there was no enemy action during this first day, there were several incidents which quickly taught us some valuable lessons. The first incident was in the morning, when a booby-trapped mine exploded and wounded a number of men. The Tellermine had been located, uncovered carefully by hand, and a cord fixed to the handle, in the usual way; but unfortunately due to familiarity and over-confidence the party remained standing while the cord was pulled. As the mine came out of the ground it was exploded by a booby trap switch fixed underneath it. It was the first booby-trapped mine we had found; many others were to follow later, but we had learned our lesson: always lie flat on the ground when a mine is lifted.

By afternoon this party was getting very tired, having worked continuously from 0200, and had to be relieved. They had also been greatly delayed as their mine detectors were continually picking up bits of metal shrapnel, all of which had to be investigated, for this valley had already been fought over before we came on the scene. The answer was to start several mine-sweeping parties working in echelon about half a mile apart. Soon every mine detector in the Company was in use, and every Sapper had a job.

Meanwhile 3 Section, less the Sub-section with the 1/6 Surreys, with Freddie Leadbeter, whose job it would be to clear the verges, had initially been repairing the worst of the potholes. Thus clearing and marking the verges with "Mines in Verges" or "Verges cleared" had lagged behind, with the result that a Gunner truck had gone over a mine and been blown up. However, by nightfall of the first day the road and verges had been cleared for about four miles. Brigade HQ moved up to Ksar Mezaour farm, and 59 Field Company HQ together with 2 Section moved into Ksar Mezaour station (see map 2 on page 28).

The following day, Monday 12 April, it was decided to start work at 0400 am, this time with 3 Section leading, because so far they had had the easier task while

1 Section took over clearing verges. We also decided to start the three remaining Sub-sections of 3 Section one mile ahead of each other, with two mine detectors to each Sub-section, thus rendering the checking and clearing of the road three times faster. This was very successful and they now far outstripped 1 Section clearing the verges.

Later in the morning Freddie Leadbeter, 3 Section, reported that two small bridges had been destroyed, leaving gaps about 30ft. wide. I promptly decided to ask Lieut.Colonel Pat Foley to release two 40ft. Bailey Bridges from 18 Field Park Company, who were now also established at Beja, and to give the task of erecting them to Peter Boston with his 2 Section. The plan was to bring up the first bridge set at dusk, and the second set two hours later.

This operation actually worked according to plan, except that the timings were a bit optimistic, the bridges taking longer to build in the dark than anticipated. However both bridges were completed and open to traffic at first light on Tuesday morning 13 April. Peter Boston with 2 Section returned to Company HQ at Ksar Mezaour station, leaving a small party of Sappers on each bridge for maintenance.

I am reminded by Peter Boston of an incident which occurred on his return to Ksar Mezaour.

"On top of the station chimney two storks were nesting, making a clattering noise with their beaks and giving a high-visibility exhibition of gross indecency. On many of these days we were buffeted by exceptionally high winds which blew steel helmets off people's heads and all papers had to be kept in place with stone paperweights. While watching the storks, Peter Boston noticed a curious thick, spiralling cloud above them, which he at first took to be a mass of small whirling birds; then he began to think it must be manna from heaven, or perhaps a cloud of enemy propaganda leaflets. The cloud gradually descended earthwards and he set off in pursuit, seizing the nearest motorcycle. When he eventually caught up with the cloud he discovered that it consisted of hundreds of unused return tickets from Ksar Mezaour to Beja (aller et retour), which had presumably been blown up out of the station by a whirlwind. He collected a handful as souvenirs but, unfortunately, circumstances prevented us from ever putting this bonus to good use."

On the Tuesday morning Sapper tasks and affiliations remained unchanged, namely 3 Section clearing the road with 1 Section following and clearing verges. It had been decided that because there was no moon and the nights were so dark, work must cease between midnight and 0400, thus giving the Sappers a modicum of rest. However at this point the flanking Battalions met with enemy resistance and the advance came to a halt, and this gave me the opportunity to recall the two Sapper working parties back to their Sections, much to their relief.

Freddie Leadbeter, 3 Section, asked for a bulldozer to assist in making small diversions where the road surface was destroyed; but unfortunately this bulldozer went over a deeply laid Tellermine and was blown up, the driver luckily being thrown clear and unhurt, though rather shaken. The mine had been cunningly laid close to a burnt out German Tiger tank at a point in the road where the surface was full of shrapnel and pieces of metal from the tank, making it impossible to use a mine detector.

Next morning, Wednesday 14 April, the Brigadier planned two attacks, one on each flank, to regain the initiative. These attacks were only partly successful, with both Battalions suffering rather heavy casualties. Meanwhile the Chief Engineer of V Corps, Brigadier Caldwell, paid us a visit accompanied by Lieut.Colonel Pat Foley. He suggested that where the verges were heavily mined, a second track be made well clear of the road through the fields. This was immediately put into effect, thus creating a two-way route very successfully. At the same time it was decided to replace the two Bailey bridges with stone paved fords; this was done during the night of 15/16 April and the bridge sets collected by 18 Field Park Company.

During the afternoon Freddie Leadbeter and No.3 Section were sweeping for mines from Sidi Ksir station towards the Brigade objective of Sidi Nsir station, but this section of the road came into full view of the enemy, and was very soon subject to enemy mortar fire which effectively put a stop to further clearing. Freddie was slightly wounded but noticed a more seriously wounded infantryman; he therefore called up one of his own Section lorries, but while they were lifting the injured man into the vehicle a mortar bomb landed and burst under the tailboard of the lorry. Freddie was now quite badly wounded in the right arm, and, together with the infantry soldier, was evacuated back to the medical dressing station. He never returned to the Company and was a great loss, for he was a good officer and popular with his men. His place was taken by Robert Hutchinson from HQ Section. No more mine-sweeping was possible until after dark.

Just before this incident occurred, the Section had run into a very thick and heavily laid minefield in the road. Some seventy mines were lifted from half a mile of road. All these mines were the yellow painted desert type, presumably diverted by the Germans from the 8th Army front. Several instances were encountered where a Tellermine was laid resting on the nose of a British 25 pounder shell, presumably to create a bigger explosion, and there were also many instances of two or three and even four Tellermines laid on top of one another. Luckily none turned out to be booby-trapped, but we had found a few antipersonnel A/P mines.

The German A/P mines were very similar to our own shrapnel "S" mines and were generally planted in verges where soldiers might tread. They were activated either by being trodden upon or by trip wires and, like the British "S" mine, jumped up a few feet to explode, creating a shower of shrapnel. They were exceedingly dangerous, often lethal, and sometimes difficult to detect. Everyone was aware of the danger and very cautious. Fortunately we did not find many in this area.

Once again verge clearing and sign posting lagged behind, with the result that an anti-tank gun truck was blown up while pulling off the road, and judging by the size of the crater it must have been one of these augmented mines. However, thanks to good training none of our Sappers was caught napping.

At dusk on this day, Wednesday 14 April, Barney moved the Company H.Q. to a ruined farm opposite Brigade H.Q. to be nearer to me while I was at Brigade. But it did not prove a very good idea, for they found themselves wedged between two field artillery batteries which attracted the attention of enemy fighter bombers whenever they came over. So what with the noise of shells continuously passing overhead, and being periodically strafed by ME 109s, the Company HQ did not get very much sleep. It was too far forward.

That same evening the Brigadier decided to use the forward Section (3) with Robert Hutchinson in an Infantry role, with four infantry anti-tank guns (6 pounders) of 2 DCLI to form a strong road block astride the Sidi Nsir road just short of "Hampshire Farm", where a previous battle involving the Hampshires had taken place. This was in order to release the 2 DCLI Company to return to its battalion, to take part in a determined attack on the left flank the next morning.

It was further laid down by the Brigadier that this Section of Sappers together with the four anti-tank guns be commanded in person by the OC of the Field Company. I took this as a somewhat dubious honour and wondered why he wanted a subaltern's command to be commanded by a major; I could only think he expected trouble. Accordingly I organised two static patrols well dug in overlooking the road, and two mobile patrols moving about in front of the static positions, including "Hampshire Farm". No incident occurred except that as the Company of 2 DCLI moved out it was spotted by the enemy and lightly mortared. We had a quiet but rather uneasy night.

Next morning, Thursday 15 April, the 2 DCLI attack went in but failed to gain much ground, as the enemy had his mortars and machine guns very well sited and well dug in, and almost impossible to reach on the bare limestone hills which commanded a perfect view of the valley. At midday the DCLI anti-tank guns were relieved by a six-gun troop of 38 Anti-Tank Battery RA and command of this little sector passed to the gunner officer, Captain Adams. The Sappers remained in an infantry role plus manning an observation post for the anti-tank guns.

Elsewhere on the brigade axis road the clearing of mines from verges was completed by Hamilton with his 1 Section, and with the help of military police, "Redcaps", the flow of traffic was greatly improved. 1 Section then undertook the task of collecting up all the lifted mines and making a dump at Ksar Mezaour station.

Wednesday and Thursday, 14-15 April were dangerous days for Peter Boston's 2 Section and resulted in several casualties and the loss of most of his Section transport. The Section was dispersed in reserve on the hillside near Sidi Ksir station and his report of the events of the two days is as follows: (see map 2 on page 28.)

"I woke refreshed after a good night's sleep in the station – the first night in a camp bed since leaving Kirkcudbright! – but the day turned out to be less peaceful. In the morning my truck B6 was following a personnel carrier which went up on a mine. My truck was rather bent about by the blast and Sappers Wilding and Brown were injured in the face. A little later I was returning to base in my PU with B7 following behind, when we suddenly saw a couple of low flying Messerschmidts coming at us. I shouted to driver Waring to stop and we all leapt out; Waring into a ditch on the right-hand-side and Sergeant Molloy and I into a flooded crater on the left. Molloy took a greater leap than I did and disappeared into the water up to his chin. When it was all over we inspected the damage and found a bullet hole through the door against which I had been sitting. B7 had also been shot up badly and Sappers Lawrence, Carter and Englefield had to be taken to hospital.

The next day, about midday, the whole Section was resting up on our fairly steep hillside, thinking of food, when we were attacked by a couple of FW 190s which came in at low level and dropped a bomb on us which finally wrote off truck B7. The planes wheeled round to have another go at us but at that point one of them was shot down by the nearby gunners and crashed with a splendid explosion out of sight over the top of the hill, when heading directly for us. Our cheers suddenly changed to cries of alarm when we saw one of the plane's engines come leaping and bounding over the hill straight towards us, wreathed in flames like a gigantic Catherine wheel. It hurtled down the hill right through us, while the chaps leapt for their lives to either side. At about the fourth bounce, it embedded itself in the side of truck B8, which rocked, leapt into the air and careered off drunkenly down the slope, crashing into B9 which in turn broke loose and crashed into B10.

Sapper Paris was brewing up lunch a few feet away from B10 and was the only man totally unmoved by these events. The roar of the pressure cooker had deafened him to all other sounds and only when B10 rolled crookedly to a halt in front of him did he look up in surprise from his calm preparation of our lunch.

Inspection of the damage revealed that the bomb which finished off B7 had also put B2 hors de combat, so that in two days I had a bullet hole through my own vehicle B1 and trucks B2, 6, 7, 8, 9 and 10 were all immobilised or written off. The FW 190 which had been shot down had done for two of these vehicles with a bomb and then, after crashing, had severely damaged three more. the dead pilot would have been highly satisfied with his morning's work!

We were very lucky not to suffer more casualties in this attack. Had we not all (with the honourable exception of Sapper Paris) been looking in the direction of the spot where the plane crashed, many of us could have been mown down by the flaming Nemesis which came at us so viciously."

Coming back to 3 section road block, at "Hampshire Farm": that evening, the Brigadier decided to relieve the Section with a company of 2 Beds & Herts, at 2000 hours, but later had to postpone the time to midnight. This alteration never got through to Robert Hutchinson and might have been disastrous, for at about 2145 hours Robert sent out two small parties to meet the infantry and act as guides. The remainder of the Section stood to, waiting for the handover. Suddenly there was a burst of machine-gun fire on the left flank, and the left patrol came running back, having seen and been fired on by the enemy. The Section was immediately split into three parties to go to either flank and straight ahead. The centre party met the enemy and each fired on the other, but the enemy were no match for the Sappers, who had practised just such a situation many times in Scotland, and sent the Germans packing. Our Scottish training was really beginning to pay off.

It later transpired that this enemy party had been quite strong and were coming over the hill to lay mines on the road behind our road block. It was a very dark night;

but our patrol surprised them and they dropped their mines and tools and fled. Perhaps they were German Sappers. Robert and his Sappers of 3 Section arrived back at Company HQ at Sidi Ksir station at 0200, having been out for 36 hours without respite. They were very weary.

On the morning of Friday 16 April, we were informed that the Americans were taking over the whole of this front, in order to free the 1st Army to join the 8th Army for the final battle for Tunis. The American units would, we were told, be moving in during the following day and night, and our job was to tidy up loose ends and be prepared to hand over next day. Our feelings were somewhat of surprise; well, good luck to the Americans; it had proved quite a sticky valley.

1 Section under Hamilton spent the day tidying up the road as far as Sidi Ksir station, 2 Section under Peter Boston improved the two fords which were now taking quite heavy traffic, and 3 section under Robert rested all day and caught up with lost sleep. Company HQ under Barney moved back to Ksar Mezaour station.

That evening, most of us officers felt that we had earned a spree, and drove off to Souk-el-Arba for the treat of civilian cuisine at a local restaurant. Imagine our astonishment when, a few minutes later, the entire complement of officers of the American unit to whom we had handed over our front-line positions that morning – some 80 miles away – marched in and sat down at a nearby table! Was this how the West was won?

During this night of Friday 16 April an incident occurred which was later to cause 1 Section some embarrassment. I, of course, knew nothing of it at the time, nor did Hamilton. One of the American units moving in set up their camp in the same olive grove as 1 Section. During the night some bright spark in the Section noticed an empty American jeep trailer and decided to "liberate" it by simply hitching it onto the cook's truck. It quickly got filled up in the morning with the cook's gear and as the Section moved out early it was not noticed.

Some days later when the Company was encamped near Medjez-El-Bab a rather worried American officer appeared, saying that he had lost a jeep trailer and that if he did not return to his unit with the trailer he would be fined a very large sum of money. He had apparently been wandering round British units until he finally identified us as being their neighbours on the night of its disappearance.

Needless to say, the American was only too pleased to take it away without any further questions. Hamilton and his Section Sergeant Atkinson had learnt a useful lesson. Next morning, Saturday 17 April, I was informed at Brigade HQ that we could move back to Beja that evening between 1700 hours and 1900 hours, but we must be clear of Ksar Mezaour station by 1900 hours at all costs. All three Sections spent the day collecting mines, fixing road signs, and gathering up the miles of white tracing tape used to mark cleared lanes, for use another day. When I got back to Beja I was delighted to find that we could move straight back into our old billets.

And so ended quite a hectic week; the time had flown, but once back in billets we all felt pretty tired, very dirty, and very hungry. Quite a few valuable lessons had been learned but, on the whole, we had come out of it well. The main lesson was I think that the rate of clearing mines determines the rate of the attack and of success. Often those behind cried "On" while those in front cried "Steady", while the Sappers took the brunt of criticism. We realised that we must therefore perfect our mine clearing drills.

This detailed account was written up immediately after the battle at the request of the CRE as I think he felt it described pretty accurately the role of a Field Company in support of an Infantry Battalion.

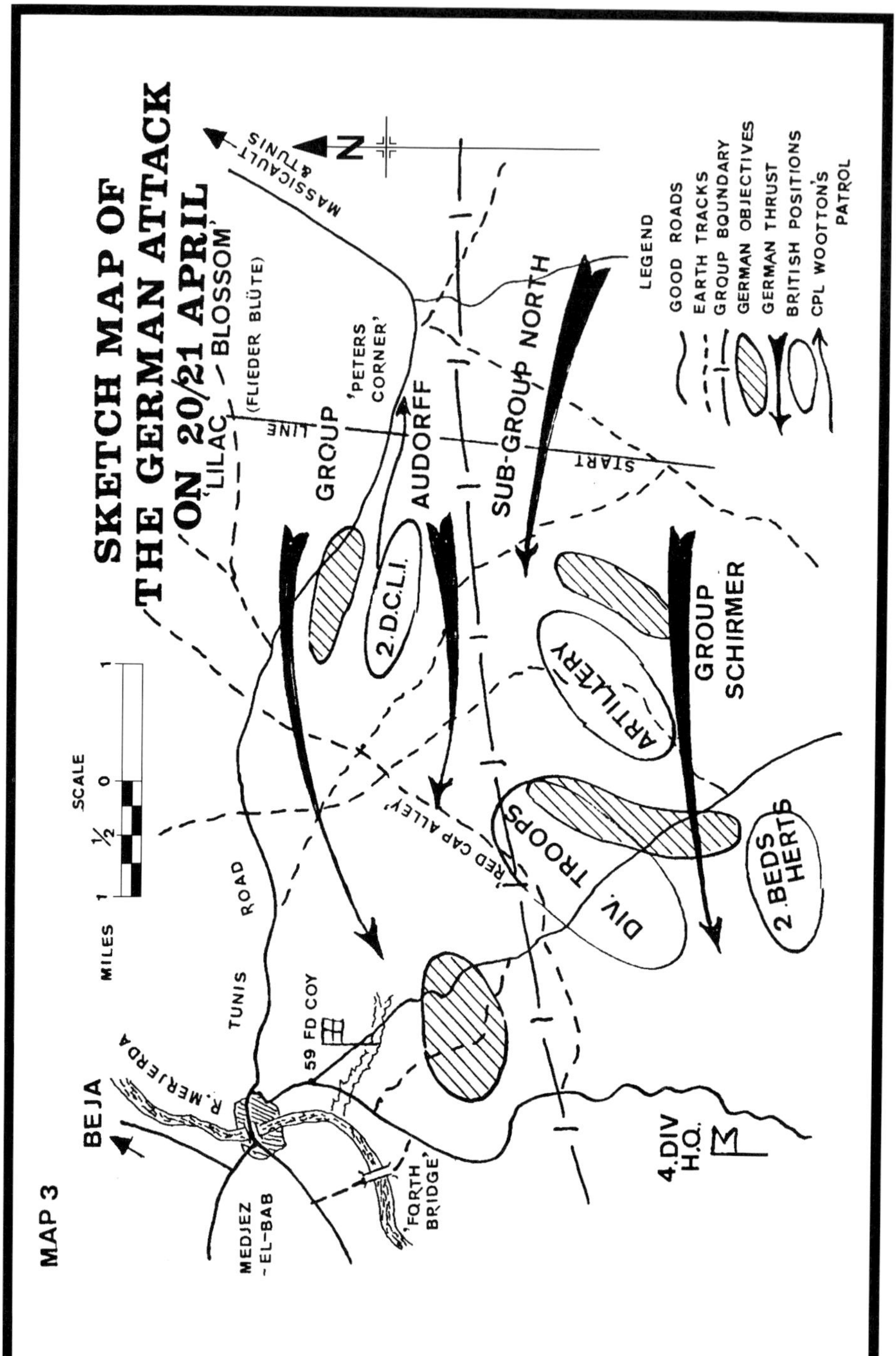
MAP 3
SKETCH MAP OF THE GERMAN ATTACK ON 20/21 APRIL
'LILAC - BLOSSOM'
(FLIEDER BLÜTE)
SCALE
MILES 1 ½ 0 1
BEJA
R. MERJERDA
MEDJEZ -EL-BAB
TUNIS ROAD
59 FD COY
'FORTH BRIDGE'
4.DIV H.Q.
MASSICAULT & TUNIS
N
'PETERS CORNER'
START LINE
GROUP AUDORFF
2.D.C.L.I.
SUB-GROUP NORTH
'RED CAP ALLEY'
ARTILLERY
DIV. TROOPS
GROUP SCHIRMER
2. BEDS HERTS
LEGEND
GOOD ROADS
EARTH TRACKS
GROUP BOUNDARY
GERMAN OBJECTIVES
GERMAN THRUST
BRITISH POSITIONS
CPL WOOTTON'S PATROL

# CHAPTER III

## Medjez-El-Bab, Tunisia

On the night of Sunday 18 April, we moved from Beja to a wadi south of Medjez-el-Bab, still in support of 10 Brigade. We moved in convoy within the Brigade movement plan. Next day we soon discovered this new country to be very different from that around Beja. There it was hilly limestone country not unlike the Yorkshire dales only steeper and with more bare rock; here we found the country round Medjez to be a flattish very fertile silt plain on either side of the Merjerda river, which gradually widened into the plain of Tunis some 35 miles away. This was to be the battleground through which the Allies were to push the Germans out of Africa. It was clearly going to be a very big "set piece" battle with 8th Army from the south and east joining forces with 1st Army from Algeria to the north and west.

The Beja hill country had been largely grass and small farms; here we were in the country of huge fields of waving wheat and sweetcorn, still very green. But there were many deep dry wadis rather like creeks leading towards the Merjerda river. This eventually flowed into the sea at Tunis. We were in one such wadi, and as things turned out it was quite a good "billet". The steep sides gave cover for vehicles and bivouacs and some shade, although by afternoon it became very hot. The Company christened our wadi "Happy Valley"; this was also perhaps because we were all together again, which everyone preferred to being split up and attached to other units in the Brigade.

At this time of year our wadi was dry. No doubt in winter it became a water-course, because there were thick beds of oleander in flower which also gave useful cover. There was a feeling of respite, but it did not last.

There was tremendous activity everywhere, all round us. Huge dumps of artillery shells were being made at night and covered by day with camouflage netting, petrol dumps were springing up overnight, in fact the whole place was in a state of sustained activity. The whole area was dissected by farm tracks. The principal of these, linking most of the units, was named "Red Cap Alley". The Military Police constantly tried to keep this clear and to keep daytime traffic down, as every vehicle movement raised a highly visible cloud of dust, giving away our positions. This was not lost on the enemy: German reconnaissance planes and bombers made many sorties although chased away by our own Hurricanes. This culminated in a savage attack upon 4 (British) Division front on the following Wednesday, 21 April. It was not surprising that the enemy reacted so violently, but it effectively put a stop to our feeling of respite and relief after the Beja battle.

On Tuesday 20 April I was ordered by 10 Brigade HQ to arrange for a small party of Sappers to accompany a patrol being sent out that night by 2 DCLI from their position just south of the Medjez-Tunis road, to explore and map the minefield situation along this road which was still in German hands. In particular the Brigadier was interested in the area where this road turned sharply north towards Tunis. This bend was codenamed "Peter's Corner" and became a focal point in the forthcoming battle. I asked Peter Boston to detail a sub-section to report to 2 DCLI and if possible of Sappers who knew the DCLI well. Peter detailed Corporal Wootton, a reliable regular soldier, with his 4 Sub-section to do the job, which might be tricky at night but not really difficult. However what none of us knew was that on this very night the German Audorff and Schirmer Groups, crack troops, were mounting a major offensive against 4 Division, hoping to catch the Division off guard. This was code-named "Lilac Blossom", in German *"Flieder Blüte"*.

Corporal Wootton's tale of this night and thereafter is best told by him when he got back to the Company, four weeks later, on 17 May, ten days after the fall of Tunis (see map 3 on page 40):

"On the night of the 20/21 April, 1943, myself and three others of 4 Sub-section of 2 Section, 59 Field Company, were detailed to go on a recce patrol with 2 Platoons of "A" Company, 2 DCLI under command of Lieut. Lehmann. Total strength of patrol:- 15 Infantry, 4 Sappers.

The object was to locate enemy minefields, estimate the depth of same, types of mine, and spacing.

We left Advance Company HQ at 2100 hours and proceeded on a compass bearing in the direction of Tunis Rd via Peter's Corner.

At approximately 2215 hours we were proceeding across country when we heard the noise of tanks and armoured vehicles immediately in front, and running at right angles to the direction we were facing.

The officer in command came back and said he thought they were our advance Recce Regiment with (mine clearing) Scorpion tanks, beating the track for mines in preparation for our attack the following evening. I asked if he was aware of the fact that they were out and vice versa and whether he knew their password. He said he didn't know for sure who they were and had no knowledge of their signals or password. I suggested under the circumstances we should avoid them or they would surely open fire if we contacted them. He went back and led the patrol in a right-handed turn, unfortunately for us the left hand man of the patrol was only about 10 yards from the track when he was spotted. The vehicles stopped, up went a Very light, which landed about a yard from us, and Jerry opened up with almost everything he had, light machine guns, mortars, GP grenades from rifles and tommy guns. (See map 3 on page 40.)

Considering the fact that we were in the glare of the Very light, which set fire to the corn very near to Sapper Cartmell, most of the fire during the first five minutes was directed at us. To move would have been suicide. I was armed with a revolver, my junior with a tommy gun and the two Sappers were not armed at all seeing they had the mine detector between them. The range was too long for us to return his fire, so we hugged the earth and waited for the fire to ease up so that we could move and see what was going on.

Sapper Kyles was wearing the container of the detector, which was being riddled with fire as he lay in the cornfield. I told him to wait his chance and then take it off so that he would be a smaller target. He did so, and the LMGs turned to the Infantry, who had by this time started to run back in the direction of our own lines.

We were plastered with mortars, some of which landed only two yards to my left. I called out to my party that I was going to try and get back, with the idea that they would follow.

Hearing voices, both in English and German, all round me, I stopped crawling and weighed up the situation. Deciding to move away from the voices I carried on crawling in the direction from which we had come. I knew that when I reached the end of the field the ground dipped in my favour, and on reaching that I would be reasonably safe. The Germans must have thought that too, because on the last few yards to the edge of the field stood a Hermann Goering paratrooper with a levelled automatic machine gun. His words were: "Stand up, Englander, put up your hands." That, and the fact that all his pals, somewhere around 100, were now completely surrounding us, just about knocked all further resistance on the head.

I was led over to the Infantry Officer, who was kneeling beside one of his privates who had been badly hit.

On reaching the track, up which the Panzer Division was proceeding, in the direction of our lines, I saw that my three other pals were prisoners too. We could not make a break away. Firstly because of the number of tanks in the vicinity and secondly, we had to carry our own wounded Infantry.

On each of the "Tiger" tanks which passed us were up to 30 men armed with LMGs, rifles and automatics.

We had to march all that night and throughout the next day until about 1400 hours. It was a German billet we arrived at where we had a little food and some awful coffee. Transport arrived and took us to a German prison camp at Tunis. After a night's sleep we were interrogated by German officers, presumably Intelligence Service. The only things we told them were name, rank and number, but they informed us as to our Division, Company and Brigade. The one who interviewed me even told me that I had transferred from the North Staffordshire Regt. to the RE. The only way that I know how he did that was by my number.

That evening we were handed over to the Italians, who marched us into a deserted shoe factory. They were civil to us but the food was only just sufficient to exist on: one-quarter of a loaf per 24 hours, one-third of a pint of coffee and a mess tin lid of spaghetti at night and three cigarettes, the like of which are indescribable. This went on for two weeks, during which time more than half of the prisoners were down with dysentery or colic. There were almost 1,000 in all. Medical supplies were scanty and hospitals being all full of English and German wounded very little could be done for these people.

On the afternoon of Saturday 24 April, one of my Sappers, Kyles by name, was taken along with a total of 150 others. We have not had any notification of his whereabouts since. He was quite all right when he left us. We were informed on Wednesday 5 May that some time that evening we would be placed on board a boat bound for Italy. The Italians must have been expecting the attack on Tunis by our forces at any time because they went as far as to say, "It won't be long now before we are in here and you will be outside guarding us."

That night 450 of us were escorted to the docks but an air raid alert was sounded as we reached the docks area. All the Germans and Italians immediately panicked and made haste to get into Tunis centre away from our bombers. It was a remarkable sight to see such chaos among them. We had a good laugh out of it. The lorries we were in were taken down the side roads away from the docks until the raid was over.

Tunis itself was not bombed much but all the docks and harbours were a complete shambles. Our bombers certainly made a good job of work.

Eventually we boarded the ship and at about 0200 hours, two hours after we were scheduled to sail, 250 U.S. prisoners came aboard. At this time, and lasting until about 0400 hours, our bombers were busy over the harbour and prevented us from sailing.

At first light a pilot boat guided us through the harbour and we anchored off Cap Bon to await escort which would arrive that night, 6 May.

A Scout plane (Kittyhawk) saw us and immediately attacked us with bombs and machine gun fire. One bomb hit the fresh water tank. He went away and brought twenty of his pals who proceeded to paste us good and proper. We survived repeated attacks all that day. Towards evening two destroyers who were to be our escort, were spotted by Fortresses who hit and left one blazing while the other turned and ran.

We stayed all night off Cap Bon without further incident, but next day, we were plastered again only this time besides Kittyhawks, our Spitfires and dive-bombers joined in the fun. Strange to relate we had only two direct hits, first down the forward hatch, which was empty, but failed to explode. The second hit a raft, hoisted above the deck near hatch 23, where we were accommodated. It exploded and completely smashed the raft but did not penetrate the top deck.

In the afternoon a German gunner was killed at his post and an American soldier was fatally wounded by cannon shellfire which penetrated through the top deck and exploded in the hold. Total number of casualties was: 6 – two dead and four with flesh wounds. There was plenty of colic and dysentery aboard.

That afternoon the German officer in command of the ship beached us about ¾ mile from shore in 18 foot of water, opposite the village of La Goullette, approximately 7 miles from Tunis (see map 5 on page 56). The near misses of the bombs had made it impossible for the ship to proceed as she was listing to starboard. Leaving one armed Italian aboard, the crew and guard abandoned ship and left us to the mercy of our own bombers. The guard gave himself up and a lieutenant-quartermaster took charge of the ship and hauled down the Italian flag. He also organised parties who put out POW signs and Red crosses on the ship's sides and decks.

During the time the German gun crew were on the ship, they never shirked their duty. They stuck it until their ammunition ran out and one of them was killed at his post.

Our own planes, when they saw us, left us alone as long as there was no movement on deck, but the American Kittyhawks still continued to hammer us.

Night came and 150 sick and wounded were taken ashore on rafts towed by a motor launch belonging to one of the French civilians in the village. The Germans in that district had destroyed all their stores and were waiting for our troops to occupy the place so that they could give themselves up.

It was decided that at first light a recce party should swim ashore and get in touch with both American and British Air Force to stop them attacking us. At approximately 1000 hours, with the help of a Frenchman, contact was made with the RAF to stop strafing us. It was not until nearly 1400 hours that contact was made with the American Air Force. We then hoisted both British and American Flags.

The French motor launch plied back and forth from the beach to the ship, taking 50 ashore at a time. The boat was emptied completely by 2000 hours, Saturday, 8 May.

At that time there were no British troops there, as far as we could see. German lorries with German drivers took us from the shore to a school in the village.

Some time during the evening we found out that a Brigade from the 78th Division had taken over the place. We stayed there a day and a night and were taken by RASC to a place just outside Medjez-El-Bab. The quartermaster there gave us what kit he had and we stayed there two more days. We had to move out so that some few thousand enemy prisoners could take over our billets.

A reception camp was our next billet until Lieut. Boston came for us on the 17 May."

That was a digression. We must now return to the Company, who were still unaware of trouble brewing on our front.

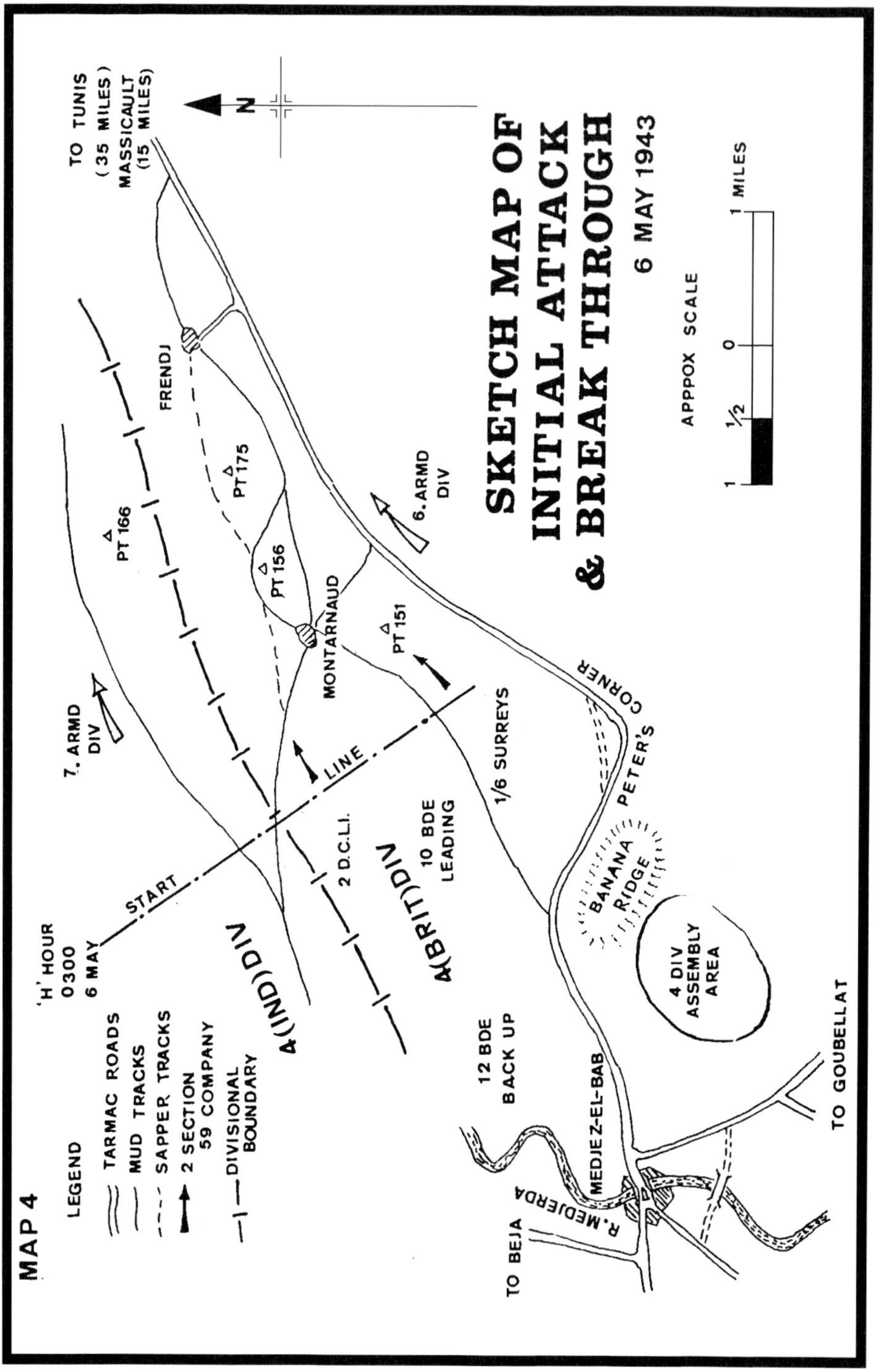

MAP 4
LEGEND
TARMAC ROADS
MUD TRACKS
SAPPER TRACKS
2 SECTION 59 COMPANY
DIVISIONAL BOUNDARY
'H' HOUR 0300 6 MAY
START
LINE
7. ARMD DIV
4 (IND) DIV
2 D.C.L.I.
4 (BRIT) DIV
10 BDE LEADING
1/6 SURREYS
PT 166
PT 175
PT 156
PT 151
FRENDJ
MONTARNAUD
6. ARMD DIV
TO TUNIS (35 MILES)
MASSICAULT (15 MILES)
N
SKETCH MAP OF INITIAL ATTACK & BREAK THROUGH
6 MAY 1943
APPPOX SCALE
1 ½ 0 1 MILES
PETER'S CORNER
BANANA RIDGE
4 DIV ASSEMBLY AREA
12 BDE BACK UP
MEDJEZ-EL-BAB
R. MEDJERDA
TO BEJA
TO GOUBELLAT

# CHAPTER IV

## The Battle for Tunis

Meanwhile Corporal Wootton's misfortune became fortunate for the Division, because a warning of the German attack was radioed back by Lieut. Lehmann to his Battalion headquarters and thence on to Divisional headquarters. This was lucky because an attack was not expected, and the Division would probably have been caught napping. As it was every unit was alerted and the German attack was held; not, however, before the enemy had made considerable inroads into the Division's sector, almost overrunning Divisional headquarters. As soon as we heard the alarm in 59 Field Company; we took up a defensive position with everyone dug in, Bren guns manned at strategic points, and mobile patrols out. Fortunately, perhaps, for us, the main thrust of the attack was to the south of our wadi. We heard and saw it all going on and kept our fingers crossed.

A copy of the German order for this attack operation was found on 11 May by Robert Hutchinson on El-Haouaria airfield at the tip of Cap Bon, left behind by the retreating Germans, and is included as Appendix I on page 165.

The following day, Thursday 22 April, IX Corps of 1st Army – ours being V Corps – mounted a strong attack on the right of our sector, which had the effect of pushing the Germans back, but not beyond "Peter's Corner" which was very strongly held. By now we feared Corporal Wootton and his three sappers must be either killed or in the bag.

It was on this day in the afternoon that we got a message from Divisional HQ to send a Sapper party to blow up, beyond possible recovery, a German Mark VI "Tiger" tank. This was a more difficult task than it sounds because a "Tiger" tank is extremely tough. However Hamilton and Sergeant Atkinson of 1 Section set off with a couple of Sappers and a case of plastic explosive. They found the abandoned tank on the track taken by the Schirmer Group the previous evening; it looked huge, and in good order. They decided to pack the explosive round the outside of the breech mechanism of the 88mm gun inside the turret, to do as much damage as possible.

Hamilton then attached a detonator and a long length of fuse, and closed the lid of the turret They lit the fuse and retreated to a safe distance, and after what seemed a very long wait there was a terrific bang which virtually split open the turret and destroyed everything inside.

Two days later on Saturday 24, 4th Division and 1st Division – which comprised V Corps – attacked in order to keep the Germans occupied. This time 12 Brigade was leading with 225 Field Company and 7 Field Company clearing mines and marking safe tracks. 10 Brigade with 59 Field Company in attendance was in reserve in case they were needed to back up 12 Brigade. But this was not required.

Next day Sunday 25 April was Easter Day, though one would not have known it, for the tempo of preparations and at the same time the business of keeping the Germans guessing was hotting up. 225 and 7 Field Companies were busy lifting mines at "Peter's Corner" which proved to be a real hornets' nest. We had orders to move from our comfortable wadi, our "happy valley", to an area east of "Banana Ridge", which hardly deserved the description "ridge" being only some 25-30ft. above the surrounding plain. It was a dreadfully exposed and draughty area. However on this day for the first time we became aware of the arrival of the 8th Army. We heard their guns away to the south and saw several small recce parties with 8th Army insignia painted on their yellow vehicles, very conspicuous in the green landscape. This was very encouraging. They were in shorts and khaki drill shirts and very weather-beaten and brown, while we were sweating in battle dress and still rather pale.

All the next week fighting continued to keep the enemy's head down while the traffic jams of yellow vehicles of 8th Army mingled with the dark green of 1st Army. To us lowly members of the Division it seemed impossible to cram any more units into the area. We wondered what sort of a battle it was going to be.

"Peter's Corner" was at last captured and Robert Hutchinson with 1/6 Surreys made and marked a wide cleared by-pass on the inside of the bend. Finally on Saturday 1 May 78th Division who had followed our 4th Division into Algiers took over the 4th Division Sector outside "Peter's Corner" to allow the whole Division some respite before the big battle.

For four days the Company was once again all together, resting, checking equipment, and generally getting ready for the battle which we now knew was scheduled to commence on Thursday 6 May at 0300 hours. On Tuesday, wonder of wonders, the Company Quartermaster Sergeant came back from the Division Ordnance park with a lorryload of khaki drill: shorts, long trousers and two shirts per man. Everyone was delighted although it was still decidedly chilly at night. Of course it became the subject of many jokes, the most popular being that it was to confuse the enemy and make him think we were a completely fresh Division, for there was little or no time to sew on the divisional insignia of the red quadrant. We certainly had very white knees compared with 8th Army. It all had the effect of putting the Company into high spirits at quite a good moment.

On Wednesday, the eve of the battle, I had a remarkable surprise. In the afternoon my brother, much older than me, and a regular Gunner colonel in the 8th Army, moved his Regiment of guns into our Sapper area in order to fire his guns on the following day when we moved forward. We had not seen each other since before the war began – he was in Egypt and 8th Army, whilst I, a T.A. soldier, had been to

France and back via Dunkirk, then to Scotland, and on to 1st Army in Algeria. Strange that our paths should cross on the very eve of the last battle in North Africa. He parked his yellow truck close to our Company HQ, complete with its chicken which had come all the way from Egypt and had, so I was assured, laid an egg every other day.

He joined us for supper in our particular hole, as we were still eating off plates and had a reasonable supply of whisky. At midnight he went off to shoot his guns while I went forward to watch my Sappers checking for mines. We did not meet again until after the end of the war.

"H" hour was 0300 and exactly on time the combined artillery of two armies opened fire. It was the most extraordinary and terrifying moment that any of us had ever imagined. It made one feel extremely small and vulnerable and at first one was gripped with an overwhelming desire to creep under a stone. But this very quickly passed and was replaced by an exhilaration and excitement at being part of something so big and important.

At this point I am going to hand over to Peter Boston who wrote this account of the night's happenings on his return to the company, two days later when it was all over.

"An account of the activities of 2 Section of 59th Field Company in support of the 1/6 Surreys and the 2/DCLI Bns who led the attack of the 4th Division on the morning of 6 May 1943 which ultimately led to the capture of Tunis and the surrender of the Axis Forces in North Africa. This account was written by Lieut. P. S. Boston, RE, who was the Section Officer immediately after the battle. To follow this account, see map 4 on page 46.

This account deals with the activities of 2 Section, 59 Field Company, in the attack in the Montarnaud Sector on the night 5/6 May 1943. For the attack the Section was split into two halves, two Sub-sections going with each of the two forward Battalions; who were the 2 DCLI on the left and the 1/6 Surreys on the right. 1 and 3 Sub-sections accompanied the DCLI and 2 and 4 went with the Surreys, the task of each party being to make and mark, where necessary, a passage for the carriers, and to undertake any RE work necessary to assist the advance. Each party had with it one 15cwt truck loaded with mine clearing stores, pole charges, and made up charges for demolition of immobilised tanks. The men themselves carried picks and shovels as well as rifles and moved on foot, one Sub-section with each forward company of each battalion.

It was anticipated that the tracks would be pitted with small craters as a result of the barrage.

I myself was to travel with the battalion HQ of the Surreys with my Recce Sergeant, Batman and PU (Personal Utility) Wireless truck and a DR (Dispatch Rider) for use in case wireless communication was for some reason impossible.

The Section, organised as above, reported to the Battalions concerned at 1900 hours on 5 May and moved up on foot to the Start Line in stages with long halts, which were very chilly as we were all wearing KD (khaki drill) for the first time. Lying in the damp grass we could hear intermittent gunfire from the direction of Point 156 to the North, and from the Peter's Corner area to the South; also an occasional cry of dismay when a thin pair of KD trousers was pierced by the ubiquitous thistle.

At about midnight a solitary plane dropped a cluster of flares about half a mile away and we all stood looking at our boots for about five minutes, feeling absurdly conspicuous. The plane faded into silence and then suddenly returned and dropped a bomb which we afterwards discovered was on the edge of the village of Montarnaud, our objective.

At a point about one mile behind the start line all DRs were made to dismount as a precaution against noise and Sapper Briggs was left pushing his motorcycle uphill with the aid of the Reserve Wireless Operator. He was not seen again for twelve hours, as he was subsequently stopped on the route by a traffic control and not allowed to proceed even after the barrage had begun. By the time he did get through nobody was able to tell him where the Surreys had got to. They had taken a different track from that originally stated.

The Barrage was due to begin at 0300 hours on the 6 May. It was difficult to say at what precise moment the noise started, but we all suddenly realised that the curtain was up, and we began to amble forward very apathetically, grinning to each other at the thought of the enemy's discomfort. The whole valley ahead of us sparkled with the flashes of exploding shells, and all the horizon trembled with a continuous thunder, which popped and bubbled like a domestic hot water system on the boil. Superimposed on this was the hiss and sharp crack of twenty-five pounder shells passing close overhead. At least, most of them passed overhead. Some of them most certainly did not, and I noticed at least two explode a bare twenty yards away. One of these was followed by a shout of pain from the darkness and much rather belated ducking by most of those in the vicinity.

Seeing that the PU was not up with Battalion HQ transport I sent my Sergeant back up the track to hurry it up. Meantime my batman and I followed on with Battalion HQ

About this time, 0320 hours, the Gunners put down a lot of smoke as a signal that the barrage was about to lift forward. As a result of the smoke everybody was completely blinded, visibility being cut down to about 20ft. This gave the effect, together with the effects of some of our own shells falling short, and a few near misses from German shells and mortar bombs, of shells apparently coming from every direction. It was now discovered that Battalion HQ was in advance of the leading companies; and also rather close on the heels of the barrage. A halt was therefore called to allow the companies to regain their position and direction. This latter need never have been lost as it was, even in the smoke, quite easy to see three stars just to the right of Cassiopoeia which marked the direction of the objective.

Taking advantage of this halt, I decided to go back along the track to look for my Sergeant and the truck which had not yet arrived. I was afraid they might have got lost in the smoke. I did find them about 500 yards back where they were held up behind some six-pounder guns which were blocking the track. However, by dint of some forcible language and rather reprehensible "cutting in" we got the PU and the tool truck through: but Battalion HQ was no longer where I had left them. All we found was a fork in the track and a horse standing petrified and paralysed with fear, but miraculously not wounded by the barrage. We could also see a fire which at first seemed about half a mile away, but soon manifested itself as a burning house one hundred yards away. We were entering Montarnaud.

Knowing that Battalion HQ had intended skirting to the right of the village I took the right-hand track, having first verified, by going down on hands and knees for a minute examination of the ground in proverbial Sherlock Holmes fashion, that carriers had recently used the track. This precaution was suggested by the fact that I had seen a minefield trace showing blocks of Tellermines in Montarnaud.

It was now about 0430 hours and just beginning to get lighter. We could just make out the silhouette of troops on the skyline of Hill 156, which was the first objective of the Surreys and half a mile beyond, that is to say east of, Montarnaud. I looked in vain for the silhouettes of Battalion HQ vehicles. While we were deliberating whether we had taken the right track, a burst of machine gun fire from the forward slope of Hill 156 came rather close, and I thought our best plan was to close up on the leading infantry and the barrage, at all costs so that we should pass any enemy survivors before they could find their feet again. So we cocked our tommy guns and drove in considerable haste up the track which skirted the right-hand slope of Hill 156. No sooner did we reach the Hill than I saw Battalion HQ transport over to our left on the other track. I told my Sergeant to get the two trucks round on to the other track somehow, while my batman and I went across country on foot. (See map 4 on page 46.)

We had not gone fifty yards when we were attracted by a figure running frantically towards us from the top of the Hill, his hands high in the air, uttering repeated cries of *"Kamerad"*. As he arrived, breathless, I searched him to ensure that he had no weapons on him. But I merely had to make a move towards his pocket and he flung out the contents for me with all possible speed. He was obviously badly shaken. He had a respirator container which, in proverbial British fashion, was found to contain all manner of personal effects but no respirator. The only article which he refused to part with, and which I did not insist on having, was a large wad of toilet paper, the function of which he made doubly plain by repeated and spirited demonstrations. My batman and I marched him off in front of us to Battalion HQ where we handed him over to an infantryman who was already marching off half a dozen other prisoners.

Having found Battalion HQ again and a passable route to it for my truck I went back to where I had left my truck to try and bring it across, if it had not already gone back. Half way there my batman suddenly became extremely cautious and started stalking round a clump of shrubbery like a poacher. I was about to assure him that there was no need for his crouching posture, when I heard him shout, "Out you come," and saw two Germans emerge from below ground. They spoke English very well and had a machine gun on the front of their trench. Judging by the position I considered it certain that they were the men who had fired at us previously and on my truck. There was also a third German, very badly wounded, who was imploring for water and appeared on the point of death. Unfortunately our water bottles were on the truck and, in any case we had no time for unnecessary delays as it was essential that I should get my truck to Battalion HQ in case there was any important information or work requiring attention. Furthermore the gathering light had brought with it a stream of tracer bullets which came intermittently very low over the Hill, at times very close. These two extra prisoners were themselves the cause of considerable delay as one could only walk very slowly and it took us three or four minutes to get them off our hands. Some of the tracer must have been 88mm ammunition judging by its size and the way it bounced from hill to hill like tennis balls.

By the time we got the prisoners off our hands, and had picked up off the ground a large and aggressive portrait of the Fuehrer and a German set of technical instruction on some sort of rocket mortar, the Infantry were at their second objective, Hill 175, which was about half a mile beyond Hill 156 and from the top of which the Union Jack was already flying. The time was now approximately 0600 hours so that the attack, in spite of the confusion caused by the smoke, had gone pretty well to time.

I set out on foot, my truck not yet being available, up to Battalion HQ with my batman plodding along behind me no doubt cursing my long legs. But I could not wait for him. As I walked up to Hill 175 the familiar clatter of Churchill tanks was heard on all sides and the objective was soon surrounded by them, and very welcome they were as moral support to help in consolidating the objective. One of them was almost immediately hit by a 105 mm shell and burned for the rest of the day.

On arriving on top of Hill 175, which was the final objective for the Surreys, I eventually found the CO of the Surreys and found that he had no job which he wished me to do. Slit trenches were available, having previously been dug by the Germans, so the task of digging in was facilitated. Having discovered members of the Sub-section which had been with the Surreys, and having ascertained that they were all present and in high spirits, I went back again to find my truck. This I found at just the spot where we had previously lost Battalion HQ. It had not been able to get on to the other track owing to the passage of Churchill tanks and was stuck while endeavouring to cross a ploughed field. With the truck we also found stragglers from Sub-sections who had got separated from their mates in the smoke.

Remembering the minefield trace, and seeing a notice saying *"Achtung Minen"* on the junction I organised these men into a mine-detecting party and searched the area. No mines were discovered at all, so it seems that the information on which the minefield trace was based was incorrect. However, the notice implied that there were mines in the vicinity so we erected some "Mines in Verges" notices to be on the safe side. At this moment a party from 225 Field Company arrived to sweep for mines the track leading south from Montarnaud. I told them the only information I had was that there were minefields actually in Montarnaud but not around it. I also said that we had swept 50 yards down the road and found nothing. I had not swept the verges.

While the sweeping was in progress I sent back information over the wireless to my Company Commander, giving my present location, the fact that we were investigating a supposed minefield, and that no other Sapper work had been encountered up to this point. Interference was so bad – heavy firing was going on all round – that this process took about half an hour, as every sentence had to be repeated three times each way, one phrase at a time.

As soon as the sweeping for mines was complete we snatched a bite of our very thick and stale sandwiches, removed our long trousers and changed them for short ones, and then returned to the vicinity of Battalion HQ to collect all that we could find of the Section. It was now about 0800 hours and 12 Brigade, who had passed through us after capturing Hill 175, had now established themselves on their own objective a mile or so further forward.

The Surreys appeared to have suffered practically no casualties, and those that were missing from our own Sections I had since brought up with me in the truck.

We were now very tired, sweaty and hungry, and it felt more like tea than breakfast time. I told the chaps to try and find a tin to brew up some tea while I went over the hill, a quarter of a mile on our left, to try and find and bring back if possible the two Sub-sections who had been working with the DCLI. I found "B" Company of the DCLI very easily; they directed me to "A" Company who in turn directed me to "D" Company. But none of them could direct me to their own Battalion HQ – with the exception of "D" Company who pointed "Battalion HQ" out to me about a quarter of a mile away across a field of four foot high corn. On arriving at the place to which I had been directed I found that there were no DCLI in that area at all but only a few Gunners.

I had by this time walked about two miles through the corn and had found nothing but growing fatigue and an appetite for the ears of corn. I therefore decided to return to Hill 175 knowing that the party with the DCLI would know that the Surreys were immediately on their right and would return as soon as the DCLI had no further work for them.

They eventually returned that afternoon. Meanwhile the rest of the Company came up to the area where we were and established itself in that location. No further work was forthcoming that day as the Surreys had reached, and were merely holding, their objective while the attack went across the plain ahead of them. The only excitement was a spell of heavy shelling which fell accurately on the top of Hill 175, exactly where the Surreys were dug in, round about 1,500, forcing them to move further down from the top of the hill, and causing far more casualties than had been incurred during the battle.

The actions of the various Sub-sections during the attack were as detailed below.

1 and 3 Sub-sections followed the track which formed the left-hand boundary of the DCLI advance. As they would have to come back to their truck for tools in the event of any Sapper work cropping up, it was decided to keep them with their truck all the time, having only a representative of each with the forward company commander to give advice and form an opinion of the men and tools required for any jobs.

The formation adopted for the advance was:– The carriers advancing along the track preceded by the Sappers, level with whom were the leading platoons of the forward Companies. In the smoke however the forward Companies became a little less forward and furthermore, became intermingled and confused. The result was that the Sappers led the attack without at the time realising it, and were actually the first troops onto the objective.

The only Sapper work they had to do arose when a track marked on the map could not be found on the ground and Sergeant Cox, who was in charge of the two

Sub-sections, was informed that what was actually a "T" junction should be a Cross Roads. He therefore decided to make it a Cross Roads and set about sweeping and marking the missing track for a distance of two hundred yards. This led the carriers up to the objective. The first troops to arrive on this objective, after the Sappers and carriers, were not the DCLI but the 6th Black Watch of 12 Brigade who were due to follow through the DCLI when the latter had captured their objective. When the DCLI did arrive they were subjected to heavy mortar fire, but the arrival of the Churchills was timed right and the DCLI were able to consolidate the objective properly. Immediately on the left of the track up which the Sub-section advanced was the 4th Indian Division with whom the recognition password was very incongruously "Canteen".

2 Sub-section advanced with "C" Company of the 1/6 Surreys. No Sapper work was encountered at all. The track along which the Surreys advanced was clear of mines and obstructions and was of passable surface. As stiff resistance was met with on the first objective, from a machine gun post, in an Arab Settlement, the Sub-section laid down its picks and shovels, fixed bayonets and with the aid of the bren gun, and a very spirited attack, helped the Company of Surreys to overcome all resistance.

They then advanced with the Surreys to the second objective, Hill 175, and dug in. It was there that I later found them. Their co-operation in the attack on the first objective was appreciated and praised by the Commanding officer of the Surreys. (The picks and shovels were subsequently recovered, with the addition of 15 brand new German shovels.) Sub-section advanced with "A" Company of the Surreys. No Sapper work was encountered. The Sub-Section advanced behind Company HQ throughout and no work was necessary, nor were they called upon to give assistance in the Infantry capacity. At the end of the attack the Section was all present, no injuries, tired, dirty, full of thistle thorns but in excellent spirits."

Next day, Friday 7 May, the Company moved to Massicault and was rejoined by Peter Boston and 2 Section. I received warm thanks and congratulations from the Battalion Commander of the Surreys for the spirited assistance given to his "C" Company in gaining their first and vital objective. Also Robert Hutchinson returned from his attachment to the Recce Regiment who had been the first troops into Tunis. Robert himself had been with the leading tanks into Tunis at 1700 hours that afternoon: a city *"en fete"* with joyful crowds lining the streets.

Next day we moved again to Mohamedia and established ourselves on a hill overlooking Tunis and the sea: what a glad sight. Mohamedia was one large farm, incredibly scruffy and swarming with flies. They formed dense clouds round the cook-house and wherever there was food. Peter swears he counted no less than 22 of them on a forkful of mashed potato about to enter his mouth. Fortunately we only stayed there one day and were glad to move on. (See map 5 on page 56.)

To all intents and purposes the North African Campaign was over. To some, especially of the 8th Army who had fought all the way from Alamein, it must have seemed somewhat of an anticlimax. After all, the combined might of General

Montgomery with his 8th Army and General Alexander with 1st Army made a formidable adversary who by sheer weight of men and armour were almost bound to win. For us, however, it was not completely over, for the German "Afrika Korps" had retreated to the Cap Bon peninsula, probably 100,000 strong, and must be rounded up. Although demoralised and without Rommel, they still constituted a distinct threat. Cap Bon was the next objective.

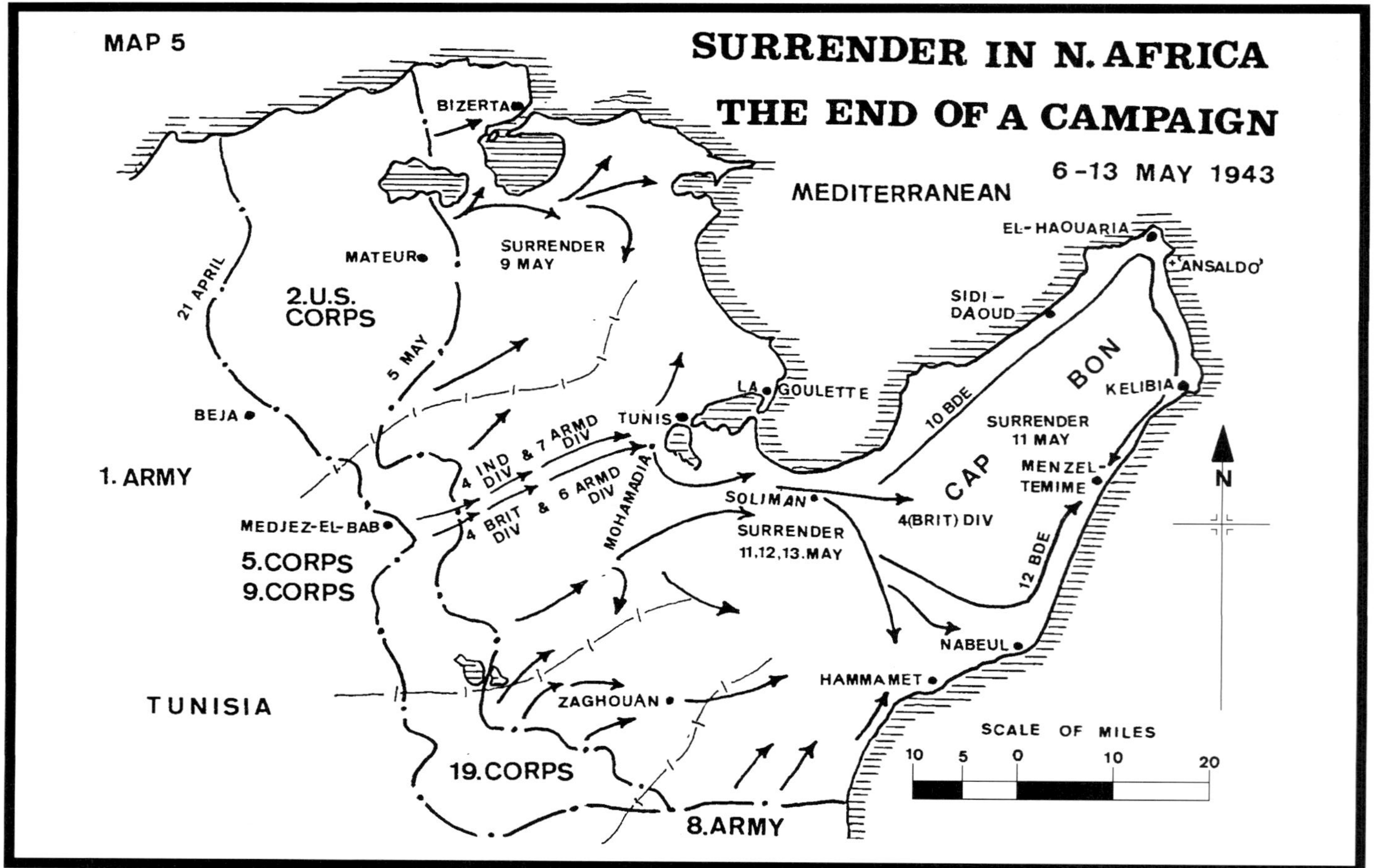
MAP 5
SURRENDER IN N. AFRICA
THE END OF A CAMPAIGN
6-13 MAY 1943
MEDITERRANEAN
BIZERTA
MATEUR
SURRENDER 9 MAY
2.U.S. CORPS
21 APRIL
5 MAY
BEJA
1. ARMY
MEDJEZ-EL-BAB
5.CORPS
9.CORPS
4 IND & 7 ARMD DIV
4 BRIT & 6 ARMD DIV
MOHAMADIA
TUNIS
LA GOULETTE
SOLIMAN
SURRENDER 11,12,13.MAY
4(BRIT) DIV
10 BDE
12 BDE
CAP BON
SURRENDER 11 MAY
EL-HAOUARIA
'ANSALDO'
SIDI-DAOUD
KELIBIA
MENZEL-TEMIME
NABEUL
HAMMAMET
ZAGHOUAN
TUNISIA
19.CORPS
8.ARMY
N
SCALE OF MILES
10 5 0 10 20

# CHAPTER V

## Tunisia – Cap Bon

The race to encircle Cap Bon was on, just in case the Germans were thinking of staging a "Dunkirk", for they had an excellent airfield at the northernmost point of Cap Bon peninsula at El-Haouaria and there were plenty of fine sandy beaches from which troops could be evacuated. At Kelibia there was even a small port.

The job of encircling the peninsula was given to 4th Division on Monday 10 May to start as soon as possible. There was only one road round the peninsula, with a transverse road across the base from Tunis to Hammamet. None of these roads was tarmaced, which meant they could easily be mined and were in fact very dusty. There were almost no tracks at all across the peninsula, which had a mountainous spine. 10 Brigade were to encircle left-handed round the west and north coasts, while 12 Brigade encircled across the base to Hammamet and up the east coast to Kelibia. In fact the two columns met half way up the east coast at Menzel-Temime at about 1500 hours in the afternoon of the next day, Tuesday 11 May.

On the morning of Monday 10 May, having had just one day, Sunday, to rest and sort ourselves out at Mohamedia, the Company, less Robert Hutchinson and his 3 Section who were already up with the leading infantry, followed 10 Brigade H.Q. and set up a temporary camp at Soliman. This was where the west coast road branched off the Hammamet road. From here it was possible to send up additional Sappers or equipment as might be required by the advancing column.

It was a race against time and very exciting. 3 Section with Robert Hutchinson was in support of the 1/6 Surreys, who led the 10 Brigade column. There was very little resistance on the west coast and no mines laid in the road, so advance was rapid. More and rather sporadic resistance was met by 12 Brigade but it was ill-organised and easily overcome. Advance on both roads continued all night, and in the early hours of Tuesday morning, 11 May, the main body of the enemy was completely surprised and surrounded. By 1100 hours 12 Brigade had taken some 7,000 prisoners on their route.

Meanwhile 10 Brigade, led by the Bren Gun carriers of the 1/6 Surreys with Robert Hutchinson and his Sappers, pushed steadily on through the night to reach El-Haouaria airfield at dawn. There were large groups of Germans and their vehicles apparently waiting in hopes of relief aircraft; but none came. There were several burnt-out ME 109 bombers and a great amount of equipment which had presumably been bombed by us. So fast had been our advance that the Germans were completely taken by surprise. About 5,000 of them were rounded up on the airfield, and they calmly sat down to await their fate. A reserve battalion was quickly detailed to look after them.

It was upon reaching El-Haouaria airfield in the early morning that Robert came across the German briefcase, carelessly cast aside, which contained the operation order for the attack on 4th Division at Medjez-El-Bab, code named "Lilac Blossom" (in German), previously described by Corporal Wootton. Robert, being a salesman, could speak German and was able to recognise the significance of the document.

By the evening of 13 May some 51,000 prisoners had been rounded up in Cap Bon. The whole operation from commencement at Soliman to joining up at Menzel-Temime took just 27 hours, during which the leading units had covered over 100 miles. It was by any standard a remarkable achievement, although by then the once-proud "Afrika Korps" had become a thoroughly demoralised crowd. The sequence of surrender can be seen on map 5 on page 56.

The GOC 4th Division, Major General JLI. Hawksworth, CBE, sent a message to all units of 10 Brigade saying:–

> "Well done all ranks of 10th Infantry Brigade and attached. You have won Cap Bon stakes by several lengths.
>
> In the Field, 12 May 1943"

On Wednesday 12 May the Company moved to Kelibia on the north-east tip of Cap Bon. On that day I drove with my batman Rodgers and driver Sullivan completely round the peninsula, a wonderfully exhilarating drive of 100 miles. All resistance had ceased and it was quite safe to drive alone. The North African Campaign was now definitely over and all that remained to be done was to clean up the peninsula and get rid of all the German prisoners back to makeshift POW camps at Tunis. There was however an enormous amount of equipment, guns, vehicles, and dumps of all sorts to be cleared.

For Rodgers the drive was like a day out to Margate and for Sullivan it was at last a pleasant drive into the country. The two of them chatted away enthralled by the sunny countryside and everywhere signs of a dejected and beaten enemy. We stopped for a picnic in some olive groves overlooking the sea. While Rodgers and Sullivan busied themselves brewing tea, I climbed a little hill to get a better view of the coast. It was just possible to see the white houses of Tunis on the horizon, twenty miles or so to the west. After our picnic we drove on through Soliman across the base of the peninsula and back up the east coast to Kelibia.

Kelibia was a pleasant little seaside town facing east with a small port, a magnificent ruined castle standing guard above its beautiful sandy beaches, and a rocky cliff rising up behind the town giving it shelter from the north and west. Peter Boston's sketch from our camp site gives a good impression of it. It was a very hot

*Kelibia, May 1943.*

little town. Our camp was on the south of the town facing due east in an old olive grove giving right onto the beach. Between our olive grove and the road was a field of sweetcorn just beginning to ripen and irrigated by channels of fresh water.

The old olive trees gave us quite a lot of shade. For the Sappers it was a seventh heaven, with plenty of fresh water for washing and the sea to bathe in after a day's work. But work there was to do in plenty, though of a very different nature to the fighting role we had pursued up to now. For the next few months we were to live a very different sort of life, but nevertheless one of many surprises.

On Sunday morning 16 May a thanksgiving service was held at Brigade Headquarters at Kelibia to which all units of 10 Brigade sent detachments. It was an extraordinarily nice, simple service, just a hollow square of men on the sand with old olive trees all round, the sea beyond, and the padre in the centre.

On this day, 16 May, censorship was lifted and all ranks were permitted to write home and tell their families all that they wanted to of what they had seen and done since arriving in North Africa. I too wrote home at considerable length and quote just a few paragraphs.

First of the surrender:

"I have never witnessed such a scene, streams of German soldiers all driving their own trucks back to Tunis waving white flags. It was an absolute and complete collapse such as we never dreamed possible for they have left a tremendous quantity of ammunition and food and could have held out for weeks. But their leaders had fled. Then came the marching column, 10,000 in one day alone. The day before yesterday we discovered an almost perfect airfield (El Haouaria) with 20 great big Junkers troop carriers all destroyed by being driven into each other – why didn't they fly them away? Many prisoners said they had waited on that airfield for days for the planes to take them away, but they never came – thanks to the RAF. A bitter disappointment for the crack Hermann Goering Jaeger Division who had successfully held us up at 'Peter's Corner' before the final battle."

Of the Company's camp I wrote:

"This is a quite delightful spot under the shade of old olive trees with a field of yellow corn between us and the shore of silver sand and deep clear water. What could be pleasanter for refitting and reorganising the Company. The men are all very happy especially this afternoon. There is an old Arab in flowing robe and red hat ploughing just beyond my tent with a camel and a bent log – at least that is what it looks like. He has been at it all day. The towns are all white and the houses vaulted. They look cool and nice from a distance but actually stink to high heaven. There is a little mosque that rings a bell for morning and evening prayers. It is all very lazy and sleepy. I wonder how long we shall stay here a week perhaps, no longer."

I then described a normal working day:

"It starts at 0600 hours with "Stand To" parade when every man in the Company gets up, goes on parade dressed with rifle, steel helmet and ammunition – an old custom but a very good one. Breakfast at 0700 hours and at 0800 hours work starts. I usually start by doing a bit of office work or an inspection. Then I go out in my truck visiting the Sections to see what they are doing. This invariably results in a chase to the CRE or Brigade HQ or Division HQ for information or stores or something.

We get all sorts of dumps of mines, unexploded bombs, cratered roads and weak bridges reported, and they always need investigation. So I go and have a look and rush back to get some men onto the job. Sometimes I get back for lunch but more often take it with me. Back for tea at 1630-1700 hours. if possible. Then the usual arrangements for tomorrow's work, daily orders, etc. Evening "Stand To" parade at 1900 hours. Then supper, our big meal, and then the BBC news at 2000 hours

After that I look at the day's post of intelligence summaries, messages, etc., and flop into bed at 2100 hours when it is pitch dark, too dark to see the earwings. There are thousands here and they get into everything. I'm sure there are lots in my pyjamas and in my bed but by 2100 or 2200 hours I really don't care. Such is a normal sort of day, the only difference in battle being that I live in my truck either at Brigade HQ or with the CRE and the days are awfully apt to go on for 24 hours. Of all the aspects of this sort of life the one that I enjoy most is our lack of possessions. I virtually live in my truck and can reach for anything I need."

A final paragraph to this letter read:

"Just received a message from Brigade. They have found a complete German "Mobile Bath Unit". Will 59 Company run it for the Brigade? Of course we will but I must go and have a look at it first."

And there my letter of 16 May ended.

The next celebration was on Thursday 20 May when a victory parade was organised in Tunis. Robert attended with twenty of his Sappers; everyone else was simply too busy. However on Wednesday 2 June, when some of the pressure of work had relaxed, the whole Company together with many other units of 4 Division lined the road from Tunis to Grombalia (see map 1 on page 14) to cheer Prime Minister Churchill as he was driven slowly by with Generals Montgomery and Alexander sitting beside him in the open car.

That was quite a thrill, the only snag being that it was a very hot day and we were on the north side of the route facing the sun. We still only had berets which gave little protection, with the result that most of us had headaches at the end of the day. This led to my purchasing about 200 straw hats in Tunis, and obtaining official agreement to allow all ranks to wear them at work. At first it was hailed as a great joke but actually avoided headaches and heat stroke. Later on we were issued with floppy hats which made a huge difference.

About this time I was instructed to make arrangements for disposal of a number of unexploded bombs in Kelibia town. I gave this task to Peter Boston and the following quotation is from his report on the mission:

"I received my instructions with interest, since none of us had had any bomb disposal training. We were, however, fairly experienced now in mine detection and lifting and I felt that we ought to be able to get by with cool heads and common sense. I chose Corporal Irons to go with me, since he was an unflappable character with a good pair of hands for mechanical problems. We were provided with an Arab guide, who had a smattering of French, to show us where the bombs were and we set off in a 30cwt truck.

We had not been into the town before and it rapidly became apparent that most of the streets were far too narrow to admit the truck, so we parked it and continued on foot, walking along a narrow alley between whitewashed plastered buildings. Eventually our guide turned in through a small doorway and we found ourselves in a sort of room full of hens and goats, with an earth floor thickly covered with straw and dung of various sorts.

A further archway led out of this into a small open yard where the bomb was lying. It appeared not to have fallen on its nose but on its side and a large chunk of metal had broken away to reveal the solid core of yellow explosive. I suppose the bomb was originally of about 100lb. capacity but by now it weighed somewhat less since the interior was occupied by three hens who were pecking away at the explosive with rather ruminative expressions, as if trying to convince themselves that they had really acquired the taste.

At this point the owner of the house emerged from another doorway in the yard and asked us to come in. We stepped in and found, to our astonishment, an absolutely immaculate cool room inside, with walls and ceiling of the purest whitewash, beautiful rugs on the earth floor, which was as spotlessly clean as an operating table. Round the walls stood priceless carved and painted wooden cupboards. Not a fly was in sight, surprisingly, in view of the farmyard conditions outside. We subsequently observed that this was the normal pattern of these little town houses – one entered from the street through the animal quarters and graduated to greater and astonishing purity within. I felt I ought to remove my boots.

We drank tea from delicate handle-less cups and then proceeded to business. We picked up the remains of the bomb with careful hands and staggered down the street with it to where we had left the truck, placing it gingerly inside, and went off to find the next one, which turned out to be a considerably more alarming errand.

The bomb proved to be of similar size, but intact, and was lying in a similar backyard, which this time also contained a donkey. The owner of the house was a muscular little man and when we had been introduced and explained our business, he suddenly bent down and lifted up the bomb, and, before we were aware of what was happening, placed it across the back of the donkey and kicked the unfortunate animals' back legs vigorously so that it broke into a trot. The donkey careered out through the farm quarters and on into the street with the owner clinging precariously to the tail of the bomb as it lurched alarmingly from side to side, while its nose narrowly missed collision with the jamb of the outer arch. Irons and I were convinced it was going to fall off and land on its nose and perhaps, on this second attempt, the detonation mechanism would operate.

I suspect that we both had a craven impulse to take cover from the impending explosion, but duty called and we ran down the narrow street with our hearts in our mouths, endeavouring to steady the thing while the donkey galloped its capricious and sinuous course along the narrow alley and in and out of various startled spectators. How we reached the truck without the bomb falling off remains an astonishing mystery.

Luckily all the bombs that we were shown were lying on the surface, so that we did not have to perform any tricky excavations.

Eventually we had collected a haul of bombs weighing a little over a ton, which we laid carefully in the truck side by side in such a way as to keep their noses from accidental contact and drove back to our lines with the most extreme caution.

We decided to unload them in a little deep wadi near the beach, where the whole lot could be safely detonated. We placed a 5lb. detonating charge on top, wired up with cordtex and a longish fuse and, having roped in a few members of the Section to act as distant sentries, lit the fuse and retired to a safe distance. Before doing so, we had, of course, observed the landscape and established that no one was in sight.

Nevertheless, when the fuse had about another three minutes to burn, I was horrified to see an Arab on a camel suddenly appear out of a little clump of trees, ambling unconcernedly towards the wadi. I ran towards him, shouting at him in French, "Explosif – danger de mort!" and similar fatuous phrases but, apart from hurling what sounded like voluble Arabic abuse at me, he took no notice and continued on his way. I could think of nothing more to do than to fire a shot across his bows from the captured Schmeisser sub-machine gun which was now my personal armoury. This stopped him for a moment only; with redoubled abuse he urged his camel on and at that moment the earth was rent asunder. The camel showed an astonishing ability to "turn on a sixpence" and disappeared like lightning in the direction from which it had come, leaving its rider on the ground. He got up unharmed, and disappeared with commendable agility in pursuit of his mount. I trust that, in retrospect, he realised that I had been acting in his best interests, and that he came to forgive me for my aggressive lack of hospitality."

On 15 June, John Barnikel was appointed Adjutant of 4th Division Engineers, under Lieut.Colonel Pat Foley. He was a great loss to the Company but it was a truly well deserved promotion, for Barney was a very good organiser. His place as Second-in-Command of 59 Company was taken by Hamilton, who was promoted to Captain. This meant that temporarily 1 Section was without an officer, so Sgt. Atkinson now took command.

Later on, on Friday 18 June, the whole Company was called upon again to help line the same Grombalia road with other units of 4 Division for a visit of H.M. the King. This was a great honour and a much more enjoyable day than the earlier occasion.

On Monday 17 May Corporal Wootton and his Sappers Vines and Cartmell were fetched home by Peter Boston after four weeks in enemy hands, a cause of great rejoicing in 2 Section.

Meanwhile, I was asked by Brigade HQ to investigate a ship beached in a cove near El-Haouaria point. This sounded interesting, so I set off with driver Sullivan and batman Rodgers to find it. (See map 5 on page 56.)

The ship turned out to be a small Italian coasting steamer commandeered by the Germans and apparently sunk in the middle of a most beautiful sandy cove, very reminiscent of Cornwall, a mile or so from the road and approached through sandhills and marram grass. We suddenly came upon a perfect horseshoe cove of golden sand and blue sea. The ship was about 100 yards off-shore with the sea just lapping the deck. Sullivan and I stripped off and swam out to her, leaving Rodgers to guard our clothes against any roving Arabs. The ship was lying on an even keel in about 18ft. of water so clear that one could easily see the bottom. Her name was *"Ansaldo"*. Once on board we moved about very cautiously just in case of a booby trap or trip wire. The bridge, which was quite small, like a fishing boat, appeared to have been abandoned in a hurry; a chart, set-square and pencils were lying on a bench under the windows as if the skipper, who I'm sure was a German, had been trying to locate his position at the moment of departure. The little set-square is on my desk to this day.

But why the sudden departure and sinking of the vessel? We couldn't find any reason, no signs of it having been bombed or strafed from the air. She must have been scuttled, but why? Perhaps her master and crew preferred the thought of an Allied POW camp to the possibility of a watery grave if she had ventured out to sea again.

However, our instructions were to investigate. We found a hatch cover just being lapped by the sea, and managed to open it – carefully. To our surprise and slight consternation we found the hold was packed full of new German Mark II Tellermines; what a splendid explosion there might have been if only the crew had booby-trapped the hatch cover. I still tremble to think of it.

We swam ashore and back to our clothes, greatly refreshed after a lovely bathe, and returned to Kelibia to report. We were later instructed to clear the ship of the Tellermines – which was rather unexpectedly deemed a Sapper task because the Ordnance Corps were too busy elsewhere, so Robert and his 3 Section did this over the next few days and thoroughly enjoyed it.

This is perhaps a suitable place to say something about these characters – my batman Rodgers, driver Sullivan, and our Officers' Mess cook, Corporal Parry, as we shall hear more about all three as time goes on.

Rodgers was a "Londoner", a regular soldier of some years' service and a married man. He was an excellent batman and a real handyman. The batman's job is that of a discreet servant whose object is to assist his officer with the chores of life, leaving the officer free to concentrate on his job of leadership. In practice a good batman will pitch his officer's tent, pack up and unpack, do his laundry, mending, and generally be on hand. All of which Rodgers loved doing and prided himself on making sure that I was always properly turned out. He must have been a wonderful husband. Unless we were out on a detachment he worked in the Officers' Mess, helping our cook, Corporal Parry, with whom he got on extremely well.

Driver Sullivan was not a regular soldier. He was called up after the war started and because he had been working for a civil engineering contractor he was posted to the Royal Engineers. He was young and intelligent, and thinking it might be of use to him, he did a drivers' course. He was posted to 59 Field Company just before we left Kirkcudbright for overseas, when our numbers were being made up to strength, and because he seemed a likely lad the CSM suggested he be the OC's driver. I liked him because he was always cheerful and he kept his vehicle, whatever it might be, in excellent order. We never ran out of petrol nor did we ever break down – his life would not have been worth living if we had. He loved driving and was good at map reading – he could find his way anywhere and, strangely enough, got on pretty well with Rodgers although they were such very different types. He would have made a brilliant Rally driver; I wonder if he ever has done any.

Corporal Parry was a Welshman, a slate quarry man from the remote village of Deiniolen in North Wales. When the demand for slates fell away in the 1930s, Parry joined up in the Royal Engineers because he understood and was accustomed to explosives. When asked what he wanted to do he replied, "I'd like to be a cook", thinking that would be the safest line to take. He did a catering course and was posted, much to his surprise, to an active field company – 59 Company in 4th Division – and found himself the Officers' Mess cook. He was a gentle, quietly spoken, man with a soft Welsh accent only too anxious to please. He thoroughly believed in the old-fashioned concept of Service. As my home was in North Wales too we had this in common. During the long slog up the leg of Italy Corporal Parry served us wonderfully well, providing hot food and tea at all hours of the day and night.

During these days Hamilton, who had not yet taken over as Second-in-Command, and his 1 Section were wholly engaged in clearing up El-Haouaria airfield, filling in bomb craters and making good the runways for our planes to use, and also rehabilitating the control tower to some semblance of order. For this job we had borrowed a bulldozer and driver from 18 Field Park Company. He was under great pressure to complete this job as quickly as possible for the RAF to move in and as an insurance against enemy raids from Sicily only 100 miles away. In fact the Germans did make a lightning raid on June 10 and dropped eight large bombs on Kelibia.

Peter with his 2 Section was instructed to build a bypass round Kelibia village. He too was under pressure to complete a passable road as Kelibia with its narrow streets, always full of donkeys, camels and goats, was in a state of constant traffic jam.

My next assignment was to investigate an apparently deserted sardine factory at Sidi-Daoud on the north-east coast of Cap Bon, not far from El-Haouaria airfield. The smell of hot sardine oil was almost overpowering at quite a distance, as the weather was now real Mediterranean summer heat. Again it was a nice little Italian factory built at the head of a rocky creek, not at all unlike many a tiny harbour on the north coast of Cornwall and, again, completely deserted. However on this occasion it had clearly been bombed and strafed by our planes.

However, what immediately caught my eye was a remarkably English looking open rowing boat or cutter for eight oars, and completely undamaged. There was very little paint left on her but at the stern I could just make out the word *"Ausonia"* which sounded very much like a P & O name; she could have been a lifeboat. But as a company boat on Kelibia beach what could be better? I could already see her in my mind's eye complete with mast and sail. My driver, Sullivan, was equally excited, but Rodgers, being a Londoner, was a bit more dubious. The problem was how to get it back to Kelibia.

Fortunately this solved itself in a rather neat fashion. We were already several vehicles under establishment due to Peter's losses in the "Hunt's Gap" battle, as indeed were many other units in the Brigade as well; meanwhile there were hundreds of abandoned German vehicles littered about in the Cap Bon peninsula. The job of collecting these in and allocating the best of them to units of the Brigade to make up their deficiencies had been delegated to Major Hugh Harben, who commanded the Brigade LAD (Light Aid Detachment – REME) whose job it normally was to repair the Brigade's vehicles. They were camped beyond Brigade HQ at the northernmost point of Kelibia bay. I immediately talked to Hugh Harben about how to recover the boat itself as well as making up our company deficiencies.

He agreed that our allocation was four three-ton lorries and that our MT Sergeant Tranter could go out and find what he wanted so long as we did not cheat, and reported correctly what we recovered. At the same time we could look for a four-wheeled trailer which could carry the boat. Sgt. Tranter was a splendid MT Sergeant, a very good mechanic and very knowledgeable about lorries. In civil life he had a small garage on the outskirts of Birmingham.

He decided that the best lorries to look for were ex-American 3-ton Chevs, probably originally captured from the 8th Army and which had mostly come all the way from the Western Desert. He and his lads soon found four reasonably good trucks, with a fifth for use as spares. In their searches they found a long trailer; it might once have carried a German anti-aircraft gun, but was now destined to be our boat-trailer. I was in a hurry to get the boat safely back to Kelibia in case anyone else

*The 'Kelibia'*

had similar designs upon it; for although Brigade HQ in the shape of the Brigade Major, Edward Ford, had agreed that we should have it, there was something of a free-for-all atmosphere abroad.

Once we got it back to Kelibia the Company carpenter soon made eight oars and a rudder. Sergeant-Major Tutton, who came from a Southampton sea-faring family, set about making a sail out of a surplus tent, as well as all the other necessary rigging. In about a week the boat was ready for launching. It was named *"Kelibia"* and was used most evenings by one Section or another. A great deal of fun and quite good training was had from it, though always under strict safety regulations, as we did not want an accident. On Sunday 13 June the Divisional Commander, Major General Hawksworth, and CRE, Lieut.Colonel Pat Foley, went out fishing in Kelibia bay, rowed by a 59 Company crew. Unfortunately they did not catch very much.

A further quote from one of my letters home dated 6 June gives some idea of Cap Bon:

"It's getting hotter and the country is changing. The corn is ripe everywhere now and the Arabs are cutting it by hand with reaping hooks. A most laborious and back-breaking task. Then it is piled up on the backs of camels and taken to a communal dumping ground where it is laid out on the mud and a camel and an ox are driven round in circles all day. The whole thing is quite incredibly primitive and cannot have been changed at all since Biblical days. But, goodness me, the Arabs are cruel to their animals, it makes one's blood boil to see them beating the unfortunate and tiny donkeys. But it's fascinating to see the life of the country going on round one again, for during the battle all the Arabs disappeared or went to ground. Now they are busy everywhere. We get lots of eggs, marrows, onions, lemons and most surprisingly excellent native wholemeal brown bread. In fact our food and standard of messing is very good now.

We have just had another of these awful gales from the north, it blew at about 60mph all day. Everything was enveloped in flying dust and sand. This tent flapped and thundered at its guys and we all got very bad-tempered. Visibility was reduced to nil all day. I went down to the sea to have a bathe, it was quite warm, I simply had to wash the dust out of my hair and ears. But the wind only lasted one day thank goodness.

Today is Sunday and it dawned the most perfect morning imaginable. Dead still, not a cloud in the sky. The sun is just coming up behind the fort on the rock and lighting the sides of some naval ships anchored in the bay in front of us. It's a wonderful moment of the day, so cool and still with a wonderful sort of purple glow round the horizon between 1700 hours and 0600 hours. Breakfast at 0700 hours and it's just ready too – bacon, eggs and fried bread with native brown bread, butter, and marmalade. It's going to be a most heavenly day. I'm delighted, for this afternoon we are holding a regatta or aquatic sports, with all kinds of swimming races, novelty events and diving. Barney has been to Tunis and got some good prizes from the NAAFI."

And there my letter of 6 June ends.

Meanwhile a lot more official work was piled upon the Company. This included extensive road works on the coastal road, which was feeling the effects of all the extra military traffic using it. We were also asked to improve a very poor cross track through the middle of the peninsula, though this actually proved rather a waste of time and effort. Peter Boston set up an elaborate Brigade water point with reserve water tanks and purification plant at Kelibia, on the stream that fed our sweetcorn field, which now suffered a water shortage, and this also curtailed the company's washing facilities.

The pace seemed to hot up along with the weather, and left no time for war training or for recreation either. However, this had not been forgotten by the powers that be, and we learnt towards the end of June that we would shortly be moving back to Bougie in Algeria for concentrated military training.

Shortly before the departure of the Brigade from Cap Bon, however, the Khaid of Menzel-Temimie, who was the most senior and influential of the local Arab rulers, issued an invitation to Brigadier Hogshaw, the Brigade Commander and some of his officers to attend a falconry party and luncheon at his farm on Friday 11 June. The invitation read as follows:-

Headquarters<br>
10th Infantry Brigade<br>
7 June 1943

Dear Dan,

On Friday 11 June 1943 the Khaid of Menzel-Temime is arranging a falconry meeting in the Dar Safi Area 7672 under the auspices of the

Chief of the Dar Safi tribe in honour of the British Army.

The Brigade Commander is attending and invites you to take part. Rendezvous at Brigade HQ at 0900 hours, 11 June 1943.

Lunch will be provided by the Chief of Dar Safi.

Yours,
Edward Ford

| | |
|---|---|
| Lieut.Col. P. G. R. Preston | Comd. 4 Recce Regt. |
| Lieut.Col. W. A. Whittaker | Comd. 2 Beds & Herts |
| Lieut.Col. G. R. D. Musson | Comd. 2 DCLI |
| Major A. P. de T. Daniell | Comd. 59 Fd Company RE |
| Major J. P. Miles | 2 I/C 4 Recce Regt. |

When I had recovered sufficiently from this remarkable feast I recorded the event at some length.

"On the morning of 11 June we assembled at Brigade Headquarters, set off at about 1000 hours, and went along the most awful mud track which got steadily worse and worse, through horrid dry dusty country, till finally we arrived at a sort of oasis of trees and shade which was the Safi's farm.

The "falconry" was very interesting but rather tame. We and about twenty Arab "hangers-on" proceeded to walk through some rather dry standing corn (rather full of thistles, in fact very prickly). We followed two ruffianly looking Arabs who had falcons on their wrists; these I think were Merlins, grey with very yellow eyes. The idea was that if a quail got up the falcon was thrown in the direction of the bird. But it was much too hot, and no birds got up at all. So in the best tradition of the French "Le Sport" some quail were released out of little baskets and the falcons flew after them, catching them in the air about 25 yards away, much to the enjoyment of everyone. I'd love to see it done properly with natural game, and they apparently do a lot of it in this part of the world.

We then returned to the farm about 1200 hours and were offered some most delicious cool fresh lemonade. After nearly an hour of drinking lemonade and smoking in a very cool and comfortable sort of vaulted Arab house the lunch was ready. This was served in another vaulted room with really lovely carpets on the floor; the walls of course were just plain whitewash. Mercifully we did not have to take our shoes off and squat on the floor as I had rather feared we might have, it being a purely Arab establishment.

We were offered aperitifs and I drank some terrifically fiery gin: it was obviously pre-war and well over-proof. The first course was hors d'oeuvres, sliced egg and wee potatoes, well doused in olive oil. Then followed an entrée of the most delicious sort of crisp pancakes, turned over with a poached egg inside and chopped-up parsley and mint, the pancakes of course fried in olive oil. But they were excellent and I had two, which was very foolish. Then followed seven meat dishes! The first, little mutton joints in sliced egg and semolina, the second again little joints of mutton with some sort of a mash and eggs.

About this stage we were drinking some quite good Tunisian wine. So far I was going strong, talking to a Frenchman on my right with Col. Preston, who was in great form, on my left, and Geoffrey Musson opposite to me, also in cracking good form. The next meat dish was roast hare followed by roast partridge. I didn't have any hare, but for fear of appearing rude felt that I must have some partridge. By now we were drinking excellent French Bordeaux.

It was now about 1400 hours. I was feeling jolly full. However, the next dish to appear was roast chicken with tiny little round roast potatoes all cooked in olive oil in the true French style – you know it well. This looked so good that I had a morsel, only to be persuaded by the Khaid, who was on Col. Preston's left, to take a proper helping. Then a most phenomenal thing occurred – the Major Domo, who was a magnificent type of old retainer, dressed in the uniform of a French sergeant but wearing a fez, brought in an enormous platter about 4ft. in diameter, of stuff that looked like aluminium but was probably silver, bearing a complete roast lamb, complete with head, ears, legs and tail covered with sliced lemon. Of course this was an incredible and magnificent sight, so everybody clapped wildly. I may say there was a large crowd of hungry-looking Arabs round the door, who were all assisting with one thing or another. They all looked frightful ruffians, but you should have seen their eyes gleam at this roast lamb.

As soon as it was "passed" by the Khaid it was carved there and then and we all received a large slice dosed with olive oil and lemon – but no veg! It was most beautifully tender and tasted quite delicious. I seem to have missed out a dish, but I knew there was another meat dish somewhere. Everything was cleared off the table and a vast tray was brought in loaded with Arab sweetmeats and bowls of a sort of trifle. The trifle was lovely because it was pure whipped cream, and the sweetmeats were so good that I had to sample at least four. They were made of honey, almonds, coconut, all frightfully sticky and sweet. At last the end appeared to be in sight, for I was feeling near to bursting! Then at last appeared fruit – the most enormous green figs I have ever seen, all at least 3" in diameter. Mine was like a peach; I had no idea they were so good.

Then to wind it up – it was nearly 1600 hours– most excellent black coffee. Of course everybody had made speeches, some in a wonderful mixture of Arab, French and English. We toasted "La France" and "Les Alliés" and of course "La Victoire", so this incredible lunch finished at 1600 hours and we could honestly only just about lift ourselves out of our seats.

In an almost unconscious coma we filed back into our trucks and set off back along that terrible bumpy track. That return drive was a nightmare. When I got back to the Company Lines I went straight to bed and could not look at food till late the following day – nor, I heard later, could any member of the party.

I shall always look back on that falconry meeting as one of the more memorable events of our very pleasant sojourn in Cap Bon."

MAP 6

# THE < GUSTAV > LINE AT THE TIME OF CASSINO. 12 MAY 1944

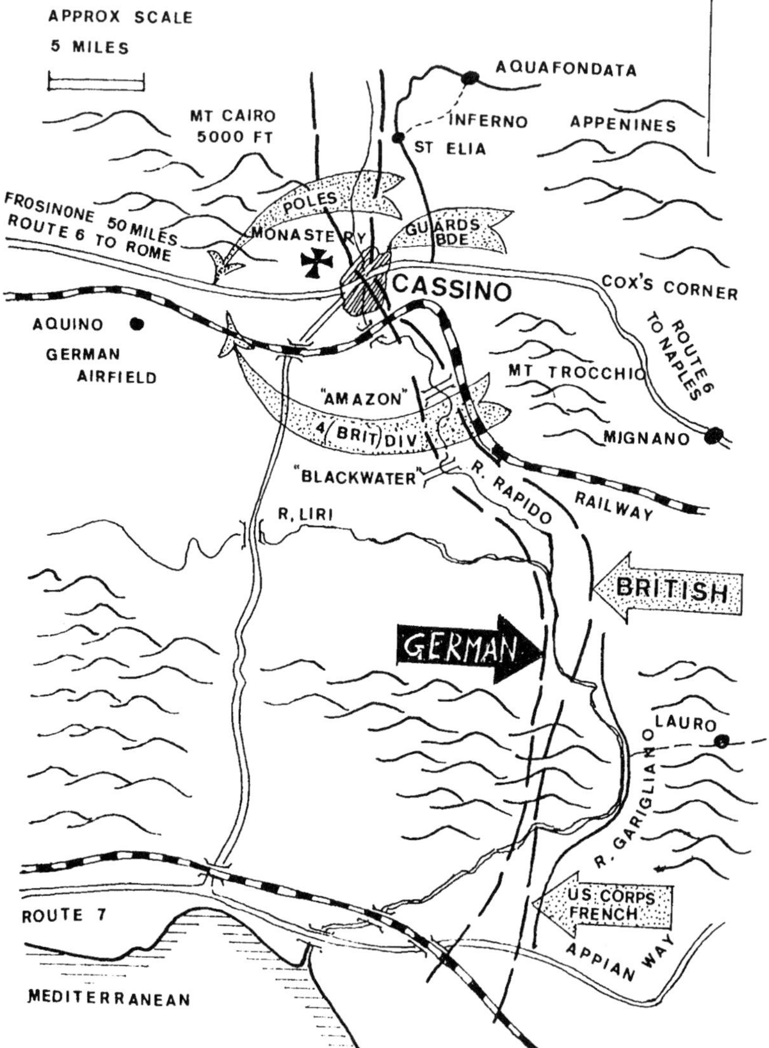

# CHAPTER VI

## Algeria – Bougie

On the last day of June 1943 we started our journey to Bougie, which was about 600 miles to the west and would take us four days. We had to lift the whole Company as well as all our equipment, and at this time of the year in North Africa it could be very hot. In fact one of the first things we noticed after leaving our comfortable olive grove at Kelibia was that the landscape had turned yellow. When we came to Cap Bon the country was green with masses of wild flowers everywhere; now, six weeks later, the countryside was burnt to the colour of straw. No flowers anywhere, and very few birds – only the colourful bee-eaters on the telegraph wires.

Just when we were on the point of leaving, a truck arrived from Divisional HQ RE with Lieutenant Ben Chubb. Ben joined us from the Parachute Regiment to take over Ham's 1 Section when he was promoted to Second-in-Command of the Company upon Barney's departure to be Adjutant of the Sappers at Divisional Headquarters. He was quite a dashing young man who had volunteered for service with the Parachute Regiment as a Sapper officer. Before joining 59 Company he had carried out an operational jump with his Regiment north west of Tunis at the time that we were engaged in the "Hunt's Gap" battle at Beja. During the jump he had in some way got entangled with a container which was also floating down under its own parachute. The result was that he and the container crashed to the ground together and Ben was slightly hurt. This resulted in his being recommended for service in a field company of Engineers.

He had been called up straight from Bristol University while his brother, slightly older, was already a pilot in the RAF. He had plenty of time to fit into the Company while we were in Bougie and very soon showed himself to be a good reliable officer and completely dependable. I remember once being driven by Ben in Italy in his Jeep. We were on a narrow road with ditches on both sides. A tank appeared ahead, coming towards us. I shouted "Look out!" Ben replied, "Let the B get out of my way." But of course he didn't and at the last moment we had to swerve off into the ditch. I could hear the tank crew chuckling. Ben was inclined to be impetuous.

Ben was a chess player and found opponents in Peter Boston and Robert Hutchinson. Peter had made a chess set out of 303 cartridge cases, suitably crimped

*Ben Chubb and Robert Hutchinson.*

and bent into the requisite shapes and, whenever time permitted they could be found deep in a game of chess, smoking pipes and surrounded by a blue haze of smoke, oblivious to all around them. It is an enormous asset in war to have another quite different interest and I think Ben, Peter and Robert found an escape in chess.

The first stage of the journey to Grombalia was easy but the next day, 1 July, was 190 miles to Roumes es Souk. It took us fourteen hours, and it was very hot, with temperatures up to 100°F; our straw hats were a godsend in this heat. No vehicle dropped out, although the captured 3-ton Chev which was towing the boat was finding the going distinctly difficult. Next day was an easier run to Jemmapes, well into Algeria, of about 100 miles which took us eight hours. My diary noted "Company transport going well". Full marks to Sergeant Tranter, our MT Sergeant. Our route can be followed on map 1 on page 14.

By now we were on the coast road and quite often close to the sea. Vegetation was green again and from time to time we drove through cork forests. We saw many of the colourful pink hoopoes. On Saturday 3 July we were making for Djidjelli and during the afternoon found ourselves driving close to the sea with only sandhills between us and a beautiful long sandy beach; so we made a stop and the entire Company had a bathe followed by a brew-up of tea. It was a wonderful break which everyone enjoyed. On Sunday 4 July we reached our destination, Bougie, and set up camp on the outskirts of the town.

The road between Djidjelli and Bougie hugs the coastline which has precipitous cliffs most of the way, with the most beautiful deep coves of turquoise blue sea and golden sand. It was a terribly dangerous road because, as a driver, one's gaze was

*Anse des Aiguades, Bougie. 10 July '43. The coastal road cut into the cliffs..*

constantly distracted by the magnificent views which opened up round every bend and corner. Peter's sketch shows the road cut into the cliff face. In fact so obvious was the danger that at each end of this scenic stretch there was a large warning notice which read:

**Route dangereuse**
**en corniche**
**Etroite et sinueuse**
**pour 35 kilometres**

Bougie was quite a big town of several thousand inhabitants, with a bustling little harbour. It was all very French. 10 Brigade HQ was also just outside the town, and soon all 10 Brigade units were established in and around the town. The country was very different from that of Cap Bon, more like the South of France; a rocky coast with deep coves, steep rather bare hills with terraced vineyards, and inland areas of dense cork and oak forest.

On arrival at Bougie we were joined by another young officer, 2nd Lieut. John Notley. He appeared, at first, to be rather young and inexperienced, but he very soon dispelled this illusion by his dedication. He had in fact come straight from the Royal Engineers OCTU (Officer Cadet Training Unit) and was full of all the latest training methods, and was keen to try them out for real. He soon won the admiration of everyone by his sheer enthusiasm and expertise. Later on when he took over 2 Section

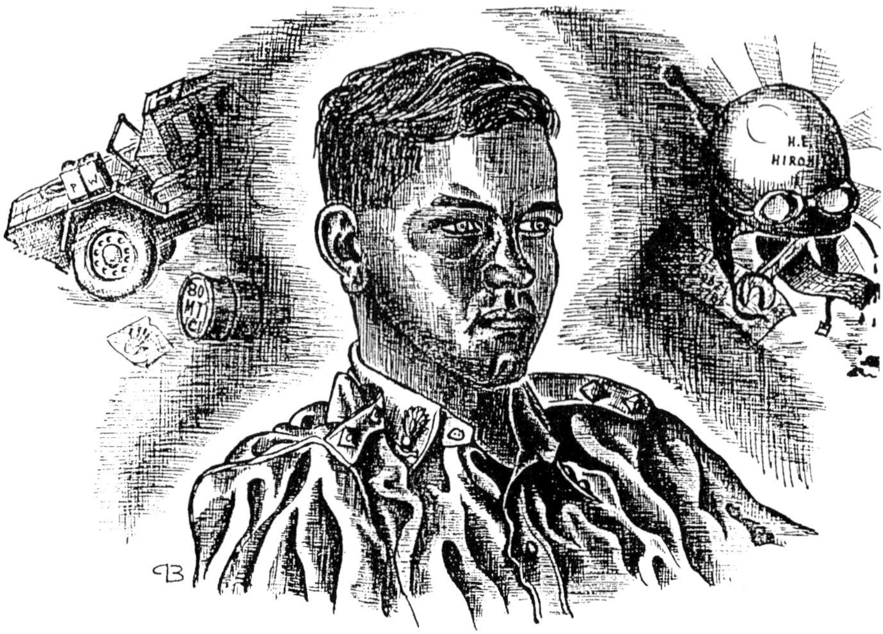

*John Notley. October 1943.*

from Peter Boston they became the most successful Section in the Company, and thereby of course tended to get the most work. John had taken a regular commission as opposed to the war time short service commission. He came from a military family and ultimately went on to become a brigadier, of which there are not many in the Corps of Royal Engineers.

At the same time we lost Sgt.Tranter, who had applied successfully for a commission and now left on posting to a REME officer training unit. We all wished him well, for he had done a wonderful job in keeping the Company on the road.

Another change had also taken place: Lieut. Col. Pat Foley had left 4th Division on promotion. His place was taken by Lieut. Col. Moberley. I missed Pat Foley, having got to know him well through our training at Kirkcudbright, and latterly in two battles. One has to get used to change in the army, especially in time of war.

On 10 July we heard that Sicily had been invaded by the Allies, which was great news. We had been expecting it, but had no idea when. Meanwhile we were beginning to do serious training for assault landings. The navy had provided a new type of assault landing craft which carried 200 men and their vehicles. We all went on board in Bougie harbour, then out to sea for a short trip finishing up by landing on a sandy beach outside Bougie.

We did this a good many times, until all the drivers had practised driving ashore. Even I drove a 3-tonner ashore, hoping the engine would not stall. It was all great fun; in fact anything which afforded opportunities to get wet was enjoyable in the very hot

July weather. We were also able to take our boat the *"Kelibia"* out for a row or a sail at weekends. She had a naval mooring in a corner of Bougie harbour.

There was good bathing and swimming in the coves around Bougie. But one of the unexpected hazards of bathing in their deep clear water was that of sea urchins on the sea bed. They were impossible to see and very easy to step on, whereupon the urchin's spines, which are very sharp, penetrated the sole of one's foot and promptly went septic. Our MO was kept busy digging them out and applying iodine and plaster.

Another irritating problem of this period, of which I was reminded by Ham, was the capacity of the local Arabs to enter the camp at night and steal anything and everything they could lay their hands on, especially on dark nights. They would even enter a tent of snoring Sappers and steal their clothes. We had to be particularly careful of rifles. The ultimate theft was 1 Section's marquee tent which was cut free and disappeared one dark night. This was too much for the CRE who stepped in and ordered something to be done about it. As a result we surrounded the camp with barbed wire to which were fixed improvised trip wires which set off 'Very light' flares. These caused many alarms and excursions, some genuine, but some of unwary Sappers coming in late.

Towards the end of July news was coming in of the successful landings in Sicily and we began to think our next theatre of war might be Italy. This would mean very different work for Sappers; whereas in Africa our main task had been mine clearing, in Italy it was more likely to be bridging and reopening of roads. So, sure enough, on 23 July I received instructions to find a suitable bridging site and establish a bridging training camp, to be run by 59 Company for training all the Sappers in 4th Division. That included 7 and 225 Field Companies and 18 Field Park Company, who would be providing the equipment.

Lieut. Col. Moberley suggested we look at the river Oued Seybouse which flowed out at Bone, 150 miles to the east; so on 24 July Robert and I established our camp in a nice shady eucalyptus grove on the Oued Seybouse about twelve miles inland from Bone. I wrote home on 26 June describing our drive from Bougie to this camp site on the Oued Seybouse.

"It was a wonderful drive of about 150 miles or so along the coast. Almost all the way on our right towered the northern Atlas mountains, quite a mighty range, cloud-capped with terrific cliffs straight down into a vividly blue sea. For the first 100 miles or so the road is "en corniche" often cut into the face of the cliff. Then we wound up a valley and over quite a high pass. It is a magnificently engineered road. Then we drove for miles and miles through cork forest where I saw quite a lot of interesting birds, lots of hoopoes and a beautiful bird rather like a kingfisher with a green breast, and of course lots of storks. Robert actually saw a Barbary ape. They are quite small monkeys which live in the cork forest."

I later in the same letter referred to the malaria scare which was then occupying the mind of the Higher Command:

"The camp site is fine and we are a very happy crowd. I don't think the malaria menace is as serious or as bad as it is made out to be. We all have to take a horrible yellow pill, mepocrine, every day and every man has to sleep under a mosquito net and when he goes to bed has to smear his face with cream. Finally, between sunset and sunrise all have to wear long trousers and rolled-down sleeves. It is quite a complicated business and must be enforced and checked daily by an officer. Anyway no one has got it yet."

For the next two weeks all three field companies worked hard at constructing Class 40 ton rafts and floating Bailey bridging capable of carrying Churchill tanks. We borrowed a Churchill tank and crew from 21st Tank Brigade and each Company built a floating bridge in turn for the tank to cross backwards and forwards. It was very good training and we all enjoyed it. The Seybouse was quite a wide slow-flowing river and provided excellent bathing in the evenings. All sorts of water sports and competitions were also carried out.

Most weekends we took the *"Kelibia"* out for a sail. It was a splendid way of teaching the senior NCOs how to sail, but we had a very strict rule of no swimming out at sea; I did not want to risk an accident. I also insisted that there should always be an officer in charge. We tried fishing, but with no success.

For the next two months we were kept extremely busy on all sorts of training exercises. Courses were being run for the officers and senior NCOs and the men were kept busy on Bailey bridging, improvement of roads, shooting – we constructed a rifle range in the hills behind Bougie – and constant practice in mine-clearing drills: we needed to perfect our mine lifting skills.

At the beginning of September a new type of work began with the news of the success of the landings in Sicily. Bougie harbour was being used as a supply base for the Sicilian campaign and we were called upon daily to supply Sappers to load ships in the harbour. This was quite hard work and the men got very fit and strong. All the harbour cranes and installations were manned by the Army; the operation of the port was extremely efficient and looked upon with envy by the French officials.

Then on 19 September we heard the depressing news that we might have to stay at Bougie for some months yet – and certainly into the winter. We were instructed to build a winter quarters camp for ourselves; this meant Nissen huts, concrete paths, a proper cook-house, mess huts, ablutions and latrines, quite a big job. So we set about designing a camp, which of course was named "Kirkcudbright Camp", and ordering all the necessary stores, concrete materials, bricks, and a concrete mixer, etc. Needless to say, as other units were doing the same thing there were delays in delivery, shortages and rationing.

However, everyone set to and worked very hard. On 28 September we had the first day of heavy rain. My diary states: "An appalling day of torrential rain. The whole campsite is reduced to a state of mud." This resulted in feverish work on concrete paths and completion of Nissen huts. On 17 October, just one month after starting work, the whole company moved out of tents into winter quarters in a completed

View (from the Dining Table) of the Officers' Mess Bath house with full steam up. John Notley like a boiled salmon within; door propped open with logs to let out the blinding fumes without admitting the inquisitive eye; Diesel oil in the water.
(OFF): "Hhhhheyy!! – Curly!! Look – she's boiling again."

camp. It also included the completion of a bath-house, which had a tendency to boil over with disastrous effect upon the unwary, as sketched by Peter. On 18 October I had my first hot bath since 9 March; it was a red letter day. We celebrated by going out for a meal in a small French restaurant in Bougie.

On 30 October an ENSA (Entertainments National Service Association) touring company put on a show for the whole Brigade in our Kirkcudbright Camp. Peter Boston's sketch vividly portrays the scene, with a rigged-up stage and borrowed benches and chairs. About a thousand men were squeezed in with the Brigadier and all the senior officers of the Brigade. It was a great success and a very fitting way to celebrate the completion of our camp, which I think was the first in the Brigade to be completed. Meanwhile 7 Field Company, now commanded by Major Mike Low, had moved into a French barracks on top of a mountain overlooking Bougie, a magnificent spot 1,000ft. up.

It was on 1 November that 2nd Lieut. Malcolm Drummond and 2nd Lieut. Eddie Meldrum joined the Company as first reinforcement officers. We now had three Scotsmen, Ham, Eddie, and Malcolm, who made a strong team from over the border.

Malcolm was a great big strong fellow, rather taciturn, but really stolid and utterly dependable. When being given a job to do, he would want to know all there was to know about it and would then sit down and plan it with his NCOs in considerable detail. From my point of view as OC this was sometimes rather time-consuming, but his men felt very secure under his command. It actually fitted in rather well because he eventually took over 3 Section, which had been Freddie Leadbeter's Section,

*4 Div. RE concert in Kirkcudbright Camp. 2 Sept. '43.*

and they had somewhat similar characters. He was sometimes inclined to be slow off the mark, but was loved by his men for they knew instinctively that he always had their welfare very much at heart. He stayed with the Company a long time and later on in Greece commanded it for a short time.

Eddie Meldrum, who joined at the same time as Malcolm Drummond, was a Highlander from the north of Inverness. He, like Peter Boston, had been training to be an architect and later on, after the war when he returned to "Civvy Street", became an architect on the staff of the National Health Service. Eddie's natural role was as a member of a team and thus the perfect Second-in-Command. For a time he worked with Peter Boston as his Second-in-Command of 2 Section, and they became a very strong team. Like Peter he was an excellent draughtsman, which for a Sapper officer is an extremely useful accomplishment. He and Malcolm Drummond have remained close friends for the rest of their lives, as indeed have most of the officers who served with 59 Field Company in North Africa and Italy.

The arrival of these two officers coincided with strong rumours that we might be going to Italy, which bucked up our spirits no end. 10 Brigade immediately put on a Mountain Warfare exercise up behind Bougie in the northern Atlas mountains, which entailed climbing Mount Toudja, just over 3,000 ft., with splendid views. It was very exhilarating and also good training for the men.

The only unpleasant aspect of these climbs into the mountains were the prickles. In addition to areas of prickly pear on the lower slopes, with their vicious thorns as one climbed, there were plantations of dwarf gorse. In flower these plantations were magnificent patches of yellow, but their thorns were awful. Higher up still were masses of a sort of ground covering bramble with equally vicious thorns, and a pretty, low, ground covering rock rose with thorns quite out of proportion to its size. In all, the whole mountain sides were a mass of prickles and, in the African sun and consequent sweat, scratches and pricks quickly became septic: an unexpected and annoying hazard for the MO.

The kind of mountain warfare training that we worked on in these hills behind Bougie consisted first of all in trying to assess the sort of help the infantry might ask for, and then in carrying it out. This boiled down to making passable tracks up steep mountains, out of sight of an imaginary enemy, and then digging or blasting out foxholes and defensive positions. It did in fact coincide with what we had to do later on in Italy.

After we had been told we might have to spend the winter in Bougie we were asked one day to accept two "AMGOT"( Allied Military Government of Occupied Territory) officers for a few days, as a change for them from kicking their heels at 4th Division headquarters. They were waiting to be posted to Italy – perhaps to Rome – when the Italian Government collapsed, as everyone expected it would when the Germans' hold over the country diminished. One was a police inspector from London's Metropolitan Police and the other was a barrister, also from London.

On joining us for a few days just to see how we lived, they found our Mess so comfortable and informal, and Corporal Parry's cooking so excellent, they felt very

*Keep it under your hat. Malcolm Drummond. 2 Oct. '43.*

relaxed and we found them good company and interesting, with their stories of London's night life.

On the second or third evening of their stay I was invited to bring them along to a local Arab party being held in a mountain village up behind Bougie. The entertainment consisted of watching a group of men, fine-looking Berber Arabs, dancing to a band of local drums and pipes. The tempo hotted up and the dance became more and more erotic as they leaped about. Meanwhile we, the onlookers, drank the local spirits and clapped in time to the band. Some joined in, but after a while we decided to return home, it was getting boring.

When we got back to camp it was quite dark, and probably about 2300 hours. The Officers' Mess was empty. Presumably the officers had gone to bed, but Parry was up and made us cocoa. We too decided to turn in.

Our sleeping hut was curiously quiet, no one was snoring, not a sound. I was a bit suspicious but thought nothing of it and sat down on my bed to take off my boots, when there was a loud explosion and my bed erupted. Pandemonium ensued as I hurled my boots at John Notley's bed, and anything else I could lay my hands upon at other beds. They had fixed a booby-trapped detonator under my bed and were waiting for our return. It was all great fun and thoroughly schoolboyish.

No harm was done. The policeman immediately entered the fray and enjoyed the joke immensely, but our barrister thought it was all rather unseemly. When calm was restored, Parry brought in more cocoa and we all eventually went to bed. Next day routine training continued as usual. Looking back one is apt to forget that we were all very young at the time and enjoyed good parties, some enjoyed them more than others. Of our three Scotsmen, Eddie Meldrum enormously enjoyed a good binge while Hamilton and Malcolm Drummond were more sober. It was during our stay at Bougie that we invented the character of the "little brown man" with his birdcage and spoon. Eddie, Peter and John Notley were his most frequent recipients of a spoonful of "birdcage" sprinkled on the tongue in the early mornings. A frequent opening gambit at breakfast at Bougie might be, "Did the little brown man visit you this morning? He did me the little blighter!" Peter depicted the little fellow as being fat and hairy with protruding nose and eyes – a throughly revolting creature.

From now on the pace of training and work in the docks hotted up, as news came in of the Allies' advance into the foot of Italy. In late October we started working night shifts in Bougie harbour loading Bailey bridging for Italy; this certainly confirmed our suspicions that, if we did go into Italy Bailey bridging would be our main task. With so many rivers and mountain roads it was an easy country to

*Lieut. The Hon. Ed Humdrum. Eddie Meldrum*

defend by demolition and the Germans were certain to do that.

Peter left by plane from Algiers for a mountain warfare course in Syria, Robert went off for a similar course in Morocco by plane to Oran, and Ham was sent on a reconnaissance trip to Constantine to find a suitable site for a Divisional Rest Camp. Later he and Robert, with a party from 3 Section, started work on this rest camp, using POW labour.

We soon learned that all ranks were to have a week's leave over the next few weeks, hopefully prior to a move into battle again. I went to visit 3 Section, now working at Constantine, and asked Lieut.Col. Moberley for permission to visit the famous Roman ruins at Timgad, and then go on to Biskra on the edge of the Sahara. I had always wanted to visit Biskra and see the desert, as my father had been there many years ago and liked it very much.

So on Tuesday 16 November, my driver Sullivan and I left at 0800 hours and drove first to Batna high up on the edge of the southern Atlas mountains. From there it was a short way to Timgad. The ruins were magnificent and in wonderful condition: beautiful colonnades and roads, a forum, an amphitheatre, and several temples, all of pink sandstone against a backdrop of the high Atlas mountains, now covered in snow. There was no one about: it was completely silent and awe-inspiring. Back to Batna and on over the Col de Telmet, 6,200ft. By now the landscape could have been anywhere in Scotland, with heather, pine trees, and grass. We were not far below the snow line and it was cold in our khaki drill shirts and shorts.

Then we dropped steadily down with a growing river on our left and the railway line on our right to the spectacular gorge of El Kantara. The country was becoming bare and parched, with prickly pear instead of heather, and palm trees instead of pines. It was an extraordinary transition. The river now became a rushing torrent, and it was hot again. (See map 1 on page 14.)

The railway which we followed down to Biskra was of course the same railway that we had met earlier at Guelma junction on our way up to Tunisia after landing at Algiers. It was a magnificently engineered railway, very steep in places, and through the El Kantara gorge it was carried on a shelf cut into the cliff face. Having followed it down from the Col de Telmet I can well understand the need for the huge locomotive that we saw at Guelma. Unfortunately we never saw a train on any of our drives.

Once through the gorge of El Kantara the scene suddenly opened out, and away in the distance was the desert, flat like a yellow sea as far as the eye could see in all directions. As we drove towards the desert the river now became wide and slow-moving, about the size of our river Severn. Then suddenly over a very few miles this huge river flowed out into the desert and disappeared, giving more than ever the impression of flowing into the sea. We drove on to Biskra, a fascinating and quite large town on the edge of the desert, full of Bedouin Arabs, camels, and open market stalls selling everything under the sun. Unfortunately we had very little time to look round, for we felt we must start back before night fell.

We camped at El Kantara railway station and left early next morning to retrace our steps to Batna, from there across the plain to Setif over the northern Atlas, and down to Bougie in time for a good supper. A drive of 280 miles in the day; but it had whetted my appetite for another visit.

On our return I found that Captain Hamilton was to leave us on 19 November for Philippeville, and thence on by sea to Egypt and Cairo. We were all very sorry to see him go.

On 24 November Captain John Heath, who had been in a County Surveyor's office in England, arrived to take Ham's place as 2 I/C of the Company. He quickly found his place in the Company. Peter Boston returned in great spirits from Syria, having had a very strenuous course in mountain warfare. On 1 December we all spent a long day up in the mountains climbing Djebel Jouah, over 3,000ft.

It was now looking more likely than ever that we were destined for Italy, and this was almost confirmed by another unexpected dispensation of leave; all officers could take up to six days' leave, as long as it was taken in relays, as the training and work programme had to go on. Most of the officers opted for a visit to Algiers to taste its night-life, but I wanted to go back to the desert. Malcolm and Robert were keen to do this too, so we got permission to set off in a 'White' Scout car to Biskra and Touggourt, 100 miles on into the desert.

We left on 5 December, with John Heath taking over the Company in my absence. The 'White' Scout car was a bulky American 4-wheel drive reconnaissance truck which had been issued to the Company, and which we felt was not likely to get stuck in sand. We took forty gallons of petrol to be on the safe side. Peter's sketch shows a 'White' scout car.

*Siesta in the desert, between Setif and Constantine. 11 Sept. '43.*

The drive to Biskra took all day and we shared the driving. Again we camped for the night at El Kantara station, taking over the waiting room for sleeping quarters. Unfortunately this time the mosquitoes were terrible and I slept very little due to the constant buzz of the little brutes, even though we had mosquito nets. Next morning we cooked breakfast on a primus stove and set off early for Biskra to spend a quiet and rather pleasant day exploring, and after much haggling I bought two Bedouin prayer mats in the market. We camped for the night outside the town under the stars in a sand-dune. No mosquitoes.

I found an extraordinary fascination in sleeping under the stars in the desert. It is very still, and in December the air is crystal clear and quite cold, though the sand is still warm. The night has a soft velvet feel and is wonderfully tranquil after the heat of the day.

Next day we drove on to Touggourt, about 100 miles into the desert. Touggourt is a truly Arab town of brown mud buildings and palm trees, once again bustling with Bedouin Arabs, camels and goats. We decided to have a night of pure luxury in the Grand Hotel Transatlantique, with dinner first; with such a name in such a place we felt we must try it, and very comfortable it was too – we had an excellent dinner. But we hadn't very much cash, so we decided to take a double room with twin beds, and draw lots for who would have to sleep on the floor. I lost; however, in the early morning Robert insisted we swop. After breakfast the hotel insisted on charging for three full bed-and-breakfasts. We resisted stoutly but ultimately had to give in, partly due to our lack of sufficiently persuasive French. This left us with very little money; it was lucky that we had plenty of petrol.

Having got so far into the desert we decided to go on south on the trans-Sahara route at least as far as the next oasis, Temacine, where we slept under the stars again in a sand dune outside the village, hoping that we had not been spotted. But this was not to be, for while we were having breakfast, an emissary dressed in a magnificent uniform arrived from the local Khaid and with much bowing and gesticulating invited us to take coffee with His Excellency.

This time we did have to squat on the floor, albeit on a beautiful carpet. Unfortunately conversation was difficult; our French was very limited and so was his, but his courtesy and thoughtfulness for us was very touching, and his coffee, thick and black, was indeed delicious. After an hour we got away, leaving with a present of the largest and sweetest dates I have ever tasted. We decided we must return home, although we would love to have gone on to Ouargla, the half-way oasis across that part of the Sahara. Discretion took over, however, and we turned for home planning to get to Biskra or El Kantara for the night. It was 9 December.

We reached Biskra about tea-time and decided to stop for a last look at the Bazaar. To our utter astonishment, we suddenly saw Driver Sullivan and my truck; he had driven nonstop from Bougie with an urgent messge to find me, to say that I must return immediately to deal with orders for the Company to move. What an incredible piece of luck that he should find me in the bazaar at Biskra having just returned from deep in the desert.

It was already late, and Sullivan had already driven 280 miles from Bougie; so we decided that we would all go back to El Kantara for the night, which was only ten miles or so from Biskra but far enough for Sullivan. We pitched our camp just outside the station and brewed up a good supper of Maconochie tinned stew, biscuits, tea, and of course the Khaid's delicious dates. We all slept soundly – no mosquitoes. Sullivan and I started early, leaving Robert and Malcolm to return in more leisurely fashion in the rather cumbersome White scout car while we hurried on in my PU truck.

We arrived back at Bougie tired but excited to find the astonishing news that we were to go overseas almost immediately, and without transport or equipment. It was 10 December and already the Company had started to pack up and paint unit serial numbers on all our personal luggage.

On Monday 13 December, we spent all day returning barrack stores to RASC, and vehicles and engineer stores to the local Ordnance Depot. We gave the cutter *"Kelibia"* to the Royal Navy, asking them to sign an Army Form 108, a standard receipt form: a sad moment in an otherwise hectic day.

On Tuesday, Eddie Meldrum left with a small advance party to join the Divisional advance party. We still did not know for certain where we were going, and we still had a pig to slaughter and eat. Next day we received the movement order to depart by rail on Monday. I was to be OC train, but where to?

Thursday 16 December was declared a rest day for all. The pig was killed immediately, and a full Christmas dinner prepared; a very happy day was had by all. Friday was a dress-rehearsal for the move, and the weekend was spent clearing up the camp.

On Monday 20 December we said goodbye to Kirkcudbright Camp. We were joined on the train by Divisional HQ RE and by 225 Field Company; it was a very crowded train but at least we had carriages this time, and not cattle trucks. We left for Rouiba, outside Algiers, at midday.

Everyone was relieved and excited that at last we were on our way: presumably going into battle in Italy, into Europe, perhaps the start of a long journey back home to Britain. We had been at Bougie for six months and by now were heartily sick of North Africa, with its flies and prickles. It was good to be on the move again.

"O Cloacena, Goddess of this Place
Wherein each morn we strain with purple face;
Smoothly to thee may all our offerings flow:
Not unduly swift — nor yet unduly slow."

Anon. IX Century.
Translated from the Chinese.

*A much contemplated scene. Bougie. 12 Dec. '43.*

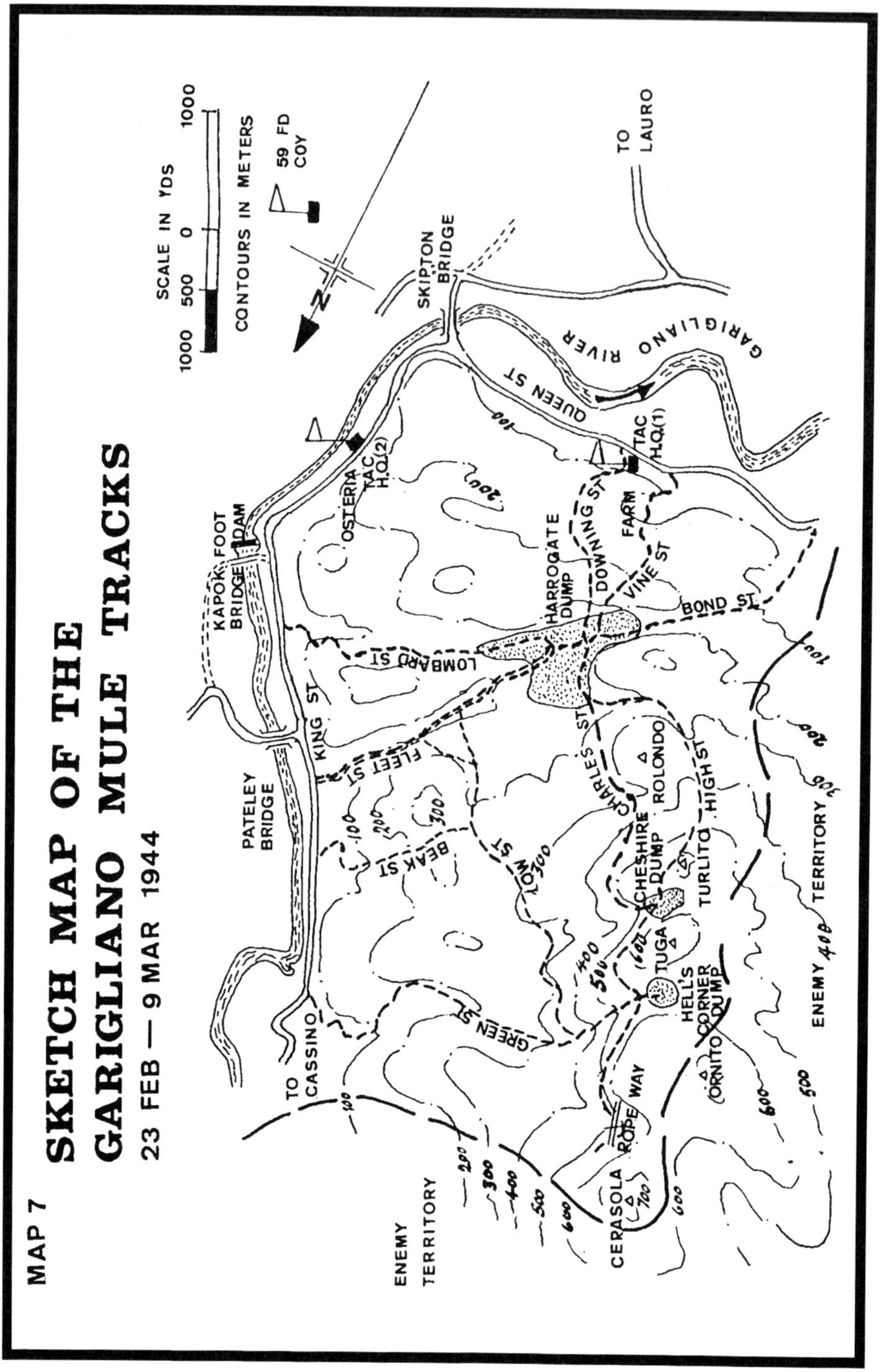


MAP 7

**SKETCH MAP OF THE GARIGLIANO MULE TRACKS**

23 FEB — 9 MAR 1944

# CHAPTER VII

## Operation "Pitchfork"

*"T'was Christmas Day in a Transit Camp whence all but we had fled."*

Barney and I sat on our beds and grumbled. My diary notes "It was a b- awful camp. All the tents leaked."

On arrival at Rouiba station we were met by guides who marched us to 'Z' Transit camp on the outskirts of Algiers. The weather was dreadful, very wet, and the camp had no drying facilities. Although Christmas Day was fine, we would much rather have been at our old friend Le Hamiz brick factory. Why should a transit camp, just because people were always passing through it, be so badly equipped and badly run? It was a depressing place, the tents leaked, it was a sea of mud, and nobody seemed to care. Obviously the camp commandant had no pride in it whatsoever.

Fortunately, however, we were not there long, for on Boxing Day we were lifted by lorry to the docks and embarked on the S.S. *'Scythia'*, an old Cunarder now turned troopship. Loading at the same time were other units of 10 Brigade. Loading onto the S.S. *'Orontes'*, a slightly younger P & O cruise ship, were 12 Brigade and 4th Division headquarters.

Our two ships sailed that evening at 1730 hours, to join a convoy of other ships from Britain. We turned east and with accompanying destroyers sailed fairly close to land. We were off Tunis at dawn, passing quite close to Cap Bon; we could clearly see the high ground of El Haouaria. We reached Alexandria on 30 December, and entered the Suez Canal.

Sailing through the canal and the Bitter Lakes was fascinating. Speed was very much reduced, to prevent wash, and the journey took two days. On 2 January 1944 we anchored in Suez bay, under the towering heights of Djebel Ataqa, and were taken off in lighters to be landed in the scruffy port of Tufiq; that same afternoon we had our first experience of a desert dust storm, everything was obliterated in a swirling fog of dust and sand.

For a few days we camped in exceedingly uncomfortable conditions on a hot dusty plain between Port Tufiq and Djebel Ataqa, before moving to a much pleasanter camp site on a hill overlooking the canal at Gebel Maryam. The canal makes a bend here, in

*Before the rains came*
*View from a tent in the world's worst transit camp. Rouiba 22 Dec. 1943.*

effect to go round the hill, which has at its top a magnificent monument erected in memory of the completion of the canal in 1869, by the Frenchman Ferdinand de Lesseps, see frontispiece.

Here we were re-equipped with American vehicles and, we noted, second-hand engineer equipment, and started combined operations training, based on Kabrit. This was the Middle East Combined Operations Training Camp on the shore of the Great Bitter Lake, just south of Ismailia. The training, with our friends the infantry battalions of 10 Brigade, consisted mainly of crossing the Great Bitter Lake in landing craft and practising assault landings on the Sinai shore. We did mine-clearing drills and route marking, and generally assisted the infantry to rush inland and get established on some rocky feature. The country was extremely barren, with no roads or habitation of any sort; it reminded me of Lawrence of Arabia's books on his desert campaign, and I would like to have gone further inland, perhaps as far as his railway, but it was exceedingly inhospitable terrain and not the sort of place to become stranded. However, the weather was perfect, dry and sunny by day and quite chilly at night.

What did intrigue us was, why were we doing so many assault landing exercises when we thought we were destined to go into Italy? We afterwards learned that 4th Division might have carried out an invasion of Rhodes; perhaps this was to deceive the enemy. The training was enjoyable, however, and kept us all very fit.

Thus did we spend the whole of January 1944, and the time went remarkably quickly. Not far from our camp on Gebel Maryam, near the village of Amrya, on the

*Desert cinema at Amrya transit camp. 12 Feb. '44.*

main road to Cairo, was one of the famous desert cinemas, which had been set up behind the lines to entertain the troops during the build-up of the 8th Army before the battle of El Alamein in 1942. They were still in very good condition, and showed excellent films. They were a chain set up by an enterprising Egyptian named Shafto and were known widely as "Shafto's Palaces". Large parties of men were allowed to go out in the evenings when they returned from exercises; we all went out to the cinema and thoroughly enjoyed it: we felt almost civilised again.

At the beginning of February Peter Boston, who had succumbed to jaundice at Rouiba on Boxing Day just as we had boarded the SS *Sythia,* rejoined the Company, apparently quite recovered.

Then suddenly, on Monday 7 February, we heard that at last 4th Division was to go to Italy almost immediately. Movement orders were received and all was frantic bustle. Once again we were to leave behind our vehicles and equipment, which had to be handed in to Ordnance Depots in the canal zone. This we all felt was no bad thing, as much of it was pretty ropey. A week later, on Monday 14 February, the Company, together with 10 Brigade Headquarters and other Brigade units, were lifted in RASC transport to Alexandria, and embarked on another old Cunarder, the SS *'Ascania'*. We were on our way to Naples.

Just occasionally the Army chooses thoroughly apt names for its exercises and operations. The code name for this operation was "Operation Pitchfork", which could not have been more appropriate in view of the speed and suddenness with which it took place. We were left almost reeling – perhaps we had got dangerously used to a quiet life.

On Wednesday 16 February we sailed from Alex at dawn, to join a convoy from Port Said. In the afternoon a terrific storm blew up; seven out of ten of the convoy's barrage balloons were blown away, the gale blew all next day, so laden with sand that it was impossible to see anything, and very rough at the same time. It was an altogether miserable voyage, especially as we thought we had left sandstorms behind in Egypt. However, by Sunday the storm had blown itself out, the sea was very blue and calm, and the sun hot and bright.

On Monday 21 February we sailed into the bay of Naples. In good weather the Bay of Naples is incredibly beautiful, with Vesuvius quietly smoking in the background and the distant city gleaming in the sunshine. On closer inspection, however, it proved less beautiful; many ships in the harbour had been sunk and all round the docks was utterly destroyed. We tied up alongside an upturned ship and disembarked over its hull to hurry ashore into a waiting fleet of RASC lorries. There was no mistaking the feel that we were entering a war zone, and there was a nasty smell abroad.

It was already evening and getting cold as we drove north through the town of Capua, over the Volturno river and on up into the foothills of the western Apennines. It was late and very dark when we reached our destination, the small hilltop village of Lauro. It had a rather scruffy central square, into which the RASC lorries dumped us, turned round, and quickly disappeared back into the night. Our advance party with Eddie Meldrum was waiting with guides to take each section to its allotted billet, mainly in the houses round the square.

HQ Section and the Officers' Mess were allocated to a tall draughty house on the edge of the village; like most Italian houses it had terrazzo floors, concrete stairs, and ill-fitting windows and doors, and had no furniture at all. After Egypt we all felt cold. Next morning we were woken at dawn by a burst of shattering explosions from a battery of heavy artillery firing from the garden at the back of our house.

It was raining, and although we did not realise it then, it was a foretaste of much worse weather to come. By daylight Lauro was even more battered and squalid than it had appeared the evening before, for it had not long since been fought over. However, it was full of Italian peasants, lots of children, goats, and chickens; everyone was immensely kind and helpful,, and patently delighted to see such a big influx of British soldiers. Eggs and chicken appeared on cook Parry's menu. One did not ask from whence they came.

There was much work for us to do. We learned that 4th Division was taking over from 46th Division; 10 Brigade were taking over from 139 Brigade; and 59 Field Company was taking over from 270 Field Company. We were to take over their vehicles and equipment as quickly as possible, and this was put in hand at once. It was an excellent arrangement for us, and proved very easy and successful.

We soon discovered that the Artillery in the garden, which fired barrages at irregular intervals throughout the day – and night – attracted the occasional and always unexpected return fire. Shells would suddenly come whistling out of the blue, landing at random in the village with a shattering explosion. We did not think much of Lauro and were soon planning to move out of it.

There had been several changes in the Division since the end of the North African Campaign, with a view to our new campaign in Italy. Major-General Hawksworth CBE had left, and his place was taken by Major-General Dudley Ward, CB, CBE, DSO, who was to command the Division for the next twelve months during its progress up the leg of Italy. The 21 Tank Brigade had returned to the U.K. to take part in the invasion of northern Europe, and was replaced in the Division by 28 Infantry Brigade from Gibraltar: 4th Division was once more a standard three-Brigade Infantry Division.

Lieut. Colonel John Nelson had flown out from England to take over as CRE from Lieut. Colonel Moberley just before Operation Pitchfork, and was to lead the Sappers throughout the Italian campaign; an experienced and very pragmatic regular soldier, he was soon to show his leadership expertise in the coming battle for Cassino.

The Germans, meanwhile, held the high ground north of the river Garigliano, including the fortress feature of Cassino Monastery and the land right across the Apennines to the Adriatic Sea. (See map 6 on page 70.) It was known as the "Gustav Line" and was very strongly held. The advent of 4th Division on the Garigliano sector was just a small part of a huge build-up of Allied strength designed, when ready, to puncture this defensive line by the capture of Cassino, which would then open the door for an advance on Rome, up the valley carrying the national Route 6. All of us had our part to play – 4th Division and its Sappers including us of 59 Field Company – in this great set piece battle to come. It would prove a long hard slog.

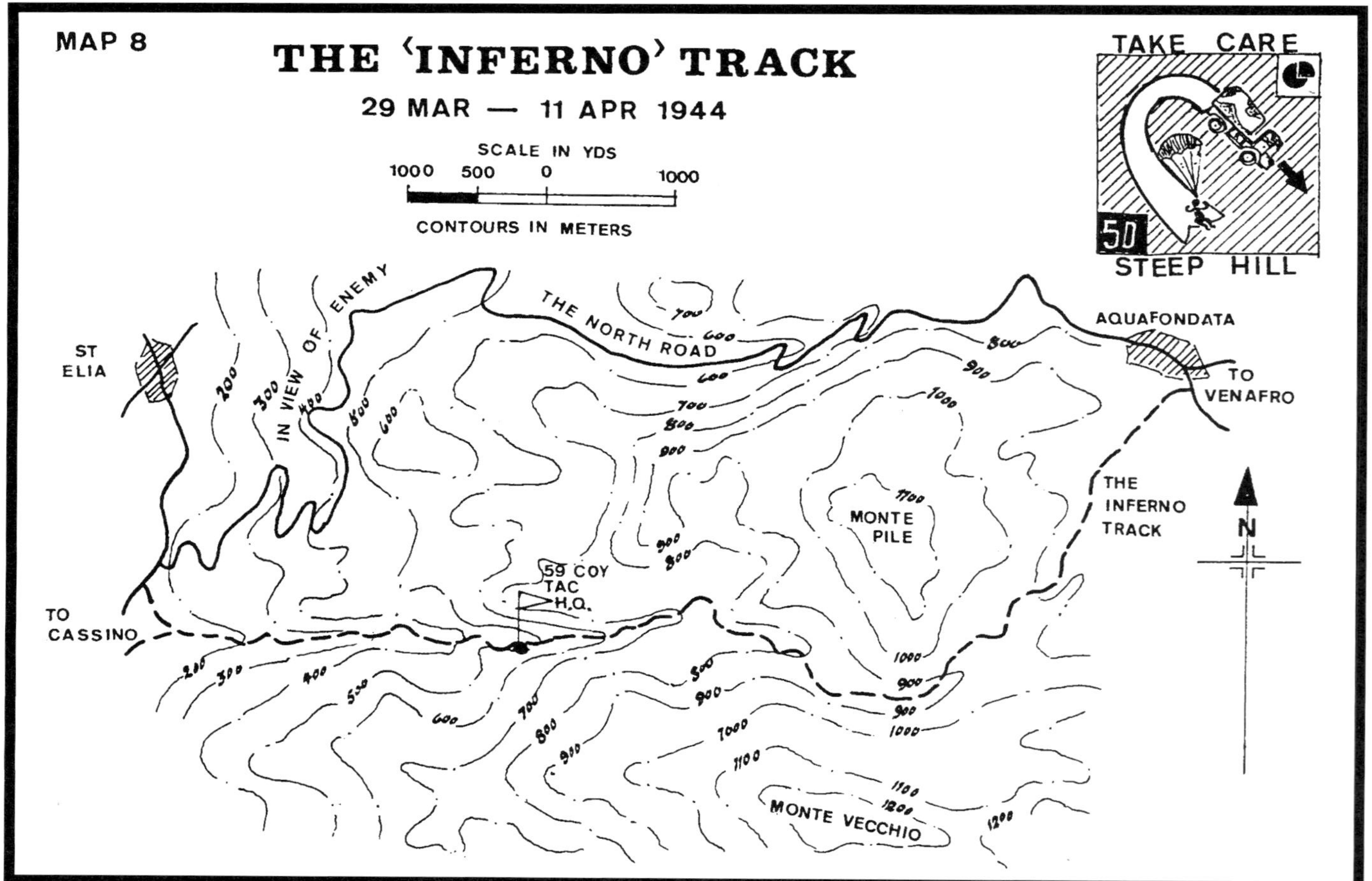
MAP 8
THE 'INFERNO' TRACK
29 MAR — 11 APR 1944
SCALE IN YDS
1000 500 0 1000
CONTOURS IN METERS
TAKE CARE
5D
STEEP HILL
ST ELIA
TO CASSINO
IN VIEW OF ENEMY
THE NORTH ROAD
59 COY TAC H.Q.
AQUAFONDATA
TO VENAFRO
THE INFERNO TRACK
MONTE PILE
MONTE VECCHIO
N

# CHAPTER VIII

## Towards Cassino

Having taken over vehicles and tools from 270 Field Company, we then took over the operational role of 271 Field Company which was moving out with 46th Division. Their role was the maintenance of mule tracks for the supply of the infantry Brigade troops holding the mountains north of the river Garigliano, the sector being taken over by 10 Brigade. It took me two days to walk these tracks with Major Gardener of 271 Company to get the hang of the work involved.

Meanwhile Ben Chubb and Peter Boston with their respective 1 and 2 Sections moved into the mountains and took over the main tracks being used to bring up supplies to the two leading Battalions of 10 Brigade.

Map 7 on page 88 shows that there are five mountain tops over 2000ft in this massif: Cerasola, Ornito, Tuga, Turlito, and Rolondo. The tops were "no man's land"; the Germans held the northern slopes and our troops the southern sides, each side periodically shelling and mortaring the other from very precariously held positions. It was a classic holding operation.

The only farms and villages were in the valley bottom; the mountains themselves were desolate, bare, and rocky, and quite apart from the enemy's attentions we were exposed to the weather – which in March was at its worst.

Our job as Sappers was to help the Infantry; sometimes blasting foxholes for them to shelter in, but continually improving the mule tracks used every night to bring up food and ammunition from the main dump at Harrogate to the forward dumps at Cheshire and Hell's Corner. All the tracks had code names and although they endeavoured to follow the easiest routes they were very steep and very rough. Mules can easily climb very steep terrain, but with several hundred of them going up and down, the tracks became terribly knocked about. And although these tracks were not in direct view of the enemy, they knew exactly where they were and from time to time shelled them quite accurately. Later on, therefore, we decided to build a completely new track.

Our work was generally done during daylight, but we had to keep a subsection on each group of tracks at night to repair any stretches broken up either by shelling or by a mule falling. Several hundred mules were held at Harrogate Dump, and their fodder too had to come up from Queen Street and King Street in the valley bottom.

Our training at Bougie was really paying off now, but there we had had no mules, nor had we taken account of wet weather. We started work on Wednesday 23 February, and it rained solidly, steadily, and monotonously, for four days. Fortunately we had changed back to battle-dress winter clothing on the ship, abandoning our khaki drill, and all ranks had been issued with leather jerkins; even so the continuous rain and wind in these mountains was very trying after our Africa experience and the men were inclined to say "Where is the Sunny Italy we've heard so much about?"

On 28 February and 1 March the CRE, Lieut.Col. John Nelson, toured the area and walked the tracks. 10 Brigade headquarters was being established at Harrogate, so we decided to upgrade the Fleet Street track from King Street road to Harrogate Dump to a Jeep track; this was a job for Malcolm and 3 section, in addition to the help they were giving to 10 Brigade to dig in to their headquarters. (Refer to Map 7 on page 88.)

Very shortly after we had taken over responsibility for the mule tracks and any other Sapper work required in this area, we received a very unusual request from the Commanding Officer of the 1st Bn. Grenadier Guards, a unit of the Guards Brigade who were holding the right hand flank of the Garigliano mountains. They had shot dead a German soldier in the narrow no-man's-land between their respective forward positions and badly wanted to know what German unit was facing them. If they could get hold of his body, his uniform and identity papers would tell them. How could they recover the body? Lieut. Col. Algy Heber Percy, their CO,being a sportsman and keen fisherman from Shropshire, asked the Sappers to make him a strong fishing rod with a rope line and grappling hook on the end of it. We made this and delivered it to the forward Company at night. After several casts the corpse was hooked and dragged into our lines.

By the beginning of March the Company was well established, with Ben Chubb and 1 Section working from a farmhouse on Queen Street. They had the two main tracks, Downing Street and Bond Street, from the road up to Harrogate Drump, the main RASC dump for the whole sector; they also had Charles Street and Oxford Street up to Cheshire forward dump. I made the Queen Street farmhouse my tactical headquarters, as being a central pivot for all the work. My diary notes that on Saturday 26 February it was hit by a German 105mm shell: this we reckoned was a fluke stray shot and indeed, fortunately, it was not repeated. But on the previous day Corporal, now Sergeant, Wootton, while working with 1 Section on one of the higher tracks, was wounded in the foot when his party was heavily shelled. It was not serious, and we only lost him for a few weeks.

Meanwhile Peter Boston with his 2 Section set up his base at Osteria, a tiny hamlet about a mile east of our farmhouse on the Queen Street road, from where he looked after Fleet Street and Lombard Street. He also took on Beak Street, which was our brand new track, hopefully unknown to the enemy. From Harrogate dump up to the forward dump at Hell's Corner via Low Street was a very long way. These high tracks all took about an hour to reach, and we did an awful lot of walking.

The only effective way to maintain them was for a Sub-section of Sappers with

*My Forward Company HQ 1 March 1944*

picks and shovels and a borrowed mule to patrol each track once every day.

On 1 March Malcolm took 3 Section up to Cheshire Dump in order to have Sappers available on the highest tracks, but he soon had to come down to Harrogate to help 10 Brigade HQ dig in, and later to take on Fleet Street, the Jeep track. 2 March was the first really fine day since our arrival, and very welcome it was too.

At the end of February we were allocated a party of a dozen Italian workmen under their own sergeant Barboni and an interpreter, Valerio Bianchini, whom we nicknamed Willie. He had been employed by the Banco di Roma and just before the war had been attached to the Westminster Bank in London for three months. His English was quite good, so he joined the Officers Mess. He rejoined his bank after the war and often came to England. Ben and I kept up with him for some years.

This little group, our "private army", stayed with us for the whole of the Italian campaign. They were all from the north, tough hard-working types; we became very attached to them, and they to us. We gave them a truck, fed and clothed them, and paid them a labourer's wage, while they in return could and did do whatever we did, except that they were not allowed to carry weapons nor to be put into a fighting role. They were all stalwart men, especially Barboni, and worked incredibly hard. Their first introduction to working with us was on these mountain tracks, where they were very much at home, and often gave a lead to our Sappers.

Each field company and many other units in the Division took unto themselves small groups of Italian workmen who similarly became their "private armies" and did sterling work in the forthcoming campaign.

*Our kit on the way up to Harrogate Dump.*

On Saturday 4 March, after more rain, the high level tracks were in very bad condition, so Peter and I decided to move to Harrogate. The Ornito – Cerasola track, which we called High Street, was a particularly difficult one with a ropeway across a gorge. It required Sappers in attendance to work on it at night. I told Rodgers my Batman to borrow a mule to take our kit up to Harrogate.

It was a horrendous experience for Rodgers, which he never forgot. He had little or no experience of mules and was ragged unmercifully about it when he returned to normal Mess duties later on in Lauro. The Arab muleteers helped him to rope on our bivouacs,bedrolls and some dry clothes, and set him off up Bond Street track. The going was rough and the mule probably obstinate, but he made it to Harrogate and there, with the help of Peter's batman Gregory, they unloaded the gear. Rodgers managed to find some mules going down and thankfully got rid of his charge. We did not think much of Harrogate but with Peter and Eddie we managed to rig up quite a cosy bivouac.

There was a heavy fall of snow on Monday night and it became very cold; but Tuesday was sunny all day and the tracks dried up quite well. Peter and Eddie, with 2 Section, moved up to Cheshire to relieve Malcolm, who with 3 Section came down to Harrogate; all this while the enemy kept up intense pressure on our Infantry who were sticking it out on the tops. They were beginning to get very tired.

On Thursday 9 March we were out of the mountains, taking on work in the Garigliano valley from 225 Field Company. I moved the Company Tactical Headquarters to Osteria as a good centre for work in the valley, while Peter and 2 Section constructed an Italian floating Kapok footbridge across the Garigliano close to a demolished dam. This was quite an exciting job, as the Garigliano is a fast flowing river, and it took all Peter's ingenuity to get the bridge across without it being swept away. Peter's task was not made easier by being subjected to a heavy bombing raid from some rogue American "Flying Fortresses" during this operation; luckily there were no casualties. He had suffered the same treatment from American bombers on the tip of Cap Bon and was always rather scathing about the reliability of the American Air Force as a result.

However, after this latest attack, he discovered that there were some hot sulphur baths in a cave adjacent to his bridging site. He decided to patronise them and, in spite of the fearful stench of sulphur, found the hot yellow waters extremely relaxing. I too had a bath in this hot sulphur water and felt a lot cleaner.

We also took over the maintenance of the other two bridges, Pateley and Skipton. Furthest forward was Pateley Bridge, which was built of folding boat equipment and took up to 9-ton vehicles, i.e. all lorries and trucks but definitely not tanks. It was in view of the enemy, who tended to shell it whenever anyone was crossing, so it was no good trying to enforce a speed limit. The technique for crossing was not to follow another vehicle but to wait and dash across independently. The Germans usually fired when they saw a vehicle crossing, too late to hit the vehicle, but might catch a following vehicle or create a pot-hole in the road in front of it. I remember once with my driver Sullivan driving along a similar stretch of road in North Africa which was in view of the enemy and was pockmarked with huge pot-holes or small shell craters. Sullivan drove straight and fast with no thought for me or the vehicle. So I said to him, "Where on earth did you learn to drive?" to which he replied, "I was a dumper driver at Elmdon Airport contract." This was a contract being undertaken by my old firm just before the war. I knew it well.

Pateley bridge was not a popular bridge but Ben Chubb took on its maintenance with his 1 Section quite philosophically and with no complaint. The other bridge was Skipton, which was a class 40 pontoon bridge, and this would take tanks. It was hidden from the enemy and was quite popular, on the direct supply route from Lauro to Harrogate. The maintenance of this bridge was taken over by Malcolm and 3 Section.

The weather remained cold and wet, but at least we were out of the mountains and could get our clothing dried. There were few buildings in the valley, and what did exist were requisitioned and used by the Army. Our Italians, under Sergeant Barboni, were employed on the main roads, and a very good job they did.

There then followed a week of rumours of a big push being mounted against Cassino, and a more local rumour that 4th Division was shortly going to hand over the Garigliano sector to a French Division; it was also hinted that 4th Division was to join the fray against Cassino. These rumours came to a head over the weekend of 18/19 March, when we heard that Cassino town had fallen to the New Zealanders under General Freyburg – but not the monastery, which dominated the whole area.

On Saturday 18 March, quite unexpectedly, we met the French Engineer officers, who announced that they were taking over from us. Their Company, 2/3 Genie Français, arrived next day and we took them on a tour of the area. This also coincided with the completion of the Fleet Street Jeep track, which greatly pleased Lieut.Col. John Nelson.

Two days later 4th Division began handing over to 4th Division Montagne Marocain, and I note from my diary that the roof of our billet at Osteria fell in, through excessive gunfire vibration. A glance at my sketch of our first billet at the farm on the Garigliano shows what poor roofs they were. Next day, Tuesday 21 March, we completed our hand-over to the 2/3 Genie Français and moved back to Lauro.

It was nice to be back in Lauro, and it did not seem half such a bad place as we had thought it a month ago. Certainly after the rigours and discomforts of Harrogate and Cheshire dumps it was indeed quite comfortable, and Willie set about finding some wine and a chicken for the Mess. At last the whole Company was all together again and united with its transport, plus the addition of Sergeant Barboni and his section of Italians. Our East Enders really did enjoy being all together again and celebrated accordingly with the help of the locals.

It was nice to re-establish the Officers Mess and enjoy cook Parry's meals again. Peter and Ben were able to continue their chess in a corner, surrounded by a blue haze of tobacco smoke. Not least, our batmen were pleased to get back to a bit of civilised living. But it did not last; within a week we moved eastwards as a complete unit, into truly mountainous country south of, and facing, Monte Cairo. We bivouacked not far from a bleak hilltop village with the formidable name of Aquafondata, at a height of over 2000ft. This village was now a major supply base.

That night, Saturday 25 March, a terrific blizzard blew up, and the Company was almost completely buried under snow. At the time Vesuvius was erupting, sending up great clouds of green ash, and it was thought that the blizzard might have been caused by the eruption. It was a thoroughly bleak place, and we looked back with nostalgia to scruffy Lauro. Peter tells me that in the middle of that night I went out into the blizzard to attend to nature and tripped over his tent guys, dislodging the pins and causing his tent to collapse upon him snow and all for the rest of the night. It was not my most popular moment.

It appeared that our next job was to construct a road from Aquafondata down a dry water-course to the village of St. Elia, a drop of nearly 1800ft. in about 6,000 yards, or three and a half miles. What a prospect! It came to be known as the "Inferno track", because on our Italian maps the river gorge was called Inferno. This can be seen on map 8 on page 94.

On Tuesday morning, 28 March, I took Peter with me to meet up with Lieut. Col. John Nelson and look at this track. Some work had been done on it, but not much; the reason for looking at it was that with the capture of Cassino town the garrison troops had to be supplied at night from St.Elia, lying in the valley opposite Cassino and immediately below both Monte Cassino Monastery,and the peak of Monte Cairo both held by the Germans. The north road down from Aquafondata to St. Elia was in full view of the enemy, whereas if we could make a passable road down the Inferno water-course, for downhill traffic only, it would be completely out of view of the enemy. The trucks could go back empty up the north road to Aquafondata base on a one-way circuit. It was a good plan.

It took two days to do a proper survey of the route and to work out how to do the work, mostly bulldozing, in such a way as to try and work on the whole length simultaneously. Our Italians were going to be in their element, and in addition an Indian Pioneer Company was made available to us.

On Thursday 30 March the whole company moved, complete and on foot, down the track to about the half-way point, where we were able to pitch our tents entirely out of sight of the enemy and nicely sheltered from the weather, provided there was not sufficient rain to flood the water-course. We left our vehicles and a good deal of our gear with a small rear party at Aquafondata. The job was of such magnitude and such a challenge that everyone was quite excited.

By the weekend work was in full swing, and the weather was improving. There was also quite a good moon, so shift work could continue at night. Every bulldozer we could get was pushing rock and earth downwards, while Indian Pioneers, English Sappers and our Italian labourers were following, trimming batters and making a reasonable road surface. We used air compressors, picks, and shovels.

The gradients were mostly 1 in 4 or 1 in 5, with three short sections of 1 in $3\frac{1}{2}$. However, it was very twisty, so if a vehicle's brakes did fail it would not go far before running into the bank; later there were recovery vehicles stationed at all the worst places. The map on page 94 gives a good idea of the route, and in the corner an illustration of the large road signs painted by Major Low of 7 Field Company, which were set up at every corner.

On Thursday 6 April Lieut. Col. John Nelson brought Brigadier Christopher Walkey, the Chief Engineer of XIII Corps, to have a look at it. Invited to drive down it in his Jeep as far as our Company area, his driver reluctantly agreed. The Brigadier was delighted with the progress so far, but the need to get supply vehicles down it to St. Elia was very great; lorries and jeeps using the north road were being shelled. We were given until 11 April to complete it for light lorries and jeeps – exactly two weeks after we had first looked at it.

Sunday 9 April was Easter Day. The weather had become quite hot, but work on the track continued with unabated energy,with only two days left to our target completion date. Then on Monday the Germans shelled the track, to everyone's consternation and irritation: they must have seen dust rising from the ravine. However, the job just had to be finished, for everyone in the Company was determined to keep to our target date of p.m. on 11 April. By a superhuman effort the Inferno track was declared open on the afternoon of the 11th, and the first convoy of light lorries and jeeps slid safely down to St. Elia that night.

There were some very scared drivers, but they all preferred it to the far more scary north road. On Thursday I handed over to the 14 Field Company Canadian Engineers, who took on responsibility for the road.

On Friday 14 April the whole Company moved back to Piedimonte d'Alife, way back on the upper reaches of the river Volturno, to get some sleep and clean up. We were to set up a bridging camp and start training with Bailey Bridge equipment for use at Cassino.

It had been a hectic two months since we left Egypt.

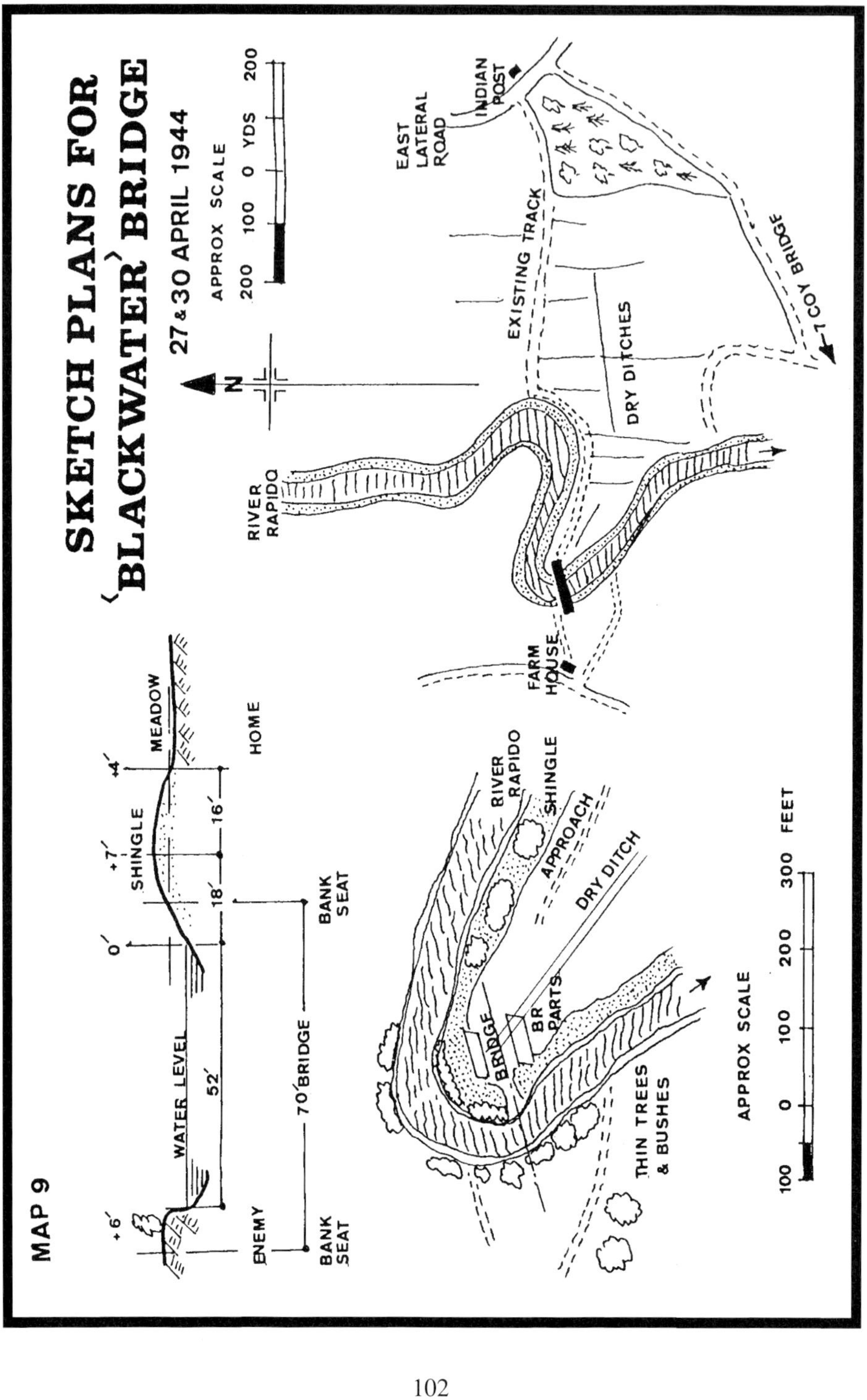
MAP 9
SKETCH PLANS FOR 'BLACKWATER' BRIDGE
27 & 30 APRIL 1944
APPROX SCALE
200 100 0 YDS 200
N
+6'
ENEMY
BANK SEAT
WATER LEVEL
52'
70' BRIDGE
0'
+7'
SHINGLE
18'
16'
+4'
MEADOW
HOME
BANK SEAT
RIVER RAPIDO
SHINGLE
APPROACH
DRY DITCH
BRIDGE
BR PARTS
THIN TREES & BUSHES
APPROX SCALE
100 0 100 200 300 FEET
RIVER RAPIDO
FARM HOUSE
EXISTING TRACK
DRY DITCHES
EAST LATERAL ROAD
INDIAN POST
7 COY BRIDGE

# CHAPTER IX

## Cassino – Planning

Piedimonte D'alife, with its rather pleasant sounding name, was a garden of tranquillity after the rigours of Aquafondata. We set up our Company camp in a vineyard of young vines. It was a very agreeable spot; but we had work to do.

It was now 15 April and for some reason which I now forget we were working with 12 Brigade instead of 10 Brigade, and therefore had to get to know the 12 Brigade infantry battalions, 6 Black Watch, 2 Royal Fusiliers, and 1 Royal West Kents.

This was made easier by the fact that the whole Brigade was billeted in the area. The Battalions were practising assault crossings of the Volturno river and our Sapper sections 1, 2 and 3 were joining them for assault crossing exercises. Capt. John Heath and I meanwhile chose a fairly narrow deep-water site suitable for launching and delaunching a Bailey Bridge.

Spring had come suddenly, and the weather was hot and sunny. Blossom and spring green appeared everywhere; it was all very refreshing and in no time at all the men were thoroughly enjoying life. Our Italians started making their own pasta, hanging it up to dry on the vines in the sun: hence perhaps the myth that pasta grows on trees.

However, before describing the detailed planning with which the Company from now on became involved, it is important to look briefly at the overall tactical situation. As described in Chapter VII, the Germans had maintained a very strong winter defensive line right across Italy, known as the "Gustav" line. On the west this followed the high ground north of the Garigliano river, where we had been, then following its tributary, the river Rapido, in the valley below Monte Cassino Monastery and Monte Cairo, and then across the high Apennines to the East Coast. The only possible gateway to the north was up the valley of the Liri river, following National Route 6 through Cassino town and north towards Rome; the east coast route was too narrow to be of any use.

The Liri valley was completely dominated by Monte Cassino, held by the Germans and rising steeply above the valleys overlooking the Liri to the west, and the Rapido to the south, with the Allies holding the land on its southern bank. Peter Boston's

*Monastery Hill Cassino from Cox's Corner at dusk. May '44.*

sketch of the Monastery hill as one rounded 'Cox's Corner' on the main road leading down to Cassino town from the shoulders of Mt. Trocchio shows vividly the extent to which it overlooked the area. Monte Cassino was the key to Rome and the whole of Italy, and must be taken before any progress could be made. The Germans knew this as well if not better than we did, and were determined to hold onto it. Any assault on Monte Cassino must first win an assault crossing of the little river Rapido, no more than sixty to eighty feet wide, but deep and fast-flowing.

The Americans first had a crack at Cassino in February, but were beaten back with fairly heavy losses. Next the New Zealanders under General Freyburg attacked on 26 March, backed up by Fortress bombers pounding the town and monastery. It was impressive, but only partially successful. The New Zealanders had a tenuous hold on Cassino town; but still the Germans bobbed up from cellars and dugouts. It was a stalemate.

General Alexander, Allied Commander, therefore decided to mount a really big assault on this sector, with each assaulting division backed up by a second Infantry division, and behind it an Armoured division. The date chosen was to be 12 May, which allowed just five weeks from the time the decision was taken to train the assaulting divisions and build up stocks of ammunition, as well as getting the guns into position. From the day we arrived at Piedimonte d'Alife we had precisely four weeks.

General Alexander's Order of Battle for Cassino was broadly as follows. Away on the right in the Appennine mountains was X Corps with 1st Canadian Division immediately on our right, and then the Polish Corps whose role was to attack the back of the Monastery in order to try and outflank the German garrison. In the centre the Guards Brigade whose job it was to contain the German garrison in Cassino Town at the foot of Monastery hill.

The main centre thrust was to be 4th Division with 8th Indian Division on our left to make the main attack to the left of Cassino Town and to try to link up with the Polish Corps behind the Monastery hill. 6th Armoured Division was poised to break through and hopefully chase the Germans back to Rome. 78th Division was in reserve to back up 4th Division or 8th Indian Division if needed.

Away on our left was an American Corps with French and Moroccan mountain divisions on our old Garigliano massif. In all it was a formidable plan designed to crack the German 'Gustav' line once and for all. I have broadly indicated this on map 6 on page 70. The code name for the battle was to be "Operation Honker".

Under the plan the Polish Corps commanded by General Anders was to attack over the mountains on the right, while 4th Division on the left would cross the Rapido and swing right-handed to link up with the Poles on Route 6, north of Cassino, then continue until they surrounded it completely. Meanwhile the Guards Brigade would contain the German garrison from the front. It was hoped that when the garrison was completely surrounded, it would surrender.

4th Division was to assault the Rapido on a narrow front with two Brigades leading – 10 Brigade on the right, 12 Brigade on the left. 28 Brigade would be in reserve ready to burst through, swing right, and link up with the Poles. Other Divisions were attacking simultaneously on both flanks. Such was the plan.

For the Sappers, 7 Field Company on the left, commanded by Mike Low, and 225 Field Company on the right, commanded by Robin Gabbett, were each to build a class 40 Bailey Bridge and two assault boat ferries across the Rapido in their respective Brigade sectors. 59 Field Company was to build a class 9 Bailey Bridge as a return route for traffic between the two class 40 ton bridges, more or less in the centre of the divisional front; this was our task.

On 26 April the CRE, Lieut.Col. John Nelson, explained the plan to me. We studied air photographs and decided on the approximate site for our class 9 ton bridge, which was given the name "Blackwater". He told me to carry out a recce of the river line, choose the exact site for the bridge, and produce an outline plan by the morning of the 28th. (See map 9 on page 102.)

Meanwhile on Sunday 23 April the complete Company had moved to Mignano, a village about ten miles south of Cassino on Route 6. All three Sections were working on improving tracks from Route 6 to a road running parallel and quite close to the Rapido; we had been given eight days to make these tracks up to Class 9 standard, and because the whole area was in view of the enemy on Monte Cassino all work was done by night. By day, the men slept.

After my meeting with the CRE we held a Company "Council of War" and decided that Peter Boston would build the bridge with his 2 Section and Ben Chubb would improve the approach and exit with half his 1 Section, while the other half was earmarked to work on ferries. Malcolm Drummond's 3 Section was the CRE's reserve, which I could not use.

We accordingly decided to carry out a recce of the bridge site and approaches the following night. On the evening of the 27th, Peter, Ben and I set off with Sergeant Cox in my jeep at dusk. We had arranged to rendezvous at the Company headquarters of the Indian Battalion, who were then holding the river. There we met Mike Low, who commanded 7 Field Company and was also doing a recce of his own class 40 bridge site further to our left. We learnt the password – an essential precaution which if I remember correctly was "rice pudding". The challenge being RICE and the reply PUDDING – and we told the Indians where we were going, and that we intended to be back in about an hour. The river itself was "no man's land" but was freely patrolled by both Allies and Germans alike.

From there we made our way in single file down the approach track to the river. It was fairly light, with a half moon, very quiet, and extremely eerie. The river had a flood bank of gravel which had at some time been dredged out of it. There was still plenty of American equipment lying about, and some very unpleasant smells. We made our way very slowly, keeping below the flood bank, towards our bridge site on a bend of the river, stopping often to listen. When we reached the bend Sergeant Cox lay down on the bank with his tommy gun cocked, as "look-out" man. We all carried Thompson Sub Machine guns. (See Map 9 on page 102).

Meanwhile Peter, Ben and I had a long argument as to who should swim the river. The point of this was, of course, to stretch a tape across the river in order to confirm the exact width, which could at present only be estimated from aerial photographs. Peter wanted to swim, but I thought it was too light, and was against it. At that moment Sergeant Cox rolled down the bank to say that four Germans were on the other side; so we all had a look, and there they were, four of them, quite clear and only 70 or 80ft. away. They must have been Sappers too, for each carried a shovel on his shoulder. What an easy shot! but we were not out to make trouble – that finally decided me: none of us was going to swim the river that night.

Instead, we quietly measured up the area for space to dump stores and build the bridge. The gravel bank was about 4ft. high, so we decided it would have to be bulldozed through, and in addition there was an annoying little dry ditch plumb in the middle of the building area. Having taken all the measurements we needed, we decided to clear out back to the road without more ado. On our way back Ben and I made notes of the amount of work required on the approach track, for it was nearly three-quarters of a mile long, with a number of little dry ditches to cross. Having reached the road, somewhat relieved, we checked in with the Indians and drove back home to the Company.

We got in at about 0100 hours, and cook Parry had hot tea and food ready for us. All three of us then got down to preparing the outline plan, working in the office truck. Peter drew a plan of the building area, Ben worked out his notes on the approach track, and I worked out the design for an 80ft. class 9 Bailey Bridge, preparing a work table, transport table, etc. At last we finished, and got to bed about 0300 hours. I felt I now had a much clearer picture in my mind of what we were up against, and how best to overcome it.

Next morning I took my plan to the Lieut.Col., John Nelson, and we discussed it together. The only real comment that arose from our discussion was that we MUST get across the river to measure its width accurately, and have a "look-see" at the far bank.

The big question of course was – who was going to swim across, an officer or a volunteer good swimmer? I decided that as there was only one officer to 68 men, I would not risk an officer, and called for volunteers. There were plenty, for morale in the Company was very high just then, anything for a bit of excitement, and I chose driver McTighe. He was the best swimmer in the Company and was Peter's own driver. We intended to go down again the following night, but when the time came it was rather light with a very bright moon, so we decided to delay for twenty-four hours. Luckily the next night, 30 April, was cloudy and just right, for it was our last chance.

That evening the party consisted of Peter, myself, Sergeant Cox, and driver McTighe. Again we set off in my jeep at dusk, and again we met Mike Low, working on the approach to his bridge. We called on the Indians again, to tell them of our movements; this was very necessary as they were extremely light on the trigger and delighted in shooting at strangers. Robin Gabbett had already had a grenade thrown at him while having a look at his bridge site away to our right. This time we all went down Mike Low's track towards his bridge as far as the river. Again it was extremely eerie, but not quite so light. The plan was for us then to crawl to the right along the bank to our bend. If we got into trouble and shooting started, Mike would come along with his Sappers to our rescue, but we reached our bend and all was very quiet.

I lay on the bank to the left, tommy gun cocked, and watched the enemy bank intently. Sergeant Cox did the same, some forty yards to the right, while Peter and McTighe in the centre prepared to measure the width of the river. McTighe took off his clothes but wore canvas shoes, dark swimming trunks, and my brown pullover to hide his pale skin. He tied the end of the measuring tape to his waist, waded in, and swam quickly across, being carried a few yards downstream. He was just making his way upstream under the far bank to get immediately opposite Peter again when two loud explosions went off over his head; he gave a tug on the tape, which was the signal for Peter to pull tight the scrap of white tape through which the measuring tape had run at the water's edge.

McTighe was untouched, and swam the 60 odd feet back twice as fast as he had ever swum in his life. Once the two men were back behind the bank we bundled up our belongings and got out of the place as fast as we could, back up our own track to the road.

Back on the road, McTighe put his clothes on again and we had a look at the tape. It only measured 52ft. which seemed a little short, but I certainly didn't fancy doing it all again. At this moment Mike Low arrived – having heard the explosions he came round to see what was up, and was delighted to find us all safe and sound. We jumped into the jeep and drove home again, to find cook Parry ready with tea for us as usual. We laced it with whisky and drank to the health of "Blackwater" bridge.

Next day of course, inevitably, the CRE would not believe our figure of 52ft. I was sure it was correct, so I asked if it would be possible to try and persuade the Divisional reconnaissance flight to fly a special air photo recce. This they did, and when the photographs came in and were enlarged they clearly showed 55ft. We were vindicated, and the CRE accepted 55ft. as the width of the water, which was subsequently found to be correct when the bridge came to be built.

The next thing to be done was to prepare the Company's final plan for the operation, and Peter and I worked together on this. The bridge was to be a 70ft. single truss construction, but Peter devised an unorthodox method of building so as to cut down to the very barest minimum of work required on the enemy bank. So began another tussle: I took Peter's side, being convinced by the calculations that it would work, but the CRE was adamantly opposed to any divergence from the strictly orthodox method of launching a Bailey Bridge, which entailed the removal of a "skeleton nose" on the far bank. Peter's method employed a counter-weight to cut out any dismantling on the other bank.

To cut a long story short, we won our case and John Nelson agreed, subject to the actual rehearsals proving successful. As a general hard and fast rule, Bailey Bridges should never be built by unorthodox methods unless there is plenty of time to rehearse, because in training the Sappers are taught the orthodox method until they can do it in their sleep. However, on this occasion there was ample time to rehearse.

Events were now working up to a climax. All along Route 6 there was evidence of a huge build-up of units of 8th and 1st Armies, and enormous dumps of ammunition and petrol. The tracks which we had been improving from Route 6 to the Rapido were finished on the night of 3 May, and the CRE was delighted with them. The weather was now set fair and getting quite hot by day. We had just received orders to go into khaki drill and were glad enough to get out of battle-dress.

On Thursday 4 May the "Blackwater" bridging team assembled. It consisted of Peter with his 2 Section. Ben Chubb with half his 1 Section, Lieutenant Williams with the bridging lorries, twenty Northumberland Fusiliers to help unload and hump stores, and a D7 Bulldozer from 18 Field Park Company. A total of 70 men, 32 vehicles, and five officers, including myself. On this occasion we were not allowed to include our Italians. We moved back to the village of Pietravairano on the Volturno river quite close to Piedimonte d'Alife, where we had been before. We chose a bend in the river as similar as possible to our bend in the Rapido and set up camp in a pleasant shady olive grove.

We had five days to build and rebuild this little bridge until we all knew the sequence so well that every single man was completely confident. On Saturday 6 May I attended a conference at 4th Division HQ when Major General Dudley Ward, the Divisional Commander, unfolded in detail the Divisional Plan for the forthcoming operation, which was code-named "Honker". On Sunday night Peter and the team built the bridge for the fourth time under a bright full moon, and on Monday we built it again as a full dress rehearsal for the last time, in exactly two and a half hours. We were very confident, and ready to go. On Tuesday 9 May the team returned to the Company at Mignano; once again we were all together, with only two days left before the battle was due to commence, at 2200 hours, "H Hour" on Friday 12 May.

50

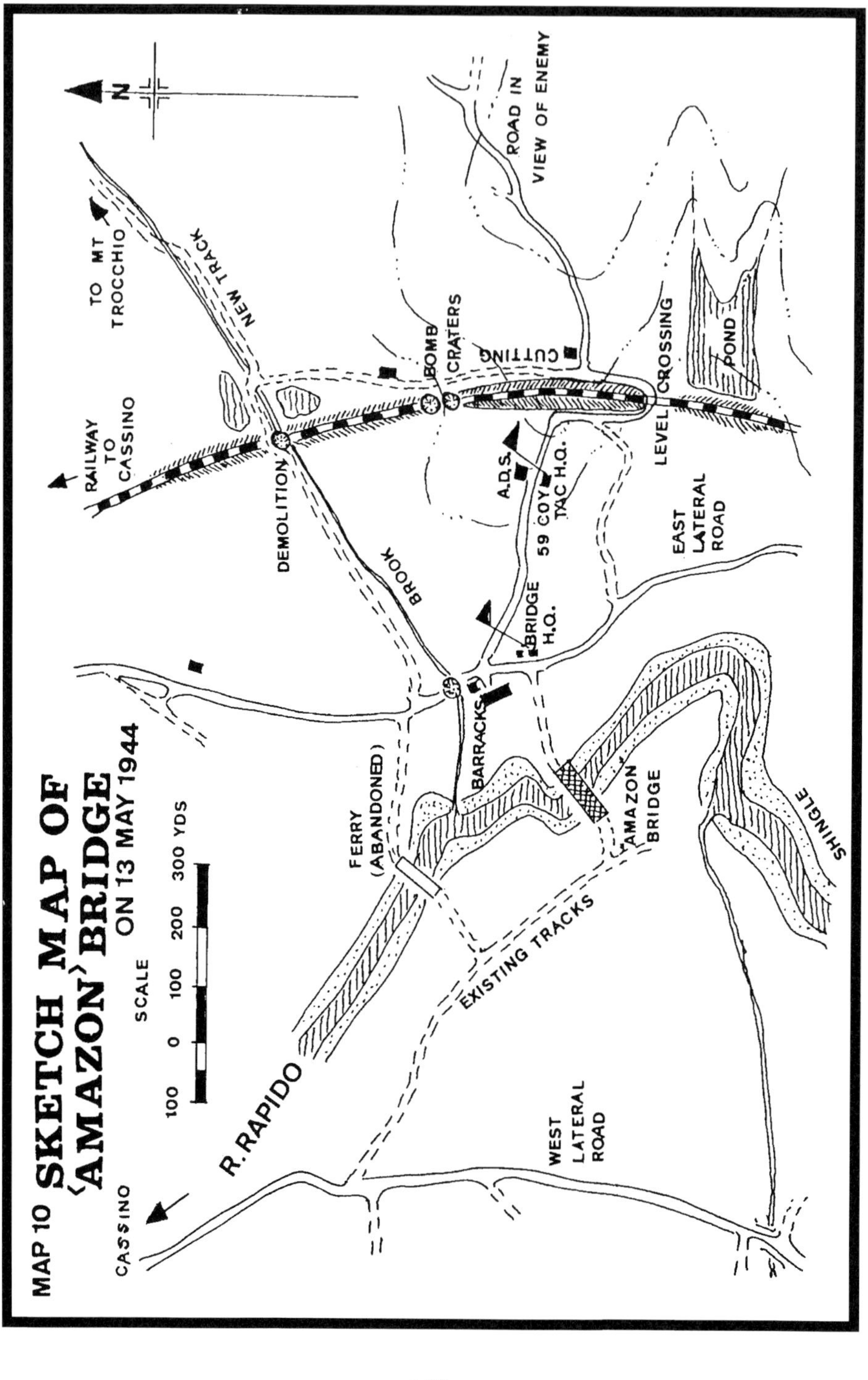
MAP 10 SKETCH MAP OF 'AMAZON' BRIDGE
ON 13 MAY 1944
SCALE
100 0 100 200 300 YDS
N
CASSINO
R. RAPIDO
WEST LATERAL ROAD
EXISTING TRACKS
FERRY (ABANDONED)
AMAZON BRIDGE
SHINGLE
BARRACKS
BRIDGE H.Q.
EAST LATERAL ROAD
59 COY TAC H.Q.
A.D.S.
BROOK
DEMOLITION
RAILWAY TO CASSINO
TO MT TROCCHIO
NEW TRACK
BOMB CRATERS
CUTTING
LEVEL CROSSING
POND
ROAD IN VIEW OF ENEMY

# CHAPTER X

## Cassino, The Final Battle

Wednesday morning, 10 May, still at Mignano. We had a free day: it would be the last for some time to come, and it was given over to chores, mainly washing clothes and writing letters, and it was a lovely sunny day. Everyone needed a rest. The bridging team had built our bridge a total of five times under progressively more difficult conditions, and the training throughout had gone remarkably well; the team had good reason to be optimistic. The rest of the company had been working for eight nights consecutively on improving tracks to the Rapido and were now feeling distinctly weary. There was the usual calm before the storm: everything that could be done had been done.

I should perhaps also mention at this point that this account of the operation and the planning for it in the last chapter were written up at the CRE's request immediately after the battle.

The following day was devoted to briefing every member of the team, Sappers, Fusiliers and drivers all included, and I read out the message of the Army Commander, General Sir Oliver Leese, to all ranks. (For the message, see Appendix II.) The briefing was done with the help of three visual aids; the first was a most excellent model of the river, including our bend and the hinterland behind it, built by John Notley almost entirely from air photos. In addition we had sufficient vertical air photos for every man to study; and thirdly, perhaps most useful of all, we had a set of low-level oblique-angle air photos of the river line looking towards the Germans.

That night the team moved up to a "Lying Up" area just behind Mount Trocchio, about a mile from the river. The whole area was surrounded by guns and was in fact a part of the "Divisional Gun Area". When I remarked upon this to some Gunners while doing a recce for the team, they said, "Oh yes, we usually get plastered about 10 p.m." Just when the team was due to arrive! Time went on, and no sign of them. I was getting very anxious: when at last they arrived, about an hour late, I was in a furious temper, and ordered them to dig in immediately. However, luck was with us, and no shells came in. I drove back to Company HQ at Mignano in the early hours of the morning, tired but relieved.

Next day, 12 May, I came up with the CRE in the afternoon as he wanted to wish the Sappers luck, etc. We were sitting on the ground with perhaps twenty-five Sappers grouped round, when suddenly shells started arriving, roaring in all over the area. All we could do was lie flat, pressed to the earth and pray, while the ground shook and heaved all round. It was very frightening, one literally bit the dust trying to make oneself smaller. In two minutes it was all over: we had had eighty shells – "10 rounds of gunfire" – from two batteries – and, incredibly, not a soul was hurt except Sapper Hughes, who was sitting on the latrine and stopped a small fragment of shrapnel, whilst our kit, motor-cycles, and the one or two trucks we had with us were riddled. So we took it as a good omen and said our luck was in.

"H" hour was at 2200 hours Suddenly the heavens were rent open as every gun fired simultaneously. There were, it was said, nine hundred guns firing in the Allied barrage. The noise was quite indescribable, and the flashes made it as light as day, but infinitely more lurid, while nearer the river itself could be heard the continuous swish of shells passing overhead. The whole effect was to make one, individually, feel extremely small.

Meanwhile the German, cunning fellow that he always was, did not retreat under the barrage but instead came forward to line the shingle bank of the river with machine guns. It was originally a still night with mist hanging over the river; but, to add to the general confusion, the Germans thickened up this natural mist with smoke till it was an impenetrable fog some hundred yards or more wide.

Into this thickest of "pea soup" fogs the Infantry advanced on a wide front carrying their boats in good order straight towards the river. "W", or Water Hour, was three-quarters of an hour after "H" Hour. But once in the fog they were lost; some went right, some went left, and nearly all went round in circles, coming back out of the fog into unfamiliar surroundings.

Meanwhile the Germans, who could not see either, fired their Spandau machine guns intermittently into the fog as well as mortaring spasmodically all along the river. All this fire was of course unobserved and therefore not very dangerous but, in the fog, extremely frightening. Some, very few, of the boats did get across; but the Infantry's main intention on landing was to get inland and seize their objectives, which they did all too easily, there being no Germans at their objectives. However, they did not clear the enemy off the far bank, nor were we able to get anybody to do this vital though invidious task. I did not want to use Sappers to do this, as we hardly had enough for our Engineer tasks as it was.

Half an hour after "W" hour I set up our Bridge HQ at the top of the Approach track and at the same time the bulldozer trundled down the track to the river. This seemed to enrage the enemy, who directed all his available fire in the direction of the sound, bringing the bulldozer to a standstill, with one driver wounded, but not until he had got almost to the bank. Every time he started up after that, a hail of bullets arrived. Next the Sappers arrived with the first of the lorries, but nothing could be done in that awful fog with bullets whizzing overhead: we simply had to get some men across to deal with those Spandau machine guns.

At this juncture the CRE arrived, and together we searched for some officers or warrant officers – but not one could we find, only dejected parties of infantry milling around with their boats. Meanwhile, however, Peter had swum across with a rope and secured both ends to trees, passing it through the bow fairlead of an Assault boat, thus making a foolproof ferry. He then found an infantry officer who raised a platoon and promised to clear out the enemy; but they soon came back, having got hopelessly lost in the fog.

All this time, of course, the bridging lorries had been arriving, strictly according to time-table, and were merely piling up at the top of the track. I stopped them eventually, but not until at least twenty out of the thirty-two had arrived. During this time Ben was able to do a bit of improvement on the track, but even that was under difficulties and several track material lorries were hit on the hill down to the river.

As the night wore on this state of chaos increased steadily, and to cut a long and exasperating story short, when dawn began to break absolutely nothing had been achieved. The Germans must have seen or sensed our concentration of vehicles at the top of the track, for suddenly they began shelling. There followed half an hour of the worst, while we tried to turn the trucks round and get them out of it. Lieut. Williams did magnificent work, finally being seriously wounded, and Sergeant Cox was also badly wounded in this jam of struggling vehicles. At this time, too, the White Scout Car, which was our Bridge HQ carrying wireless links to Company HQ and the CRE, received a bit of shrapnel the size of a fist through the radiator – much to the consternation of Company Sergeant-Major Tutton inside.

Things looked pretty bad; it was full daylight now, and the Germans had started putting over "Minenwerfers" in salvoes of six. The river was clearly in view from the Monastery, and so were we. I asked for the CRE on the wireless, explained the situation, and asked for orders; to our relief he said "Get everybody back to the Lying Up area". I sent the White Scout Car off at once and passed the word round to all the men to return individually to our field of yesterday, behind Trocchio. Finally Peter, Ben and I walked slowly back together. None of us spoke a word, our tails could not have been lower. How could it have failed after all our planning and training!

We did not know until later in the day that both the other bridges had equally failed. There was no bridge across the Rapido, and although the Infantry were across and holding their objectives, the situation was very serious. On our left flank was 8th (Indian) Division. Their Sappers had also tried all night to put a Bailey bridge across the Rapido further downstream by launching it balanced on the chassis of a Sherman tank, but this also had failed.

In the original Sapper plan for operation "Honker", each field company was to build a bridge across the river Rapido on the night of 12 May, immediately after the Infantry had crossed in assault boats and secured a bridge-head. Unfortunately this bridge-head was never secured in sufficient strength to allow any of the bridges to be commenced.

Therefore, since all attempts to bridge the river Rapido on the night of 12 May had failed, the CRE decided to make an "all-out" Divisional Sapper attempt to bridge the river on the next night, 13 May, employing each company in turn with the intention of getting a bridge across at all costs which would be capable of carrying tanks. The site chosen was the original site of 225 Field Company's bridge "Amazon". The plan adopted was also 225 Field Company's own original plan, and OC 225 Field

Company – Major Robin Gabbett – was therefore put in charge of the operation. The companies were to relieve each other as each became exhausted, in the order 225 Company, 7 Company, and lastly 59 Company. The bridge was to be an 80 feet – orthodox – Double Girder Bailey Bridge Class 40. (See map 10 on page 111.)

We were advised that due to the action of our own infantry who the previous night had taken and were still holding key positions behind the enemy lines, some half a mile or so beyond the river line, there was likely to be less effective enemy interference on the far bank. This was indeed found to be the case although enemy shell and mortar fire continued unabated.

Work began soon after 1700 hours by 225 Field Company on the near bank and near approach. 7 Field Company moved from their "lying up" area to the railway cutting, arriving about 1900 hours. 59 Field Company moved up next to an area behind the railway cutting, arriving in at about 2000 hours. I went forward with Peter and Ben to report to Robin Gabbett at about 2030 hours; on the way I met Lieut. Hobson of 7 Field Company who was just taking his men down to the bridge site to relieve 225 Field Company; the latter had had a difficult time owing to enemy observation in the fading light. I also met Lieut. Severn of 225 Field Company on his way back from the bridge site. He told me that he had finished bulldozing and had the launching rollers in position. We then went on to report to Robin Gabbett at his bridge HQ near the "Barracks".

It was decided that I should bring 59 Company Sections down to the railway cutting as each section of 7 Field Company went out, so as to be as near as possible to the job, and at the same time to set up my tactical HQ in the small building opposite the Advanced Dressing Station. On my way back I met the Commander of the Section of 586 Field Company RE, who were also to be available to finish off construction if necessary and to take over the bridge when complete; in the event, they were not used. We then went on back to bring up the Company.

The railway cutting referred to is the subject of a sketch I drew when we were working on these tracks well prior to the battle. But it does show very clearly the extent to which the Monastery dominated the whole area. It can be located on the map (Map 10 see page 111) by reference to the two bomb craters on the railway line. Also it is interesting to note that all the sleepers of the left hand track had been broken by means of a huge ripper cutting hook dragged behind a heavy locomotive. This would have disturbed the track bed so much that the same operation could not have been repeated on the track the other side.

Going back up the lane we saw the bulldozer grinding slowly across the fields, back towards the railway cutting, with the driver walking crouched behind his machine. This field was in full view of the opposite bank and was periodically swept by fire from an enemy Spandau. When he got to the cutting I asked him how he had got on; he told me he had finished the job, but that his blade elevating gear had been hit and put out of action. There was still a smaller D4 bulldozer on the site, which was working.

At the Advanced Dressing station I heard bad news, that Major Mike Low – OC

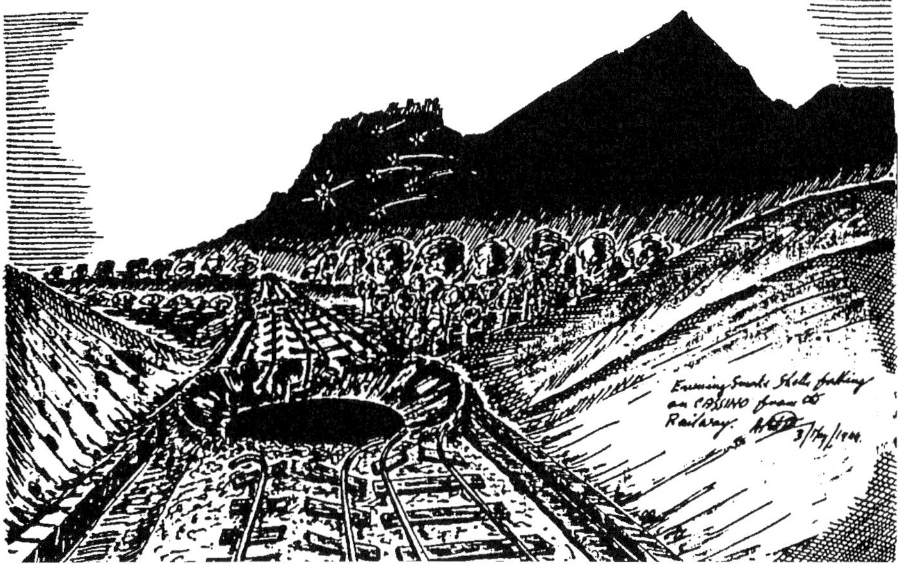

Evening smoke shells falling on Cassino. 3 May 1944

of 7 Field Company – had been hit in the legs by this same Spandau on the track just to the south of the one we had come up. Apparently he and the CRE had gone down this track to see how things were getting on; at a rather open stretch the CRE had doubled across, with Mike Low following him. Suddenly the Spandau opened up and hit Mike in both legs: whereupon the CRE carried him back up the track to the railway. From there he was taken to the Advanced Dressing Station on a stretcher, and had just left the Station when I arrived.

By the time the men were down in the cutting it was dark, about 2130 hours. I left John Notley and Company Sergeant-Major Tutton at my Tactical HQ to collect the men and despatch them down to the bridge site as required. Lieut. Barnes of 7 Field Company then arrived and asked for a Section to assist in unloading, as the remainder of the bridging lorries had been sent for. Malcolm Drummond with 3 Section of 59 Field Company was detailed and went down to the bridge, at about 2145 hours. Peter and I joined Robin Gabbett at Bridge HQ It was now quite dark, and building had commenced. Bridging lorries were also arriving quite fast, despatched by vehicle control. As bridging lorries were required at the bridge site, a demand was sent over the air to vehicle control, a channel of communication which worked extremely well right though the job.

Throughout the operation Robin Gabbett was in charge. He set up his Bridge HQ in some slit trenches just off the road behind the "Barracks", and installed in it his own wireless set direct to CRE and his Company wireless set to vehicle control. He had with him his own personal runner and one or two Company runners. Communication with the bridge site was originally by "Walkie Talkie" wireless sets, but later on the set at the bridge was damaged and communication was by runner. This chain of communication was maintained without a break throughout the night until after the tanks had gone through, in spite of Bridge HQ's quick move to a culvert under the road some 50 yards away. This was when a lorry belonging to the smoke people was hit on the road beside Bridge HQ, at about 0200 hours: it immediately caught fire and blazed furiously for about two hours, its load of smoke canisters contributing substantially to the flames, and attracting fire from the enemy. Efforts were made to put it out, but failed effectively as it was too hot to approach. At the same time enemy shelling set fire to some hayricks at the top of the field, adding to the conflagration. Our culvert proved a nice safe place for the rest of the night.

Shortly after returning to Bridge HQ at 2200 hours, Lieut. Hobson of 7 Field Company, who was Officer in charge of construction, asked me for a party to work on the far bank. Peter went down with two Sub-sections of 2 Section, the remaining two Sub-sections following shortly afterwards. On arrival several attempts were made to get a ferry across, but failed due to enemy snipers on the far bank. The plan to build a ferry was therefore abandoned for the time being, and Peter with his party assisted in the construction of the bridge.

By this time the Launching Nose was nearly finished and the bridge proper was ready to be commenced on the building rollers. This was actually delayed until all the lorries had been unloaded; there were not enough men to unload and to build at the same time, as it was not considered wise to have too many men on the site. However, due to the high shingle bank the building site was comparatively immune to small arms fire from the far bank, although the lorries were very vulnerable to mortar fire. It was therefore essential to get them away quickly, and all bar one got safely back.

Meanwhile the bridging lorries were arriving somewhat irregularly, due to the traffic regulating system having broken down so that empty lorries were meeting full ones in the narrow lanes. I despatched John Notley to sort it out, which he did, and the remainder of the bridging lorries all arrived and were unloaded by 3 Section by about midnight.

A small incident occurred shortly before midnight which is worthy of note. One of 225 Field Company's lorries stuck in the narrow lane leading down to the "Barracks", with broken front wheel steering, completely blocking the lane and preventing the last of the bridging lorries from getting through to the site. To clear this Peter brought the D4 bulldozer up from the bridge site, and coupled it to the front axle; after much straining and slithering, the lorry was pulled clear into a field.

By midnight the position at the bridge site was that the skeleton nose was complete, all stores unloaded on site, and all was ready to commence building the bridge proper. At this juncture Peter took over complete control of the building from Lieut.Hobson of 7 Field Company – who still remained at the site to assist in spite of being very tired. Peter, who already had his own 2 Section and 3 Section (who had just finished unloading), asked for Ben Chubb and the two remaining Sub-sections of 1 Section of 59 Field Company. Two Sub-sections only of this 1 Section were available, the other two being away with Infantry Battalions. These two Sub-sections went down with Ben to the bridge. Most of 7 Field Company now left the site. I was at Bridge HQ at this time, and reported probable time of completion as 0200 hours.

However this was not to be: enemy shelling and mortaring became rather more intense, and tended to be accurate. The enemy also developed a trick of firing Verey Light flares behind the building site, which silhouetted the men against the white mist and made them an easy target for enemy snipers. I therefore called for counter battery fire, speaking direct to the CRE on the wireless, and in a very short while it came over in great strength, from 6 Army Group RA, consisting of 5 Medium Regiments and 2 Field Regiments. But at the same time a number fell short, sounding terrifyingly near; a call to "pitch them up" was immediately put through to CRE, giving the approximate bearing from whence they came. This had the desired results in a very few minutes, and no more fell short. This magnificent counter battery shoot did in fact virtually silence the enemy shelling for quite a while.

Meanwhile a large mine-clearing party of two officers and 39 sappers from 8th Field Squadron of the Armoured Division, which was to follow up, arrived to clear a tank lane on the other side; but as no ferry yet existed and the other side was extremely unhealthy, we advised only a small recce party to go across at first, and for the remainder to go further back and wait. This recce party eventually crossed by the bridge; later, unfortunately, the officer stepped on a "Schu" mine and lost his foot.

At about 0100 hours Sherman tanks were heard coming down the road, presumably expecting to cross the bridge at 0200 hours. Fearing that the noise would attract fire, Robin Gabbett asked me to try and stop them. I ran off up the road, and stopped the leading tank about 200 yards off; but the damage was done, and shelling of the area increased considerably for a short while.

Meanwhile building went on steadily but slowly, due to periodical enemy interference. First of all the time of completion was amended to 0300 hours and later, out of sheer desperation, to 0500 hours. Eventually, at about 0300 hours, the bridge was pushed forward partly by hand and partly with the help of the D4 bulldozer (the D7 having long since left the field with its blade elevating gear out of action). For some time one particular Spandau on the left had been causing almost continuous interference and quite a few casualties; so Sergeant Parry of 59 Field Company decided to go across on the Launching Nose and deal with this man. He lay full length on the leading transome until it grounded, and at once ran a few yards along the bank, throwing himself on the ground to take cover. When the Spandau opened fire he got the direction and made a dash towards the spot, firing two magazines of his Tommy Gun. The Spandau did not fire again, and Sergeant Parry returned to organise getting the Launching Nose onto rollers. The 8th Field Squadron Recce Party went across at about this time.

When the job of lifting the nose on to rollers was done and the bridge moved forward again, more Spandau bursts appeared to be coming from directly inland. Once more Sergeant Parry, but this time with Sapper Halliday, decided to go after it. They were going straight towards the Spandau when they heard cries to the right; on going to investigate they found two wounded men, an officer with his foot blown off by a "Schu" mine, and a badly wounded sergeant. Sergeant Parry took the Officer back to the bridge on his back, while Sapper Halliday and Sapper Coombs carried the

Sergeant back; they were the 8th Field Squadron recce party. Sergeant Parry and Sapper Halliday then returned to shoot up the Spandau, which they must have succeeded in doing, as his fire ceased.

Occasional strafing from the "moaning Minnie" multiple mortars continued intermittently and about this time Peter received a lump of shrapnel in the biceps of his left arm. However, he was not at the time in serious pain and continued to take charge of the bridge.

As far as I can recollect, I recommended Sergeant Parry for a Military Medal in recognition of his courage and dedication during the launching of Amazon Bridge. But I never heard if he received it posthumously, as unfortunately he was killed a month later beyond Palombara.

The bridge was built complete by 0400 hours, with only the last four bays decked, and the decking of the other four bays piled on the last bay as counterweight. Every available man plus the D4 came round to push it into position; this required a considerable effort, as it was an up-hill launch.

All went well until, with 20ft. to go, the bulldozer seized up and gave out completely; both radiator and sump had been punctured some time before.

This was a major setback, as, owing to the high floodbanks, the tail of the bridge was about 7ft from the ground and it was obviously impossible to push it forward manually at this height. Peter decided that our only salvation was to find a tank to come and push in place of the bulldozer. He ran off to find one while I went to the wireless set to report the delay and the action which we were taking.

Peter's report read as follows:

"There was nothing further which anybody could do till we found some means of mechanical propulsion, so I ordered everyone to take cover where they could find any and ran off towards the area where we had previously heard the tanks taking up their positions. It was not totally dark and I could run fairly freely, and after quartering the semi-darkness for a few minutes I was exhilarated when the unmistakable black shape of a Sherman loomed up ahead of me. I fumbled my way round it, shouting I don't know what, but all the hatches were closed and there was absolutely no sign of life within. I redoubled my shouts and beat on the armour with my fists till my knuckles bled, but could raise absolutely no response. It was like a nightmare, and I felt as useless as an ant on the hide of an elephant. In desperation, I was reduced to the inanity of kicking the tank with my toecaps – a procedure which appeared to produce absolutely no noise whatever. It was agonising to have salvation so near at hand and yet to be totally unable to make myself known. They were evidently all asleep inside, and separated from me by 2" of steel. Finally I clambered up on to one of the sprocket wheels, took out my revolver, and, with the butt, beat a furious 1-2-3, 1-2-3, on the armour plate of the turret and continued this for a minute or two. Eventually, to my unspeakable relief, the driver's visor opened and I was aware of a dim light coming through from the interior and a sleepy eye regarding me. I explained our predicament, asked for his help and without a moment's hesitation the driver agreed to help us out.

*AMAZON BRIDGE*
*The crossing of the River Rapido on the night of 12/13 May 1944 painted by Terence Cuneo and hung in the Headquarters Mess of the Corp of Royal Engineers at Chatham. Peter Boston on the bridge. Reproduced by kind permission of the Corp.*

I clambered on to the front and grasped the gun barrel for support and guided the tank up to the building site.

Everybody had clearly heard us coming and they were all on their feet in keen anticipation. With the aid of the tank we yanked the bulldozer unceremoniously out of the way and I guided the driver carefully up to the bridge. We applied the muzzle of the gun to the centre of the last transom. We were lucky in having a splendid driver – he took to the job as a duck to water, pushing gently at exactly the right speed and stopping and starting with great precision according to my shouted instructions."

When I got back to the site the tank had pulled the bulldozer out of the way and was slowly pushing the bridge forward. The enemy took extreme exception to this, and put down a number of well-aimed mortar rounds, causing several minor casualties. It was therefore decided not to waste time jacking down, but to push the bridge clean off the rollers onto the ground. It did in fact fall nicely on to the base plates; but the far side still had to be jacked up to remove the plain rollers. Once this was done the launching nose was dismantled and the ramps were quickly built. I returned to the wireless set to report this excellent progress.

In Terence Cuneo's picture of Amazon Bridge, (see book jacket illustration and photograph of picture on page 119) which was commissioned by the Corps of Royal Engineers and which hangs in their headquarters mess at Chatham, the figure standing on the bridge is Peter Boston.

When the rollers were removed from the far end, the bridge rested simply on the shingle bank, and in fact only one of the two girders on each side was carrying the load, as it had been impossible to build a proper bank seat. The bridge was therefore not strictly a Class 40 bridge; however, as speed was so essential, it was decided to leave it in this condition and trust to luck. It did in fact hold up to a squadron of tanks and considerable traffic without showing any signs of failure. Two days later it was jacked up and correctly finished off.

Meanwhile there arose a very considerable risk of the enemy staging a local counter-attack and rushing the bridge, for by this time every available Sapper was working and unarmed, and there was no one available to form a covering party. Therefore Robin Gabbett, who knew the whereabouts of the Infantry Battalion, went off to get an infantry party as protection for the bridge. At almost exactly 0500 hours a runner arrived, rather breathless, from Peter, to say that the bridge was open. A runner was immediately sent along the road to pass this information on to the tanks and, at the same time, I reported "Amazon" open to traffic to the CRE. At approximately 0520hours the 17th/21st Lancers Squadron of tanks was across.

The bridge was completed, having taken close on 12 hours and the whole resources of the 4th Division RE to build it. Credit is due to Robin Gabbett for having made the plan, laid on the organisation, and controlled the operation throughout; and credit is also due to Lieut. Severn of 225 Field Company, Lieut.Hobson of 7 Field Company, and Peter Boston of 59 Field Company, for their part in the actual building, which could never have been completed without their fine leadership and complete disregard for personal danger. Finally, great credit is due to a small mixed party of NCOs and men from all three Companies, who worked unceasingly from the beginning to the end of the operation.

Unfortunately during the night quite a number of Sappers were wounded, mostly by shrapnel from bursting mortar shells. I do not recollect how many because most of them returned in due course to the Company. However, we did lose four Sappers seriously wounded by a mortar bomb which landed right in their midst and who later died from their wounds. When the bridge was finally complete Peter went off to have his arm dealt with and was sent away to hospital in Bari. We did not see him again for a month or so. He had the satisfaction of seeing the bridge completed before allowing himself to be taken to a dressing station.

To: GOC 4th Division

HQ, XIII Corps
18 May 1944

"Now that Cassino has fallen to your Division I would like to let you know how well I consider they have done. The assault across the Rapido was undoubtedly a most formidable undertaking, as the river, so aptly named, is swift and deep and the defences were well prepared and strong. The over- running of the enemy's position was a magnificent effort, the work of your Sappers on the second night was first class, and the building of the bridge which allowed you to pass over your tanks was a turning point in the battle. Each subsequent advance which you were asked to make has been quickly and successfully carried out. What has been achieved will long be remembered as a credit to the 4th Division."

(Sgd) S. C. KIRKMAN
Lieut. General Commanding

This operation was neatly summed up in the 'Eighth Army News' under the banner headline AMAZON BRIDGE EPIC by journalist Fred Redman, and is reproduced as Appendix VI.

Next day, Sunday 14 May, the Germans were pushed back and the far bank of the Rapido cleared of enemy, which would allow the building of a second bridge as originally planned. So it was that John Notley, with 2 Section, as Peter Boston had not yet returned, was able to build Blackwater bridge without incident. The next two days were spent improving the track over Blackwater to join up with Route 6 beyond Cassino town.

Meanwhile fierce fighting was still raging on Monte Cassino Hill, and around the ruins of the monastery. 78th Division passed through 4th Division and finally cleared the hill, linking up with the Polish Corps on Thursday 18 May. The remnants of the garrison surrendered once they were surrounded.

I met a Pole coming down the hill on the morning of 18 May. He had two roses in his cap and some parchment books in his hand which he had found in the wreckage.

As he passed me he said "We have not met the Germans since Tobruk but we have not forgotten those days."

The battle had taken six days from the initial assault to breaking the "Gustav" line. It was indeed a memorable week, and a turning point in the Italian Campaign.

A bronze plaque depicting the launching of Amazon bridge based upon Terence Cuneo's picture and sculptured by Mr. David Norris FRBS was placed and dedicated in the Priory Church at Christchurch, Hants on 14 September 1989 as a memorial to Sir Donald Bailey who died in 1985.

Sir Donald invented and developed the Bailey Bridge at the Military Experimental Establishment at Christchurch in the early days of World War II, which later made an immense contribution towards final victory by maintaining the momentum of mobile warfare.

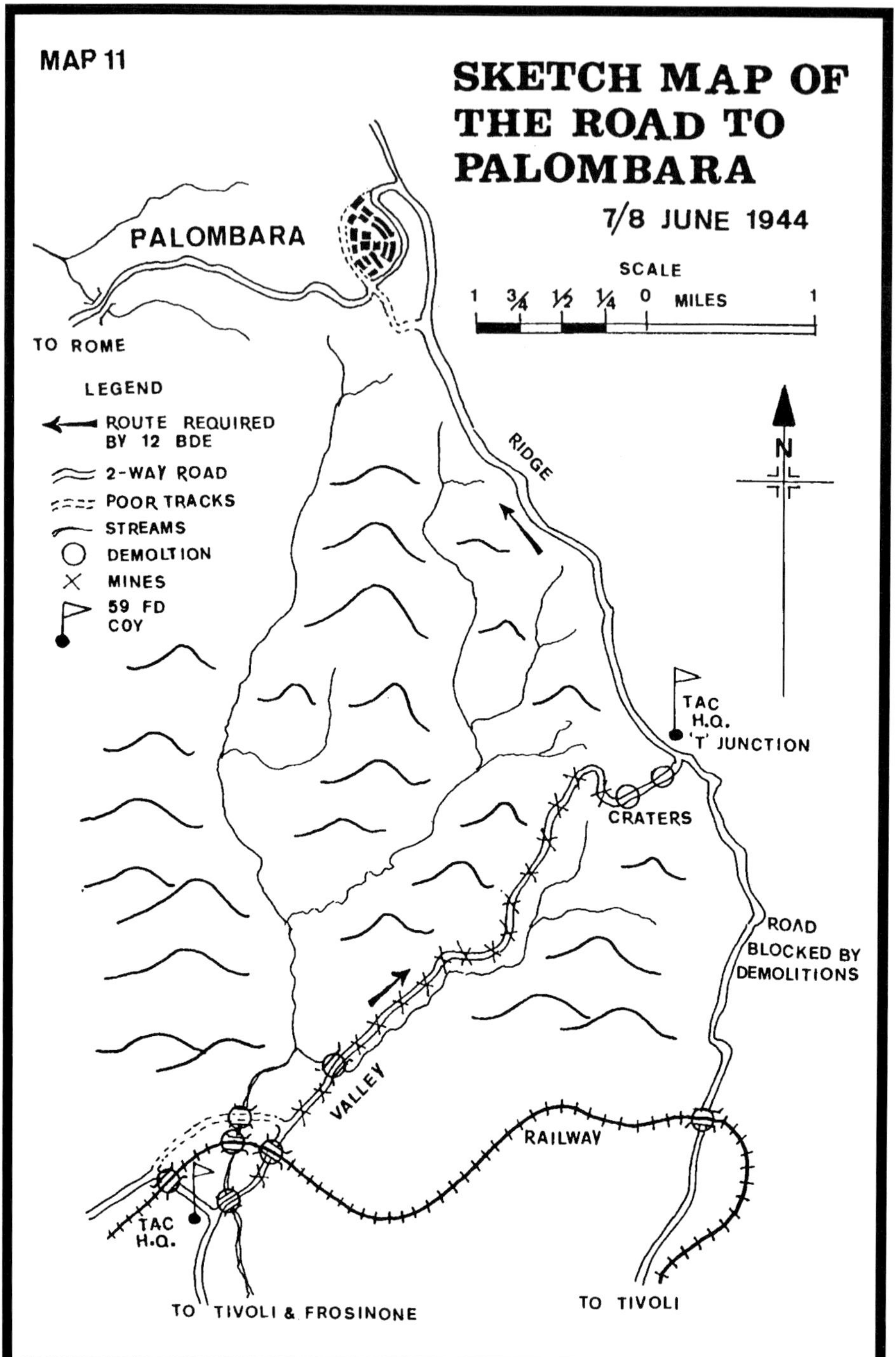
MAP 11
SKETCH MAP OF THE ROAD TO PALOMBARA
7/8 JUNE 1944
SCALE
1 3/4 1/2 1/4 0 MILES 1
PALOMBARA
TO ROME
LEGEND
ROUTE REQUIRED BY 12 BDE
2-WAY ROAD
POOR TRACKS
STREAMS
DEMOLTION
MINES
59 FD COY
RIDGE
N
TAC H.Q.
'T' JUNCTION
CRATERS
ROAD BLOCKED BY DEMOLITIONS
VALLEY
RAILWAY
TAC H.Q.
TO TIVOLI & FROSINONE
TO TIVOLI

# CHAPTER XI

## Palombara and Beyond

Now the chase was on. The Germans probably had not expected to be so decisively thrashed at Cassino and therefore were forced to drop back quite a long way before they could make a determined stand. Also, as before in Tunisia, our follow-up was very rapid. Not, however, for 4th Division, for after the fall of Monte Cassino it was the turn of 78th Division, who had gone through 4th Division, to complete the encirclement of the Monastery hill. They in turn were soon passed by 6th Armoured Division who took up the chase to Rome and the North.

On Saturday 20 May we handed over both bridges, Amazon and Blackwater, and their respective tracks up to Route 6, to XIII Corps Sappers and pulled back with other units of 4th Division to Piedimonte d'Alife to rest and refit, except for John Notley and 2 Section who had gone forward with 12 Brigade, helping them to check and clear Route 6 as far as the town of Aquino some ten miles on. They returned to the fold there next day, Sunday, which by mutual consent of all was declared a rest day. John was temporarily looking after 2 Section while Peter, who was slightly wounded at the end of the Amazon bridge building, was still away.

On Wednesday the Company was visited by Major-General Dudley Ward with the CRE, John Nelson. The Divisional Commander was making a tour of all his divisional units during this lull. The visit was very much appreciated by everyone, for he talked in a very friendly and relaxed manner to all the NCOs and Sappers whom he met, including our Italians. The weather was perfect, fine and sunny, and we all felt thoroughly refreshed.

A week later, on 1 June, we received a warning order that the division was to move up to the area of Frosinone, half way between Cassino and Tivoli on Route 6, about 50 miles on. The actual movement order arrived in the middle of the night, quite a usual occurrence. However, luckily, having been warned, we were partially packed up and moved as a company convoy after breakfast.

Next day, Saturday 3 June, we took over a very large 150ft. span Bailey Bridge carrying Route 6 across the river which flows through the middle of Frosinone. We in fact took over from XIII Corps Sappers, to whom we had handed over the Rapido bridges just two weeks previously.

This bridge, which was codenamed "Barnes Bridge", was built as a triple girder single storey Bailey Bridge; but in view of the huge amount of traffic it was likely to have to take on Route 6, the main highway to the North, including perhaps tanks on transporters, the Chief Engineer of XIII Corps advised that it should be strengthened. This could only be done by providing a second storey of Bailey panels, thus making it a triple girder double storey bridge. This was a difficult job, as it entailed a tremendous amount of lifting and humping Bailey panels. There were no mobile cranes available in those days, so we requested a twelve-hour night occupation with no traffic in order to do the job.

This was agreed, and the equipment ordered for the next night. There was a good moon and we were able to use vehicle headlights. The job was undertaken by Ben Chubb and Malcolm Drummond, with 1 and 3 Sections, and was completed by first light just ahead of our deadline.

The organisation for the supply of Bailey bridging equipment was the responsibility of 18 Field Park Company Royal Engineers, who were under the direct command of the CRE at divisional headquarters. Hence orders were always made to the CRE. However, when ordering equipment it was up to the user field company to specify exactly how much equipment was required and in what order. This was then loaded on to 3 ton Bedford lorries and sent up to the user field company. On the whole the system worked extraordinarily well, but it did depend on the user company unloading and returning the empty lorries as quickly as possible. This also suited the drivers who always helped with unloading. No lines of demarcation at the front.

Next day, Sunday 4 June, the Sappers were able to catch up with sleep in a bivouac area outside Frosinone. Unexpectedly, Peter Boston returned to the Company, from

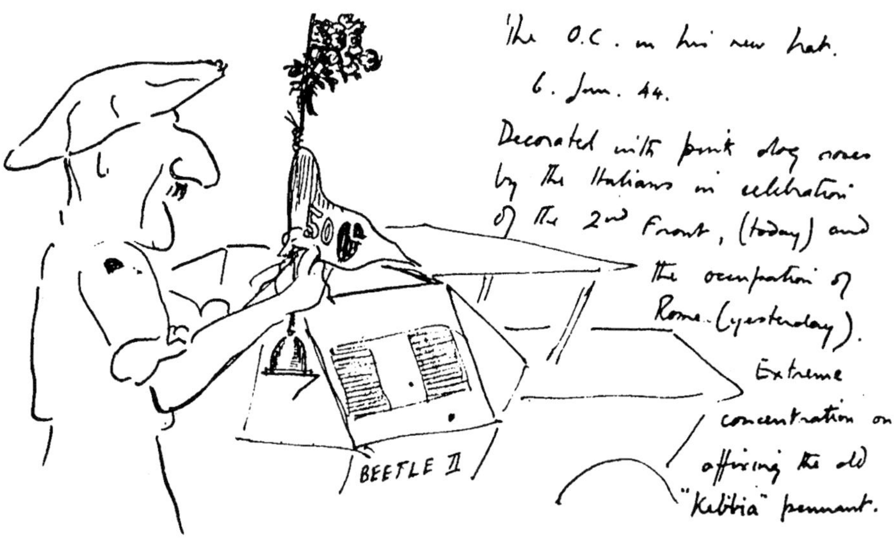


*The OC in his new hat. 6 June 1944*

hospital. There he had found himself in the next bed to Mike Low of 7 field company, and was able to give us news of his progress. Peter's return was a cause of great rejoicing in the Company. However his return was to prove short-lived.

On his return Peter related a small incident which had cheered them all up one day when the weekly ration of cigarettes was distributed. The ration consisted of 50 Players cigarettes in a round tin sealed with foil under the lid. The lid had a cutter which, when the lid was rotated, cut out a disc of foil. Mike Low with his nail scissors carefully cut the foil disk into the profile of a little elephant which he stuck down the plaster of his leg. Shortly after he went for a routine X-ray. All hell was let loose when the film was developed to show an elephant where his fracture should be. This was met with gales of laughter from his fellow patients, which did them all a lot of good. It was quite typical of Mike Low, who has an impish sense of humour.

The day following, Monday 5 June, gave us an even greater reason for rejoicing, for we heard that Rome had fallen to the Americans. They had been advancing parallel with us up the coastal road – the Appian Way. Our Italian labourers were so delighted that they picked bunches of wild flowers and tied them to all the Company vehicles. Willie and Sergeant Barboni tied a lovely bunch of flowers to the wireless aerial on my "dingo" scout car; it was a charming gesture. There were nevertheless some misgivings that the triumphal entry into Rome was given to the Americans. Our rejoicing was continued, for on the next day, 6 June, we heard of the Allied landings in Normandy.

It was on this day that a minor incident occurred which cast an amusing light on the pitfalls of the Cockney dialect. We were advancing along the old Roman Via Prenestina – a road which had escaped the modernisation of more important contemporary routes, and on which there were still considerable stretches of the old Roman paving, consisting of large roughly hexagonal blocks of granite of slightly convex profile, unkind to modern suspension systems.

We had stopped for a short rest and a group of Peter's men was sitting on the stone wall which bounded the north side of the road. While they were chatting together in a desultory manner, a rather dishevelled figure in battledress came shambling along the road from our rear. We all assumed that he was some tired and battle-worn straggler on his way to rejoin his unit and he passed along unchallenged until one of Peter's chaps gave him a friendly "Wotcher, cock?". The poor straggler was completely flummoxed by this form of address, believing, unhappily, that it required some sort of reply. Had he merely given a tired wave and passed silently on, he might have been home and dry; instead, he dug a pit for himself by stopping and saying "Excuse, pliss". In a moment the Cockney antennae were twitching with suspicion and he found himself politely but firmly surrounded. In due course we handed him over to the Military Police and another German failed to make the long walk home.

I have already mentioned that Peter's return to us was to be a brief one. When in hospital in Bari he had been visited by Eddie, who was enjoying a few days' leave down there. As he was feeling thoroughly fit, he seized the chance of a quick return to us in a Company vehicle, summarily discharged himself, and drove back with Eddie, thus short-circuiting the normal channels of 2nd Echelon and Army Movement Control.

Alas! Higher authority had earmarked him for promotion to a staff appointment and were not a little offended to find that he had slipped through their fingers. A few days later I received a perfunctory signal to despatch him immediately to Allied Army HQ at Caserta. I sent him off in a jeep with his batman, Gregory, for company and to drive the jeep back.

Meanwhile the Division moved forward into Tivoli without resistance, but it was rumoured that the Germans were digging in to hold a line in the hills north of Rome and Tivoli. The roads were crowded with traffic all moving North; it was as if the whole Allied army had developed a momentum which nothing could stop. We were glad enough to get off the road into the harbour area on Tivoli aerodrome, for we felt the traffic must end up in one huge traffic jam: which sure enough it did, that very night.

The following account, like the two previous chapters, was recorded at the time as being a very typical Sapper operation. Reference can be made to map 11 on page 124.

"Early on the afternoon of 7 June the CRE sent for me in order to give me orders for a special task in support of 12 Infantry Brigade Group. The Brigade had followed the retreating enemy as far as Tivoli with hardly any resistance. From Tivoli north to Palombara there were two roads. The main road was to the East on high ground, the lesser road entered a defile and wound up in a twisting valley with a stream on the right hand side up to a point where it joined the main road, just short of the village of Palombara perched on the top of a hill at the head of the valley. It was known that the enemy had blocked the main road with demolitions and so the lesser road was chosen to be the route forward. It was also out of view of the enemy. Palombara was an important town as it commanded a large area of the plain below and had, incidentally, been a German Corps Headquarters. It was known that the enemy had blocked the road with three demolitions and had laid scattered mines in the road surface. The Brigade column, led by tanks and self propelled guns, was to proceed up the valley towards Palombara, starting at 0500 hours on the morning of 8 June. The CRE gave the Company the task of opening this road for the Brigade Column by 0500 hours.

Two Sections only were available – Ben Chubb's 1 Section and Malcolm Drummond's 3 Section. John Notley, with 2 Section, was already up with 12th Brigade and already in the Brigade Column to help them later on. In addition the CRE put at my disposal a D7 Bulldozer and arranged with the Commander of 12th Brigade to give me a Platoon of the 2nd Battalion Royal Fusiliers as protection. Speed was essential so I returned at once to the Company to get things moving.

Having given my orders and got things under way I set off with Ben and Malcolm to have a look at the obstructions. We arrived at the first demolition at about 1800 hours. The first was a demolished bridge over a stream. The stream was dry and the abutments could be bulldozed down quite easily.

The second demolition presented rather more difficulty, as it was a partly demolished railway bridge over the road. The roadway was blocked by a mass of rubble containing large blocks of concrete. However, it was again decided that with the help of the bulldozer and a compressor and perhaps explosives a way through could quite easily be cleared. Some Teller mines had been laid on the road between these two obstacles, but had been lifted before we arrived. The general road surface was tarmac and the mines had been cunningly laid in the potholes. Curiously enough three had been exploded when the bridge had been blown, by falling lumps of masonry, leaving quite sizeable craters in the road surface.

I gave the clearing of these two obstacles to Ben who returned to bring up his men. Malcolm and I then walked on to the next bridge shown on the map. We stepped carefully, keeping to the tarmac surface, as there were several hastily laid Teller mines in the potholes. These were very obvious as, instead of a pothole, they appeared to be filled with loose stones. Sure enough the next bridge had been blown. But again the demolition had been only partially successful, leaving half the roadway intact.

We decided that if this portion was clearly marked with handrails it would take wheeled traffic, while a diversion could be bulldozed down and up the other side for tanks, the stream being dry. I gave Malcolm the task of clearing mines in the road surface and making this tank diversion with the bulldozer when it finished working for Ben. Telegraph poles would serve as handrails and the job seemed straightforward. We didn't go further but returned to the Company, Malcolm to organise his Section into mine-sweeping parties etc, and I to report my plan to the CRE

Ben, with 1 Section, arrived on the scene at about 1900 hours and immediately made a start on the first demolition with two sub-sections and a compressor. The remaining two sub-sections, with half a dozen of our Italian workmen, started work by hand on clearing the bridge. Here one of the rails was hanging across the gap and had to be cut with two slabs of guncotton. The bulldozer arrived about 2000 hours and immediately got to work on pushing down both abutments of the first demolition. It took one and a half hours to complete this first job, making an easy ramp down and up again. The bulldozer then moved on to the railway bridge.

Here quite a lot of work had been done by hand and the larger blocks were now uncovererd. It was decided to try and drag these out of the way with the bulldozer and a cable. This proved most satisfactory and all the big blocks, some weighing several tons, were dragged clear. It was then an easy matter for the bulldozer to clear away the small debris and a way through was made by midnight down to the original road surface. The bulldozer then went on to 3 Section's demolition, and 1 Section broke off for tea.

Meanwhile Malcolm had met the protection party of Fusiliers which consisted of only two Sections under a Sergeant, and had brought them up with his Section. He divided his Section with one Sub-section to clear mines from the railway bridge to his demolished bridge, one Sub-section to erect two telegraph handrails, and the remaining two Sub-sections, with the protection party, to proceed straight on up the road clearing mines.

The protection party was to proceed in bounds about a quarter of a mile ahead of the mine-sweeping party, one Section leap-frogging the other. All went well so far, the countryside being completely deserted and very quiet. When the bulldozer arrived about midnight at the third demolition the moon was up and it was quite light. By

0100 hours both the handrailing and the tank diversion were complete and the mine-sweeping party were getting to the "T" junction, having found scattererd mines all the way. They had lifted about 100 Tellermines.

We had just been issued with "Dingo" scout cars which were small two men vehicles, four wheel drive with an automatic gear box and armoured all round to shoulder level, made by the Daimler company. Behind the seats was a compartment for a wireless set. There was no windscreen. The driver could either look over the top or lower his seat and look through slits. There were no doors, one got in over the top like a miniature tank. They were excellent as a static command post but most people still preferred the jeep as being so much easier to get out of. We had four in the company, one for the Company Commander and one for each Section officer.

Our communications were as follows: I took my Dingo scout car with a No.21 wireless set up to the first obstacle and was in constant touch with Company HQ From there messages were relayed to the CRE by a more powerful No.22 wireless set on the Royal Signals net. This channel of communication proved completely satisfactory and I was able to pass hourly reports on the work straight through to the CRE My Dingo, which was in effect my Tac HQ, had, necessarily, to remain at the first demolition until this part of the road was opened at about 0100 hours. We were then able to proceed up the road to the forward mine-lifting party.

During this period of waiting some heavy demolitions were heard and seen away to the right on the parallel road from Tivoli. This meant that the Germans were still blowing demolitions on this road and that we were therefore likely to meet them at the "T" junction. The Germans evidently thought we were going to use this road, whereas in fact we were not; so the more effort they wasted on it the better. I was most anxious to get on up to the "T" junction to find out how things were going.

I drove the Dingo myself with some trepidation as the road had been mined spasmodically throughout its length and, although it had been cleared, I was the first British vehicle to drive up that particular stretch. However nothing occurred. I reached Malcolm with his men just short of the "T" junction. They were working on two craters which had only been blown by the enemy about half an hour before. In fact, when the explosion occurred, pieces of earth actually fell near the Sappers who were then working about a quarter of a mile further back.

The mines too had only just been laid ahead of the Sappers. As Malcolm was telling me this an excited group of Sappers arrived with a prisoner. He had apparently been surprised and taken by Sapper Curtis, Malcolm's batman. This appeared most satisfactory and I decided to take him back to Brigade HQ straight away in the Dingo, in case he might have some useful information. I ordered Malcolm to hold the "T" junction with his protection party until my return. I was anxious to reinforce this party in order to prevent any interference, and, if possible, to prevent any demolitions or mining on the road to Palombara, which appeared to be still open and in use by the enemy.

On the way down I met the bulldozer trundling up the road on his tracks to be of assistance to 3 Section if required. I told him to stop and await my return. We got to Brigade HQ at about 0200 hours where I handed over the prisoner, and at the same time told the Intelligence Officer that the Germans were still using the Tivoli-Palombara Road, which meant that it must still be intact. The Intelligence Officer, who was on duty in the Command Vehicle, was delighted with this news, and promptly sent for the Brigade Major, who arrived a moment later in his pyjamas. The prisoner was then closely questioned by the Intelligence Officer. He was very young, a little frightened, and appeared quite willing to talk. He belonged to 3 Company of 1 Paratroop Regiment. The Company was only about 60 strong and was engaged in laying mines and blowing demolitions in order to impede our advance. After which they expected to be withdrawn to the Florence-Pisa line.

He was on guard at the "T" junction and had no idea that British Sappers were working on the road. He thought the leading Sappers were Germans returning, as not one was wearing the unmistakable British steel helmet. He stated also that there were about forty of his Company still working on the Tivoli road. This confirmed my desire to reinforce my protection party and I promptly put my request to the Brigade Major. He agreed and ordered the remainder of the Company of the Royal Fusiliers to move in Transport to the "T" junction where I would have a guide to meet them. The paratrooper was handed over to the Military Police and I returned to Malcolm, telling the bulldozer driver on the way to proceed on slowly.

On meeting Malcolm at the junction I learned that during my absence two lorry loads of Germans had passed by in the direction of Palombara. The first lorry had passed so quickly that everyone was taken by surprise and no shot was fired. The second, however, received two Bren magazines and several Tommy Gun bursts. It had not been stopped but considerable damage must have been done as cries of pain were heard. This presumably accounted for the remaining forty or so paratroops. It was now getting late, being about 0330 hours, and we still had six miles to go before reaching Palombara, and only one and a half hours left. I ordered Malcolm to push on with all speed, checking the road for mines.

Almost immediately the Company of Royal Fusiliers arrived at the "T" junction where I had now set up my Tac HQ I explained the situation to the Company Commander, stressing the importance of pushing on but at the same time to guard against interference as the enemy now obviously knew our intention. He quickly organised his Company into a Vanguard and Mainguard, with Infantry Sections on either flank. He stationed himself with Malcolm with the mine sweeping part. It was now well after 0400 hours and getting light. Ben, with 1 Section, had now arrived at the "T" junction together with the bulldozer. I kept them here as a reserve. Meanwhile this force proceeded up the road in the direction of Palombara without interference and without meeting any obstructions or mines.

As it became light several Italian civilians appeared from the direction of Tivoli and with gestures made it quite plain that the Germans had done considerable damage and also apparently laid mines. They added that two Germans had been killed in one of their own explosions. Just before 0500 hours a Sapper came back on a borrowed Italian bicycle to say they were within half a mile of the town. I immediately reported this over the air to the CRE The next report I received, shortly after 0500 hours, stated that they had reached the village but had been fired on by a Spandau machine gun, and had therefore taken cover to await the arrival of the tanks. Again I reported this over the air and likewise waited for the head of the Brigade Column which was expected at any moment.

Precisely at 0530 hours the Reconnaissance Honey tanks leading the Brigade Column appeared rounding the corner to the "T" junction. I told the officer in the leading tank the situation and they promptly drove off down the road to Palombara. They drove straight into the village without any further opposition. The Spandau obviously did not like the look of them and beat a hasty retreat. Brigade Column rolled steadily by and was a most impressive sight. Behind the Reconnaissance Honeys came Eddie Meldrum in his Dingo, acting as RE Recce Officer. With him were two Honey tanks of the Armoured Brigade Sappers. Then followed a squadron of Sherman tanks with a Company of the Royal Fusiliers riding on them.

That comprised the Vanguard which was followed almost immediately by the Advance Guard, led by the Command Group with Gunner OP vehicles, a protection troop of anti-tank guns and a troop of self-propelled field guns, and then John Notley with 2 Section of 59 field company. All told, the Vanguard, Advance Guard and Main Guard consisted of some 183 vehicles, representing a very strong force capable of delivering the enemy quite a hard knock.

When John reached Palombara he took over the responsibility of the road from Malcolm, who returned on foot with his 3 Section to the T junction. All were a little weary after walking nearly twenty miles. Meanwhile their transport had come up. They piled into trucks and returned to the Company location to eat a hearty breakfast. I reported over the air to the CRE and returned myself, bringing Malcolm with me. Ben, with 1 Section, had already returned. It was just on 0800 hours by the time we had all got back."

The clearing of this road to Palombara was almost a "model" Sapper task, and for this reason I was asked to record it in some detail, but even so there were a couple of very valid criticisms: in the first place the infantry protection party should have been stronger. If the German paratroops had wanted to they could very easily have disrupted the operation, as the Sappers working on clearing demolitions and mine sweeping were relatively few in number and not able to protect themselves adequately.

Another serious criticism made was that insufficient signs such as "Mines in Verges" were posted by the Sappers. The verges had not been swept and later in the morning a 5.5 medium gun was blown up by a mine in the verge when passing another vehicle, which rightly annoyed the Gunners. As always, there were lessons to be learned and by looking at an operation in detail they can be pinpointed. However, the Brigadier congratulated the company and thanked us for a good job done.

Meanwhile the Brigade column had reached Palombara, but was held up by the enemy in the hill country north of the village and by demolitions on the road leading north. One particular major demolition of a bridge over a river on a sharp bend which would need a Bailey Bridge was being investigated by Eddie Meldrum and Sergeant Parry when they suddenly came under machine gun fire from the opposite hillside.

Both were wounded, Eddie slightly but Sergeant Parry more seriously. They were quickly got back to the Advanced Dressing Station where Eddie was patched up and soon returned to the Company.

But we learned a few days later that Sgt. Parry had not recovered and had died from his wounds. This was a tragic blow to the Company, and particularly to 2 Section, for Parry was very popular, a very good soldier, and a fine leader. Eddie Meldrum was very upset, they were good friends, and because Parry was in front at the time they came under fire he felt guilty; but because of the pace of events just then he soon recovered. I have found a letter which I wrote home on 16 June 1944 describing this incident which is indicative of the Germans' predicament:

59th Field Coy, R.E.
June 16th C.M.F.

Not far from the mountainous region of Cassino.

Life is very hectic these days. The weather for a week has been perfect, though perhaps a bit hot mid-day. Standing outside my little Tent this morning shaving as the sun rose, it was a dream of beauty. I heard from the Officer who was with Eddie and Sergeant Parry when they were wounded – they were hit together and are now in a big Hospital in Naples. He told me this strange story of their capture and release.

Two Boche stretcher-bearers, and the Boche Doctor who picked them up, stopped the firing while examining them and helped them to their own truck, explaining they could take no prisoners now for they could scarcely get their own wounded away.

After a day of shelling and infantry attacks the enemy dropped back in the night and next day, 10 June, we were able to tackle this demolition and another even wider gap which could not be seen until the Germans retreated. These and all subsequent Bailey Bridges are listed in Appendix III.

Both bridges were built by Ben Chubb with his 1 Section without interference. The first was 70ft. and bridged by a single girder double story supported span. A very straightforward job completed in daylight. The second bridge which was round a spur of the hill and hidden from the first was a wider but shallower gap of 110ft. The design and planning for this was done while the first was being built, but construction could not start until the first was built to allow the bridging lorries to cross it.

In this case it was possible to build a pier of Bailey Bridging equipment in the centre of the gap to support the bridge, thus in effect reducing the gap to two equal gaps of 50ft. These only required single girder construction and although a longer bridge was easier and quicker to build, it was built during the night and completed on the morning of Sunday 11 June.

Our earlier suspicions that Bailey Bridging would be our main task in Italy were being fully justified. From now on as we fought our way up the leg of Italy it was demolitions rather than mines which held up the forward movement of supply columns. Our bridging training at Bougie was coming into its own. We were to build

27 bridges in the next six months.

During these two days Malcolm Drummond and 3 Section had taken over from John Notley and 2 Section and had gone on ahead on foot with 12 Brigade trying to keep up with the retreating Germans. However it was clear that this particular battle was over, and we learned that 8th Indian Division were taking over in this very hilly country, while 4th Division was being switched further west to chase the Germans up National Route 3 towards Florence.

For the rest of Sunday we had a rest, camping in a pleasant grassy field overlooking Rome in the distance. We all needed a bit of sleep and a wash. Not for long, though, for later that night we were on the road again as a Company. We crossed the Tiber and drove through the middle of Rome by moonlight, and on up Route 3 to Civita Castellana, some twenty miles or so further on.

From Monday to Thursday we camped just off Route 3 in a nice shady olive grove while Ben with 1 Section worked on a by-pass round Civita Castellana to relieve the congestion in its narrow streets. The rest of the Company helped with additional shifts so that everyone had a good rest while the work still went on under the responsibility of Ben and 1 Section.

It was on Tuesday of this week that Eddie returned and told us of Sergeant Parry's death. This was a bitter blow to the Company, as Parry was very popular. A further blow to all of us was a posting order for Peter Boston, who was posted to Allied Headquarters at Caserta. It was promotion for him, but a loss to the Company.

By Thursday our by-pass was finished and open, though still a bit rough, and we heard that the Division was to make a huge leap forward of sixty miles to Orvieto. This would surely put us behind the enemy! Next day, Friday 16 June, we took to the road again with other Divisional units and reached Orvieto by nightfall, exhausted but thankful to have arrived safely. (See Map 14 on page 162.)

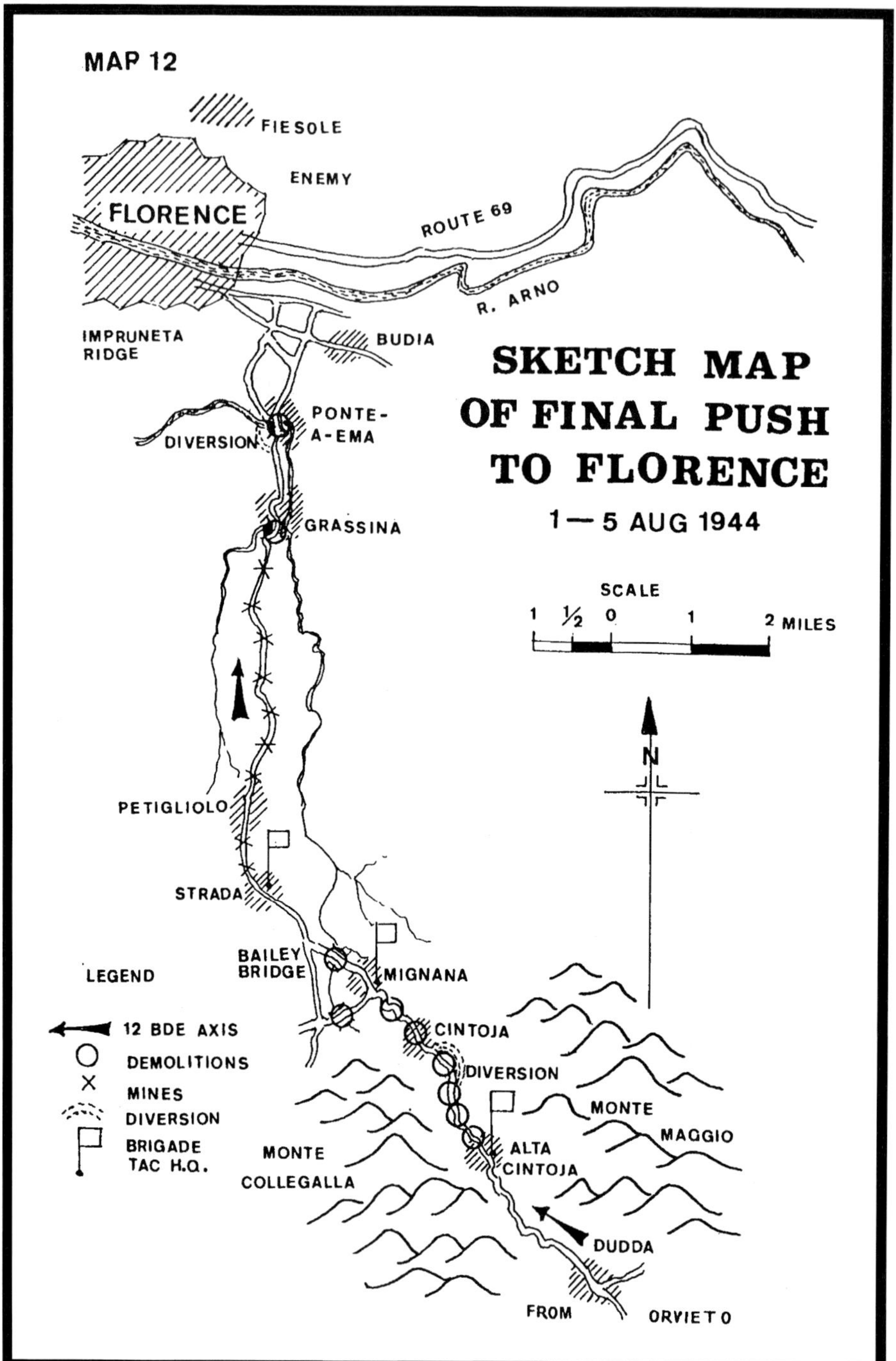
MAP 12
FIESOLE
ENEMY
FLORENCE
ROUTE 69
R. ARNO
IMPRUNETA
RIDGE
BUDIA
SKETCH MAP
OF FINAL PUSH
TO FLORENCE
1—5 AUG 1944
PONTE-
A-EMA
DIVERSION
GRASSINA
SCALE
1 ½ 0 1 2 MILES
N
PETIGLIOLO
STRADA
BAILEY
BRIDGE
MIGNANA
LEGEND
12 BDE AXIS
DEMOLITIONS
MINES
DIVERSION
BRIGADE
TAC H.Q.
CINTOJA
DIVERSION
MONTE
MAGGIO
MONTE
COLLEGALLA
ALTA
CINTOJA
DUDDA
FROM
ORVIETO

# CHAPTER XII

## Orvieto to Florence

Orvieto is the centre of a wine growing district and so the first thing we did was to send Willie, our interpreter, into the town to buy wine, which he was very happy to do. The country was very quiet; there did not appear to be any Germans about. We were camped in a nice clean hayfield and the sun was shining: it was Sunday 18 June, a day for washing and chores.

On Monday the weather broke, with continuous torrential rain turning everything around into slippery mud. John Notley took 2 Section on to Ficule to work on the road, which was giving way with the amount of traffic using it. Our Italians went with him. Malcolm took 3 Section on to make a bypass round the lovely little village of Castiglione del Taverina, so far untouched by enemy action. Our break was shortlived: by the end of the week 4th Division was to join the battle again taking over from the South African Armoured Division with 12 Brigade and 7 Field Company, in close contact with the enemy near Chiusi. The next few weeks of fighting can be followed on Map 14 on page 162.

Now began a hectic period of fighting the Germans and fighting the weather. My diary notes that on Sunday 25 June report that we had a terrific thunderstorm which completely washed away the road just below our camp site at Piegaro, a village south-west of Lake Trasimeno. While we were working on this we heard on our wireless link with HQ RE at 4th Division HQ that Major Dawson, OC of 7 Field Company and Brian Roberts, who were doing a reconnaissance in a Daimler "Dingo" scout car, had gone over a mine which exploded, turning the Dingo completely over. Both Dawson's legs were badly wounded and Brian lost his right hand.

This was the reason why the Daimler "Dingo" was not a popular reconnaissance vehicle; if it turned over its occupants could be trapped inside and underneath, whereas if a Jeep was hit or blown up on a mine its occupants stood a good chance of being blown clear. I much preferred a Jeep and so did Sullivan. Appendix V shows a sketch of a Daimler "Dingo" Scout Car.

The gap in the road caused by the thunderstorm had to be bridged and was tackled by John Notley with 2 Section in a great hurry to get the road open again. It required a single girder Bailey Bridge to bridge the 40ft. gap in the road.

We now took over from 7 Field Company in support of 12 Brigade, who were chasing the Germans very hard along the west shore of Lake Trasimeno. Malcolm with 3 Section was up with the leading infantry and Ben with 1 Section was following, opening up the road for supplies. By now they had reached Castiglione del Lago. Company headquarters and 2 Section were still at Piegaro.

On the night of 29 June, the enemy withdrew. 12 Brigade advanced rapidly in pursuit to Pozzuolo, where it dug in. 59 Company was now fully stretched checking for mines and repairing the road. We were now off Route 3 and on a minor road which was much easier for the Germans to disrupt with mines and demolitions. But on 1 July they withdrew again. We were working nonstop round the clock on the road to Foiano with John Notley and 2 Section leading.

In this flat and rather featureless country the Germans could not make a stand but they could and did hold up our advance with mines and demolitions which kept the Sappers very busy.

After a day of heavy fighting and shelling at Foiano they withdrew again, allowing 12 Brigade Headquarters and 59 Company to move up to Foiano. The advance now took a cross-country route to Monte San Savino across low-lying rather boggy land, which was not made any easier by the rain. I was first into Monte San Savino to recruit some local labour, to help us keep the Brigade supply route open, and got a great reception with bunches of flowers and lots of willing hands to help us on the road.

From Monte San Savino the advance slowed to a halt as the route went into a defile in difficult hilly country. It was now 6 July and it was clear the Germans were determined to make a stand, having reached a much easier terrain to defend. They dug in and held the village of San Pancrazio on a ridge overlooking the rather tortuous road up which the Brigade must advance.

This road with steep hills on either side followed a stream. The Germans had little time to lay mines but succeeded in carrying out two hefty demolitions where culverts crossed under the road. The first created a gap of about 60ft. and was tackled by Malcolm with 3 Section, and a bridge was built during daylight hours. This bridge was a 60ft. double girder single storey Bailey bridge and was completed by late afternoon on 6 July. Fortunately the bridge site was out of the enemy's view and although there was sporadic shelling no damage was sustained.

The second bridge, which could not be started until the first was completed, was taken on by John Notley and 2 Section who were now getting very proficient in building high speed Bailey bridges. It was only a small bridge of 40ft. single girder construction, but was very close to the forward troops and had to be built in the failing light of dusk, and in complete silence. It was finished by dark, which allowed the Brigadier to bring up his tanks for a dawn attack.

The real trouble was Monte Altuzzo, which was firmly held by the Germans, and like San Pancrazio overlooked our valley. The Brigadier wanted to attack the hill, for that is all it really was, with carriers supported by tanks; but that meant another small Bailey bridge over a demolished culvert. John and 2 Section went on to deal with this in darkness and again absolute silence – just in time before another terrific thunderstorm which almost washed it away. The Brigadier was delighted and congratulated John on his and his men's performance. Still the Germans held on to San Pancrazio and for a few days there was stalemate. It was tragic to see this pretty little village being steadily reduced to ruins.

It was during this lull on Tuesday 11 July that I received a message from the CRE to go and investigate a house called 'Fabbriche' at the village of Lucignano, a few miles south-west of Monte San Savino. It was reputed to have been a German headquarters. I set off with driver Sullivan in my Jeep in the middle of the afternoon. The sun was shining again and it was a lovely day. When we got to the place we drove up a twisting drive which opened out onto a gravelled sweep before a large beautiful country house covered with bougainvillia and other creepers. We drew up a little way from the porch and wondered what would happen.

To our surprise a charming and very good-looking young lady in a cool summer frock came towards us, saying "Hallo, how very nice to see you. Do come in and have tea, we are just going to have it on the terrace," in perfect English. She led us through the hall and sitting room of a very English looking country house on to a terrace looking across the valley to Lucignano on the hill opposite. Under an old pine tree was a circular stone table with deck chairs, and laid upon it were plates, cups and saucers, scones, jam, and a silver teapot. We were introduced to her children, a boy and a girl, I think. It was quite unreal, like Alice in Wonderland, and I could not believe it.

*The house of Paulo Manchini "FABRICHE" Lucignano.*

While we ate scones and drank tea she told us that she was English and that her husband, Count Paulo Manchini, was unable to get home. The house had been requisitioned by the German command, luckily only for a short time – just a few days – and they had only just left in a hurry. She said they had been waiting so long for the Allies to reach them that it was wonderful to see us. She also told us that they had been harbouring some escaped British prisoners of war, but they had left just before the German officers arrived and were probably safely back in our lines by now. Above all she wanted news of England and the progress of the war. Had we got a spare wireless set that we could lend her so that they could listen to the British broadcasts? The Germans had taken away their set. It was a fantastic episode and we were loth to leave, but return we must.

When we got back to the Company I reported this remarkable tale to the CRE, and no doubt driver Sullivan had much to tell his incredulous audience. That evening I made a sketch from memory of the terrace and tea table at Fabbriche. We managed to find a civilian wireless set which John Heath and I took over to Fabbriche the next day, to the delight and joy of the Countess and her family. On Friday she gave us a dinner party which was a farewell, for on that day we heard that 6th Armoured Division was attacking in strength on our right and was likely to dislodge the enemy from San Pancrazio. Sure enough, on Saturday night the enemy withdrew. He had held us up for a week, but it had given me a very memorable interlude.

On Sunday we heard that Arezzo had fallen to 6th Armoured Division and 4th Division was on the move again. As we drove up the road to San Pancrazio the inhabitants came out of the ruins and cellars to welcome us. It was a very humbling moment to be cheered and welcomed by those whose homes and possessions we had been destroying; but it vividly demonstrated the extent of the hatred felt towards the Germans by the Italians.

The Company moved up to Capponnole in difficult hilly country. With the fall of Arezzo it became clear that the best route to Florence would be up the National Route 69 from Arezzo to Florence, but to get to Route 69 would mean opening up a cross country track. This was our next task and taken on by Ben Chubb with 1 Section, soon to be helped by John Notley and 2 Section because of pressure to get it opened as quickly as possible.

This country lane, for that is really all it was, had been denied to us by the retreating Germans and required a total of six small Bailey bridges hastily put up across culvert demolitions. Thus over the next three days, from 16 to 18 July, the whole Company was involved – three small bridges between San Pancrazio and Capponnole by Ben and 1 Section, and a rather larger 60ft. double girder single storey at Levane built by John and 2 Section. Two much bigger bridges, one of 90ft. and one of 70ft., were built jointly by 2 and 3 Sections at Civitella. This really taxed the Company to its limit, with everyone working flat out to open up the Divisional access. However it meant the Division was able to advance rapidly to Monte Vacchi only about twenty miles from Florence.

On Thursday 20 July the advance was halted once more at Monte Vacchi, where the Germans had decided to make a stand. This gave the Sappers a welcome rest, for the last week had really been hectic and we were all short of sleep. The next day I was unfortunately smitten and restricted to bed with an attack of dysentery; however, after taking quantities of pills and what looked like chalk, dispensed by Angus Bellairs, our doctor, and with twenty-four hours of sleep, I was quite fit again.

During this week we were called upon several times to carry out first aid repairs to Route 69, although on the whole it was a good road and only needed repairs when hit by shells. Once again it was stalemate, with the Germans holding a ridge overlooking the road which was then the Divisional axis.

Then, completely unexpectedly, another most unlikely episode unfolded for us. On 25 July I was instructed to take a Section of the Company back to Monte San Savino to line a road next day to see and cheer H.M. the King who was visiting the Allied Armies in Italy. I took a mixed party with Ben, John, and Malcolm.

We camped in a pleasant pinewood and next day took up our allotted position lining a secondary road at the tiny village of Gargonza. When the King, who was in uniform, was driven past in an open staff car with General Alexander beside him, he received a great cheer from all the men lining the route. It was a great honour to see him, and it made a deep impression on everyone that he should come out from England in the middle of the battle to see what his army was doing. It was the second time in just over a year that the King had visited 4th Division. We returned to the Company at Monte Vacchi greatly encouraged.

On 27 July the battle moved on with 12 Brigade leading and 59 Field Company in support. Thus began the final drive to Florence. It marked the end of a three month campaign beginning with Cassino and hopefully ending with Florence, a distance of some 300 miles. The route decided on for 4th Division from Monte Vacchi to Florence was a direct line by a minor road to the west of, and parallel to, Route 69. The distance by Route 69, which took a big curve, was greater and might well be very heavily defended.

Thus on our right flank with Route 69 as its axis was 6th Armoured Division and on our left was 6th South African Armoured Division. It would obviously be a hard fight as the Germans were determined to hold the high ground of the Chianti mountains south of Florence. The following detailed account was, as in previous chapters, written down after the battle with the help of John Notley who was up with the leading infantry all the way to Florence. See map 12 on page 136 for this last push to Florence.

"By the 28 July the Brigade had reached the last high ground some twenty miles south of Florence and dominating the approaches to it. Here the enemy made a very determined stand which completely held up the Brigade for four days, from 28 to 31 July. The road from Dudda, which was by no means a main road, wound up a valley to a saddle between Monte Maggio on the right and Monte Collegalle on the left. The Black Watch and the Royal West Kents held Monte Maggio and the Royal Fusiliers Monte Collegalla, but neither was able to move on the forward slopes due to heavy enemy mortaring.

On the road one could not move by day beyond the saddle. Just above the saddle was the church of Alta Cintoja in which was sited Brigade Tac HQ, having a commanding position with an excellent view of the road, winding up the valley towards Florence. The Company at this time was back in the area of Dudda, with 1 and 2 Sections forward, ready to support the Brigade when it was able to move. I spent much of my time with the Brigade Commander at Alta Cintoja.

On the night of 29 July John Notley and 2 Section with a small party did a recce of the road from the saddle to the next village, Cintoja, a distance of about two miles. Cintoja itself was occupied by the enemy. There were six demolitions on this road, five being blown culverts in re-entrant folds and one a blown retaining wall on a shoulder. It was decided to try and deal with these during the next night with a D7 bulldozer. The first culvert and the blown retaining wall were successfully dealt with in the fading light. It then became too dark and work was suspended until early morning, when it was resumed by the light of a waning moon.

All went well until the last blown culvert was tackled. This was wet and boggy, with the result that the bulldozer became completely bogged down trying to make a diversion round the demolition. All efforts to get it out failed and when it became light John Notley had to return with his men, abandoning it, as the site was too close to Cintoja and in view of the enemy. Luckily the bulldozer itself was just out of view in the fold of the re-entrant. The Fusiliers were asked to keep an eye on it from above and prevent the enemy from tampering with it. The next night, 30 July, John Notley got hold of a Churchill recovery tank and again had a try at pulling the bulldozer out. This brought down a few scattered shells and mortar bombs, but being well in the fold of the hill they were quite safe.

Again all efforts failed, the recovery tank snapping its winch cable. It was therefore decided to abandon the machine altogether until the Brigade advanced, allowing recovery work to be done in daylight. Some bundles of faggots were placed over the machine to camouflage it and protect it from flying shrapnel; however before leaving John Notley reconnoitred and marked with tapes a diversion round to the right of the demolition. It was not a very good one, being rather steep, but did at least provide a route of sorts which would get tanks and vehicles round. Thus it was that by 31 July there was a possible route from the saddle forward to the village of Cintoja, but which could not yet be used in daylight.

On the night 31 July – 1 August the enemy withdrew, breaking contact with our infantry. Early in the morning of 1 August the Black Watch and the Royal Fusiliers were ordered to follow up to the Strada-Impruneta Ridge. The Brigadier himself moved his Tac HQ to the Monastery of Mignana. The immediate task which was of great urgency was to recover the D7 bulldozer and improve the rather poor diversion round the demolition. John Notley took this in hand forthwith, bringing up a D4 bulldozer which after a good many hours' work made a ramp down and up in the alignment of the road. Meanwhile part of the Section were digging out the D7 and the remainder were making a start on two craters in the road between Cintoja and Mignana. This made a total of seven demolitions since the saddle.

Late in the afternoon the ramp down and up was finished and the D4 was able to pull out the D7 and go on to complete the two craters this side of Mignana. During the day our Troop of anti-tank Gunners, attached to the Company, worked on and improved the four demolitions already bulldozed. By evening the road was open to all traffic as far as Mignana and in fact a considerable volume of transport had already moved up to the Mignana area. I ordered 1 and 2 Sections to move up and find a suitable camp site in the olives just short of Cintoja.

During this period of very concentrated road works, our Italians under their leader Barboni were doing sterling work. They were extremely good at road repair work, being strong as well as experienced. They also managed to pull in any locals they could get hold of who were glad of some pay and food. But we did not increase our basic group, who by now had given enormously valuable service.

During the day, 1 August, the Black Watch had reported a blown bridge between Mignana and Strada. The gap was reported as 20ft. and the depth 15-16ft. It was in fact a small masonry bridge with the complete arch being blown away. It was quite clearly a case for a small Bailey Bridge; but the site was in full view of the Germans and therefore could not be attempted before dusk. 2 section was still the leading Section and John Notley said that he was game to bridge the gap that night. I therefore ordered up 40ft. of single girder Bailey which arrived at Brigade Tac HQ at the Monastery at about 1800 hours. The Section by this time had moved to Cintoja and was therefore able to have a good dinner. At about 2100 hours John Notley went down to the site of the demolished bridge with an advance party of a sub-section to prepare the banks.

It proved a very easy site. The existing parapets were removed and the base plates sunk into the existing road surface at a span of 40ft. It was a fine night and very quiet. At 2200 hours John Notley sent for the bridging lorries; they arrived and were very quickly unloaded. The Bailey was built in the almost record time of two hours and in almost dead silence, as it was extremely eerie with occasional machine gun fire and the added crump of shells. The enemy obviously had the demolition registered from observation of his shelling during the afternoon, and I was afraid he might bring a concentration down on the bridge at any time. However, luck was with us and nothing happened. The bridge was complete at midnight and the Section returned to have a good sleep.

Next day, 2 August, the Brigade attacked the village of Strada at dawn. The village itself was empty but the slopes of the Impruneta Ridge behind were stoutly defended. Almost as soon as the Infantry had consolidated in the village, the enemy brought down very intense mortar and shell fire on the whole area and in particular on the road into the village. From Brigade Tac HQ in the Monastery we had a wonderful view of the road and the village.

As the day wore on the Infantry were able to make little headway and every vehicle which went up the road ran the gauntlet.

Ben Chubb, with 1 Section, had now taken over the lead in close support of the Infantry to allow 2 Section to rest. However, 2 Section were called upon to carry out one small task during the afternoon, which was to establish a Water Point for the Brigade Group, John Notley chose the spot where the D7 had been bogged, as there was a good stream of fresh water at this point.

When the infantry became pinned down in the village of Strada it was clear that tanks were required to clear the slopes beyond the village. A squadron of Churchill tanks was therefore sent in to assist. This was about mid-day. Unfortunately the leading tank hit a mine in the road just north of the village and lost its track. The second tank following tried to find a way round and also blew up on a mine, and lastly a carrier drawing up behind the first tank hit a mine. It was therefore clear that there was a minefield astride the main road which we required as an access. Ben Chubb went up with Sergeant Chetwood and a sub-section to try and clear a lane round the tank and carrier which were blocking the road. At first they were pinned down in a house by heavy mortaring. When this let up a taping party with two detectors went forward to do the job. Just as they rounded the tank a burst of Spandau fire down the road stopped them and they took cover in the ditch. Ben Chubb and Sergeant Chetwood then did a recce on their stomachs and discovered that the fire was coming from a house some 400 yards away. They decided to try going through the hedge behind the carrier and clearing a lane through the vineyard, using the cover of the hedge as protection. This proved most successful. A number of Tellermines was lifted and a safe lane taped round the carrier and tank.

This took quite a time to do owing to the Sappers having to work on their stomachs. However by 1600 hours it was done, leaving the tanks to knock down the hedge and flatten out the track. Ben Chubb then returned with his men, once again running the gauntlet, on the road back to the Monastery. At about 1700 hours the tanks went through and mopped up the offending Spandau. It was a good job of work and well carried out, though all were a little shaken as shelling of the area had been fairly continuous.

Again during the night the enemy withdrew and at dawn on the 3 August the Brigadier ordered the Black Watch to follow up. It was 3 Section's turn to support the Infantry and Malcolm Drummond with 3 Sections organised into two mine sweeping parties followed as closely as they could, clearing the road. Mines were found laid spasmodically almost all the way, some in potholes and some in the verges. The Section must have lifted some forty to fifty mines in the day.

By evening the road was reported clear to Grassina and not much resistance had been encountered. The Brigade Tac HQ had moved up to the Ridge just above Strada and 3 Section had taken over an empty house close to Brigade Tac HQ Late in the afternoon the Black Watch positions overlooking Grassina were shelled and it was not until after dark that Malcolm Drummond was able to get back with his 3 section.

During the day at least two big demolitions had been seen to go up in Grassina. The Brigadier therefore asked me to organise a recce patrol of the road and if possible to open a route through by daylight. The Black Watch was ordered to detail one Section as protection. I decided to give the job to Ben Chubb and ordered him to take two sub-sections, on foot with Pioneer tools. We all assembled at Battalion HQ of the Black Watch at 2200 hours. Ben Chubb set off with his party, taking with him his Dingo to keep in wireless touch with me at Battalion HQ At 2300 hours he asked me to come down as the Infantry Section would not go further.

It was deadly quiet and very eerie, and obviously German demolition parties were still at work as a big explosion took place while we were discussing the situation. At length Ben Chubb and I decided to go down with one Sapper to have a look at the bridges, the Dingo to follow fifteen minutes or so later. As the Dingo rounded a bend of the road he was shot at by an Anti-Tank gun from comparatively short range. He stopped and backed round quickly. Six shots in all were fired which were near misses and extremely frightening, but did no damage. We found one bridge intact and the next blown, giving about an 80ft. gap. However in view of the extreme quietness of the night and of the presence of this Anti-Tank gun we decided it was impossible to work. The party therefore returned, having achieved little more than a useful recce.

The next day, 5 August, the Black Watch went into Grassina to clear it up, but found it empty. Immediately the Royal West Kents were pushed through to occupy the high ground dominating the River Arno. This meant that the Sappers were immediately able to work on the road through Grassina. The task was taken on by Ben Chubb and 1 Section. The obstacles were first a partially blown retaining wall which was an easy bulldozing job for the D4. The next was the blown bridge recced the night before. This it was decided could be ramped down and up as the CRE was anxious to conserve all Bailey equipment in case it was needed to bridge the Arno. The D7 was therefore put to work and completed the job by the afternoon. The third obstacle was a blown bridge at Ponte-A-Ema. Here the civilians had already made a start at a diversion. Therefore Sergeant Cornfield with two Sub-sections of 1 Section got to work and with Lieut. Valerio as interpreter there was soon an army of civilians working as well. After this the road was clear to the river with apparently no demolitions or mines, with the result that by about 1700 hours the Divisional Axis was actually open to the river Arno although the last mile was in view and could not therefore be used.

Simultaneously during this day, 5 August, Malcolm Drummond with Willie Valerio and the redoubtable Sapper Curtis, undertook a recce of the river bank and the possible bridging sites. They set off early from Grassina, calling in on the way at the Royal West Kents Battalion HQ on the hill overlooking the river. From here they could not use the road as it was in full view of the enemy on the opposite bank and therefore had to resort to clambering from one back garden to another until they reached the last house. Here they met with a remarkable piece of good fortune by dropping into the garden of the City Electrical Engineer, a charming man who spoke good English and was very ready to assist in any way. The party repaired to a top storey window from which Malcolm Drummond obtained a fair view of the demolished Trinita bridge.

However, there were certain items of information which could not be obtained, whereupon the electrical engineer readily volunteered to go out as a civilian and obtain all details and, being an engineer, he brought back very exact and valuable information. He further volunteered to take a walk along the embankment and note the most likely fording sites. After several glasses of wine and toasting the Allies, Malcolm Drummond and Willie Valerio returned to Brigade HQ by the way they had come, with extremely valuable information for the CRE It is probable that Malcolm

Drummond was the first British officer to reach the River Arno on this Sector, and very proper that it should have been a Sapper.

Thus it was that by the evening of the 5 August the Royal West Kents were in possession of the slight ridge which dominated all the ground to the River Arno just on the Eastern side of the city of Florence. By the evening also the road was open for the Battalion's administrative vehicles as well as their carriers to come up and join them, thus solidifying the position. There were in fact no enemy left on the south bank of the river. To my mind the extremely rapid advance of some twenty miles in five days was in part due to the speed with which the Sappers overcame the enemy's demolitions and mines, once the infantry were able to push the enemy back, and open the road for the supporting tanks, carriers and guns. Each Section of the Company had its full share of work, and all the officers contributed to the success of the operation by their determination to get to the river.

*Congratulatory Message*

The following message from the Army Commander (General Alexander) has been received by the Divisional Commander and will be made known to all ranks:

> "Please convey to all ranks our appreciation of the great contribution made by the 4th British Division to our success at Florence. Their hard fought advance through the extremely difficult country on our right flank exerted a decisive influence throughout the operation. My best congratulations to you all."

(unsigned)
Lieut.-Colonel

8 August 1944 General Staff 4 Brit Inf Div

I, too, on 5 August looked down on the City of Florence from the high ground behind San Miniato. It looked very beautiful and very peaceful; but the Germans were holding Fiesole on the high ground opposite to us and probably watching our every movement. It was a fragile peace. Next day, Sunday 6 August, we spent all day working on a plan to build a Bailey bridge across the Arno on the site of the destroyed Trinita bridge, and that night Malcolm Drummond, again with our interpreter Willie and his batman Sapper Curtis, did a detailed reconnaissance of the bridge site. It was very quiet: no Germans and no locals about at all. However the next day we heard that 1st Division were to relieve 4th Division, who were to be pulled back to a rest area for a thorough rest and refit. Almost three months to the day from Cassino.

Fortunately, I think, for the city of Florence, no further advance was to be made, and by mutual consent no shelling of the city took place. While 1st Division on the San Miniato high ground and the German Division in Fiesole watched each other and occasionally shelled each other, a kind of peace was maintained. The Ponte Vecchio was intact but all the other bridges across the Arno had been destroyed. The English DAILY MAIL of Saturday 12 August 1944 reported under the heading "GERMANS HAVE QUIT FLORENCE"

> THE DAILY MAIL, Saturday, August 12, 1944
>
> GERMANS HAVE QUIT FLORENCE
>
> The Germans have abandoned Florence. This was announced yesterday by the German News Agency, which said that their troops in the city have been withdrawn from the north bank of the Arno to the northern fringe of the city.
>
> No change in the military situation in the Florence area is reported from Allied sources. East of the city Eighth Army troops clearing the Upper Arno valley are now two miles from Pontassieve, where the river takes a sharp turn to the West, nine miles above Florence.

Meanwhile, 4th Division prepared to pull out. In 59 Field Company we prepared to hand our plans for a bridge across the Arno over to 23 Field Company of 1st Division. I believe in fact it was built, as sketched by Peter Boston, some time after.

On Wednesday 9 August the Company with 12 Brigade moved from Florence to Foligno via Arezzo and Perugia, a very long drive through the night from 2200 hours to 1000 hours. By now everyone needed a good rest – but for how long, we wondered.

*Breakfast time on the Arno.*

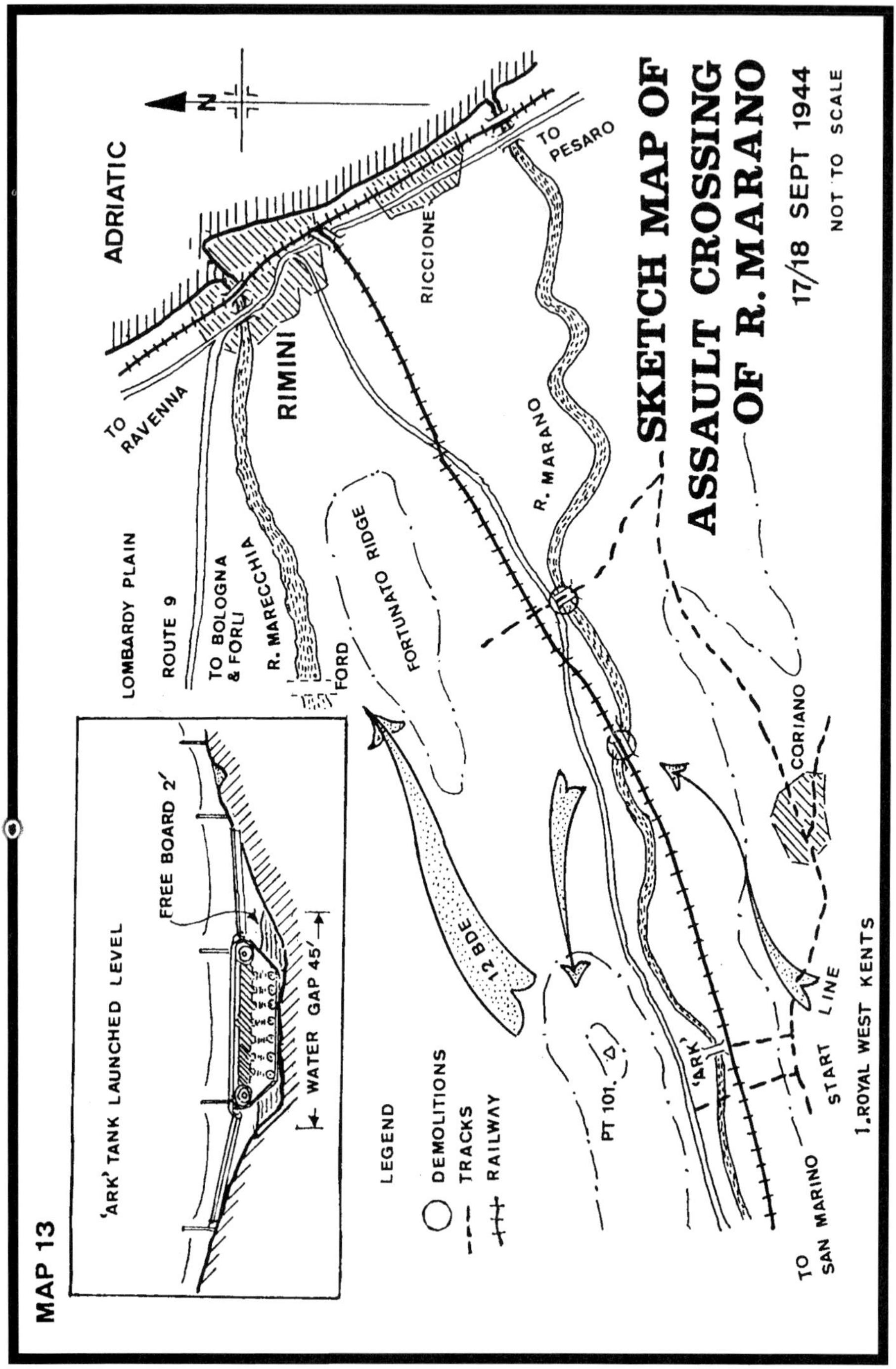

MAP 13
SKETCH MAP OF ASSAULT CROSSING OF R. MARANO
17/18 SEPT 1944
NOT TO SCALE
'ARK' TANK LAUNCHED LEVEL
FREE BOARD 2'
WATER GAP 45'
LEGEND
DEMOLITIONS
TRACKS
RAILWAY
ADRIATIC
N
TO RAVENNA
TO PESARO
RIMINI
RICCIONE
LOMBARDY PLAIN
ROUTE 9
TO BOLOGNA & FORLI
R. MARECCHIA
FORD
FORTUNATO RIDGE
R. MARANO
CORIANO
12 BDE
PT 101.
'ARK'
START LINE
1. ROYAL WEST KENTS
TO SAN MARINO

# CHAPTER XIII

## Across to Rimini

The prospect of Foligno was very pleasant. It was a nice little country town, quite untouched by the war, full of local farmers and peasants coming in to market from the surrounding countryside. The weather was fine and warm, and the topic of conversation was the forthcoming wine harvest. The war might have been a thousand miles away.

10 Brigade was allocated an area of high ground to the north of and overlooking the town, and 59 Company settled into a pleasant shady olive grove. The first thing the men needed was a really good meal followed by twelve hours' sleep. For the rest of that week we did little else. On Thursday afternoon Ben Chubb and I visited Assisi; I had always wanted to see it and this was a good opportunity.

It is a beautiful little town overlooking a wide plain to the south with high mountains to the north and east. There were no tourists and only a few British soldiers on leave. The church of St. Francis was pleasantly empty and quiet.

Next day I set out in the afternoon with driver Sullivan to visit Perugia. We had come through the town on Wednesday morning on our drive from Florence to Foligno and it looked an interesting place, although much bigger than Assisi; it too was quite untouched by the war. We drove through very narrow streets to the central square where we chose a nice looking café, parked the Jeep, and ordered wine.

To sit out in the sun and do nothing was an extraordinary luxury after the weeks of stress and strain since Piedimonte d'Alife at the beginning of May. I felt restless and found it difficult to relax. Sullivan went to sleep, which was not surprising. I was asked by the proprietor how the war was going, almost as if it was in another country.

Fortunately for Italy the war to chase the Germans up the leg and out of Italy was fought over quite a narrow swathe, only a few miles wide. Within this swathe from Naples through Cassino, round Rome, and up the west side of the Appennines to Florence, the damage to villages and destruction of farms and roads was very extensive, but beyond this swathe the country was almost untouched.

As the Germans retreated there was great rejoicing and, as with all country people, a speedy return to a normal civilised way of life. Thus August in Foligno was like a relaxed and agreeable holiday. But there was an air of unreality too, for the war was still being fought with no let-up in ferocity, and not so very far away.

On Sunday 13 August, Padre Munro, a Scot, came over from Brigade headquarters and held a memorial service for the six men of the Company who had lost their lives in the recent campaign. We were lucky not to have lost more. None in North Africa; four Sappers among quite a number who were wounded at Cassino during the second night when Amazon bridge was launched. Sergeant Parry was shot by a sniper after we had gone through Palombara, and 2nd Lieutenant Ian Innes had been hit by a sniper when we were struggling beyond San Pancrazio not far from Monte San Savino. He had only very recently joined the Company and perhaps had not had time to develop that sense of awareness and cunning so essential to stay alive in battle. At the time I had felt his death very deeply and hated writing to his mother, for he was so young and inexperienced. It was a simple and very moving service conducted in the open air under ancient shady olive trees. I think everyone was grateful for it.

We spent another week in this delightful spot. The men were allowed into the town every evening in groups; some got drunk and some made friends with the local girls. By and large everyone had a good time and the war seemed far away. Surprisingly enough there was no trouble: perhaps this was because CSM Tutton made it very clear indeed to all ranks that there was still a war on and anyone misbehaving himself would be very severely dealt with. It simply wasn't worth crossing the CSM.

At the end of the week Malcolm and I took driver Sullivan and set off for the island of Polvesi on Lake Trasimeno where a luxury hotel had been taken over as an officers' "Rest Camp". It was a very beautiful place with excellent swimming, lovely food and comfortable beds, and the same accommodation was also made available for drivers and batmen. For young Sullivan it too was a most enjoyable weekend. John Heath and Ben Chubb remained in charge of the company, agreeing to take their leave on our return.

When we returned on Tuesday evening to our astonishment and horror the Company had gone. There was absolutely nothing left: no notes, no arrows, no indication whatsoever of where they had gone, no litter even, and nobody to ask. For a while we were totally at a loss which way to go. We drove hurriedly into Foligno and searched for someone to ask. As luck would have it, we found a lone military policeman who told us that 4th Division and 10 Brigade had not long moved up the main road to the east coast, towards Pesaro, and that we might catch up with them by about Pergola not far from Urbino.

I looked on the map and said "But that's miles away!" "Only a couple of hours or so," he replied. It was already getting late. Our vision of a nice hot supper cooked by Corporal Parry vanished as we drove off north-east. I was now in a considerable panic, wondering what on earth had become of the Company. It didn't worry Sullivan in the least, who merely said, "Don't worry, we'll soon find them". "Better had," mumbled Malcolm, who hated uncertainty.

From Foligno the national route 3 north through Fabriano to Pergola was narrow and twisting for about fifty miles through mountainous country. It wound its way through the spine of the Appennines. There was quite a lot of traffic and one could not hurry. It was quite dark by the time we got to Sassoferrato, a small village about five miles short of Pergola. Here at last there were plenty of troops about, and 4th Division signs were appearing. There were also plenty of signs of recent enemy action including a huge bridge demolition in the middle of the village. The traffic was having to make a difficult by-pass by fording the river to get round it. I could not help looking at it critically, wondering who would be ordered to bridge it.

In due course we found the company encamped just off the main road and just outside Pergola. Everyone spoke at once. Dear old Rodgers was delighted to see me, saying he had bagged a pitch for my truck and tent alongside the office truck. Cook Parry had a meal ready for us. But far more important was the fact that the Company had that evening received orders to go back to Sassoferrato and build that bridge that we had looked at. Ben Chubb and 1 Section together with 3 Section were lined up to do the job next day, Thursday 24 August. Fortunately Malcolm had returned with me and would therefore be available to work with Ben. John Notley, who was in charge of 2 Section, was still away on leave; so I decided to hold 2 Section in reserve. After catching up with the news and making plans for the morrow, we got to bed about 0200 hours.

It appeared that 4th Division, now under command of V Corps, had been hurriedly brought into the battle to clear the Germans from Pergola where there had been some quite heavy fighting. We were now on the east side of the Appennines, opposing strong resistance from the Germans who had made a very heavily defended line from Urbino to Pesaro on the sea, which they called the 'Gothic Line'. The defences were based on the River Foglia which flowed into the Adriatic at Pesaro. Beyond this line the coastal plain narrowed still further until it was only a few miles wide at Rimini, before opening out into the Lombardy Plain. It was clear that the Germans were determined to hold this defile. V Corps with 4th Division as well as the 46th Division, 1st Canadian Division, and 1st Armoured Division was given the task of breaking through this gap. It looked a bit like another Cassino.

We got up at 0500 hours and had a good breakfast, then Ben and I with his Section sergeant and a small advance party of Sappers set off back to Sassoferrato to measure up and plan for the bridge. Bridging lorries were already ordered by the CRE to start arriving by mid-morning. The gap created by the demolished bridge was well over 100ft. We decided to order 130ft. of double girder double storey Bailey equipment; it was our biggest bridge yet and we were determined to make a success of it.

The men went to work preparing bank seats for the bridge to rest on and rollers on which to build it. I asked Sullivan to find a parking or harbour area for the bridging lorries to come to and from which it would be easy to call them up to the building area as required. Sullivan was young and intelligent and could do all manner of back-up jobs, which he thoroughly enjoyed. Later in the day, the bridging lorries started coming in and bridge building began.

It was in fact a very easy bridge to build. The site was level, there was no enemy interference, and plenty of strong men who were press-ganged into unloading and humping the bridge parts. Our interpreter Willie and those of his men who were still with us came into their own and worked very hard. Construction went ahead very well and by 1800 hours the bridge was complete and open to traffic. Ben and Malcolm with their men returned to camp and a hot dinner, tired but well satisfied that they had done a good job.

Meanwhile I had received a message by despatch rider Horseman to go and survey a demolished viaduct on the Pergola by-pass. This turned out to be a very different and much more difficult project. We were still on national route 3 to Urbino and Pesaro which bent round Pergola, spanning a deep gorge which had been bridged by a massive brick-built viaduct of four or five spans. These had been demolished, leaving the centre span and two columns intact. Our task would be to bridge the demolished spans onto the central intact span. The sketch which I drew at the time shows this clearly.

The problem was how to get on to this central span, which was much too high for ladders, and in those days we did not have the use of helicopters. The only way would be for a couple of men to ride across on the launching nose of the bridge as it was built and gradually pushed across the gap.

Next day therefore, Friday 25 August, we spent all day surveying the separate bridges required and planning how to do the job. We decided to work from both ends of the viaduct and hopefully to meet up on the central span. It would require four separate bridges: a 30ft. single girder, an 80ft. double girder, a 90ft. triple girder, and a 40ft. single girder. A total of 240ft. run of Bailey equipment.

The only snag to this plan was that in order to get to the northern end of the viaduct there was another small, quite separate, demolition of a culvert which would require a simple 50ft. single girder bridge. The Germans had made a good job of their

*Demolished viaduct, Pergola, 28 August, 1944*

demolition at Pergola. Thank God we had plenty of Bailey bridging equipment, held and delivered by 18 Field Park Company.

Next day, Saturday, Malcolm with 3 Section built the 50ft. bridge in the record time of about three hours. Ben Chubb and John Notley, just back from leave in Rome, with 1 and 2 Sections, started on the viaduct. It was going to take all our resources and several days. On Sunday, therefore, the CRE ordered a Section from 7 Field Company to help us. This made a big difference as it meant that work could continue without a stop on all four separate bridges which made up the final bridge.

It was finished on Monday evening and opened immediately to traffic. However, its more than 250ft. length with gaps between the separate bridges meant strictly one way traffic at a time under the control of the Military Police. It was a good job done and greatly eased the traffic flow to forward units. In the six days since Malcolm, Sullivan and I had returned from the luxurious leisure of Polvesi island the company had built some 430ft. run of Bailey bridging.

It was now Ben Chubb's turn to have a short break of leave and he decided on our recommendation to go to Polvesi. He had worked hard and done well on the Pergola viaduct, so I decided to let him go although I knew we were on the brink of a lot of work and might miss him.

Sure enough, next day shortly after Ben and his driver had left, we received orders to move on to Fossombrone to open up route 3 northwards to Urbino. The road here ran though very hilly, almost mountainous, country, and was relatively easy for the Germans to destroy when they wanted to by prepared demolitions. After all they had had plenty of time to do it while the Allied threat had been on the west side of the Appennines towards Florence.

I have found another letter written home on 2 September 1944 which graphically describes this period of chasing the Germans through this mountainous country towards the Rimini gap:

59 Fd Coy RE

2 Sept.1944

CMF

Life is a little hectic just at the moment as everything is moving so fast. It very much affects us as it has almost developed into a Sapper battle to get the roads opened. The Germans have done terrific demolitions everywhere on a scale that is almost unbelievable. It will take Italy years to get her communications, railways, power and water supplies working again. There should be no unemployment for twenty years I should think, and she will have to be assisted both with technical engineers and finance by us after the war is over.

It is rather tragic to see the extent of devastation in some towns. So you can imagine it is producing a lot of work for us just now. But the autumn is coming on us fast. I notice the days are getting very much shorter. Just now we have a lovely full moon, I hate the periods when there is no moon, the roads are so dark and perilous with traffic all driving with no lights at all.

However the grapes are getting ripe and it looks like being a very good crop.

For the next three days, we worked flat out on this road. It entailed building two 80ft. double girder, single storey Bailey bridges where masonry bridges had been demolished, and numerous blown culverts to be bulldozed down and up. The infantry were well ahead and in contact with the enemy. The bridge sites were no longer in view of the enemy, but his artillery knew exactly where his demolitions were and from time to time sent over a few shells. These were, of course, fired on chance and thus not very accurate and totally unpredictable. They were a bit frightening but we ignored them and fortunately suffered no casualties.

On Friday we moved again to just north of Urbino which looked a really interesting little town within a great perimeter wall including a huge fortified palace. I badly wanted to explore it but had no time to do so. fortunately it had not been damaged much by either side. We had to start work immediately on the Urbino – Pesaro stretch of the road.

Pesaro is quite a large town on the Adriatic coast. Once it reaches the Foglia river the road follows the river down a widening valley to the sea, a matter of about ten miles to the river and a further ten miles or so to Pesaro on the sea.

Next day John Notley with 2 Section built an 80ft. Bailey bridge across the Foglia. It was a rather difficult bridge because the road on either side of the old masonry bridge, now demolished, was on quite a high embankment – probably against flooding. This made construction of a replacement Bailey bridge rather difficult because there was so little room for unloading the bridging lorries and building the new bridge; and in addition the Germans had laid huge numbers of "Schu" mines on the verges of the road, hidden in the grass.

A "Schu" mine is a deadly little contraption consisting of a small wooden box 5" x 4" x 2" deep, containing one pound of high explosive. The lid is hinged and balanced like a mousetrap on a pin through a spring-loaded detonator. A weight of only a few pounds on the lid dislodges the safety pin, which releases the detonator to explode the mine. These mines were designed to blow the foot off the unsuspecting soldier walking in the grass, and were extraordinarily effective. The mine box being made of wood and the detonator of copper and brass, could not be detected by a mine-detector. The only way to be sure was to step very carefully. At night it was impossible to spot them.

The Germans had laid hundreds of thousands of the little beasts in the Foglia valley, together with masses of barbed wire and lines of elaborate anti-tank fences secured in concrete. It was a horrible jungle of obstacles raked by machine-gun fire from pill-boxes, and our advancing infantry had a particularly nasty job in getting through it. Our job was to try to open the road immediately behind them. Fortunately the Germans too had used the road until the last moment and thus our job was mainly to fill up and level numerous craters and a few major demolitions. It was all very reminiscent of the Liri valley below Cassino.

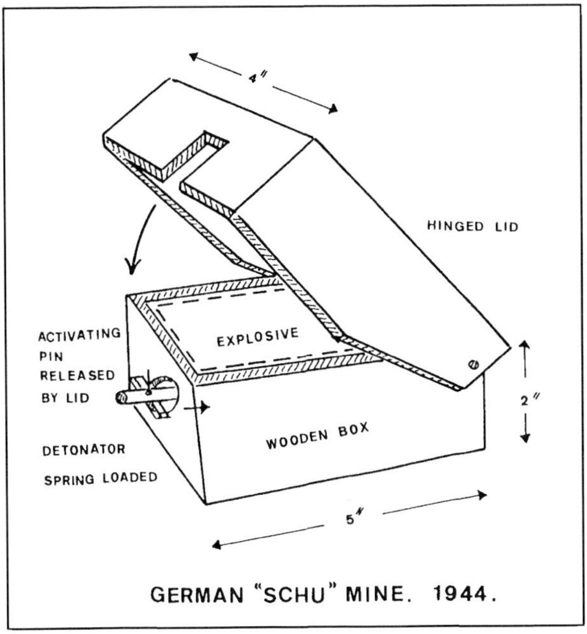


*German "Schu" mine. 1944*

We spent the next three days, Sunday to Tuesday 3 – 5 September, clearing and repairing the road to Pesaro. On Tuesday the Division was in the area of Fano just south of Pesaro on the Adriatic coast. Now, unfortunately, the weather broke, and for the next three days it rained continuously. We had orders to move up to the outskirts of Pesaro to support 12 Infantry Brigade. We had only to move the company a few miles, but it took all day and half the night, as any movement off the road on to the land meant becoming bogged down immediately. The fields were more like soup than dry land.

By the weekend, Sunday 10 September, we learnt that a really big attack was being launched and the disturbing news, perhaps rumour, that the Germans had eight divisions defending Rimini. We had 4th Division, 46th and 56th Division, 1st Canadian Division, 10th Indian Division and 1st Armoured Division, all under the command of 1st Canadian Corps. We felt that should be enough because the gap was so narrow. The next three days were spent preparing for this big attack. We were to support 12 Brigade, mine-clearing and keeping tracks open for their support, the latter a somewhat dismal lookout in this land of rain and mud.

On Tuesday 12 September, we moved up again to a concentration area just north of the river Conca, midway between Pesaro and Rimini. Concentration was the right word, for the whole area was chock full of units, vehicles and guns, all trying to get into position in a sea of mud and rain. We were all shelled intermittently but fortunately suffered no casualties.

On Thursday 14 September, 12 Brigade was involved in heavy fighting. Malcolm with 3 Section was in close support and spent much of the day trying to build quite a small bridge at Coriano, but was continually shelled off the site. He completed it that night for next day. Ben and John with 1 and 2 Sections were working at night trying to keep roads and tracks open for the Brigade supply column – difficult, because the ground was water-logged, and we had to collect and transport rubble from shell-torn farms and villages.

On Sunday 17 September, the Company moved up to Coriano. In this awful weather and conditions it was essential to keep up as close as possible to the infantry. That night, the main attack on Rimini began at about 2100 hours, when it was quite dark and raining hard.

As the Infantry attacked and the guns opened up in support, a line of searchlights was switched on behind the guns, directed towards the enemy at a very low angle. It was the first time in Italy that searchlights had been used in this way, and it was most effective, particularly as the rain continued all night and the light was reflected down from low cloud. It was a tremendous help to us and must have been very dazzling for the Germans. There were enough lights to enable them to be switched on and off and to move them about alternately, and thus avoid being shelled. It was an extraordinary night.

The following account of this battle was recorded afterwards by Malcolm and John Notley.

"For this attack 12 Brigade was leading the Division. The first phase of the Brigade plan was to obtain a bridgehead over the River Marano. This task was assigned to 1st Battalion Royal West Kents with a squadron of the North Irish Horse (Churchill Tanks) under command, 3 Section of 59 Field Company, and one troop of Assault Sappers from 1st Armoured Division with two ARK assault bridge tanks for the actual river crossing. The ARK was a Churchill tank, with the turret removed and replaced by a level flat form and two hinged ramps, which could be driven into a crater or canal to enable vehicles to be driven over it. (See Map 13 on page 148.)

The plan was that the Infantry would ford the river and secure the high ground at point 101 and hold the far bank of the river to enable the ARK assault bridge to be launched at first light, which would allow the tanks to cross and support the Infantry position against counter-attack. The Sappers were then to improve the ARK bridge with its approaches to take all traffic. The site for the bridge was chosen from air photographs to be at the end of a lane leading directly to a railway which ran parallel and very close to the river. It was a straightforward simple plan which everyone understood. (See Map 13 on page 148).

The first setback occurred when the Infantry were moving up to the start line, which turned out to be very strongly held by the enemy. Everyone got involved in the ensuing battle, which continued all night with the result that Malcolm with his Section and the troop of assault Sappers and the two ARK tanks were unable to reach the river. However the righthand company of the Royal West Kents was able to swing right-handed, cross the river, and swinging left, were able to dig in and defend themselves on the far bank of the river. The ARK Commander, a Sapper subaltern, decided to drive and launch his ARK assault bridge blind, just at first light.

He had to drive straight down the lane and at the railway where the lane turned sharp left he drove straight across the rail track, over the bank and into the river exactly opposite a possible exit to another lane. This worked precisely as planned, and with complete success. Shortly after first light the squadron of Churchill tanks of the North Irish Horse crossed over the ARK and joined the Royal West Kents to hold their bridgehead all day. Next night John Notley with 2 Section joined Malcolm to improve the approach and exit with loads of rubble, marking tapes, etc. By first light on Tuesday 19 September, the crossing was taking all comers, from Jeeps to lorries. The German paras withdrew and a breakthrough seemed imminent.

Map 13 on page 148 shows how the ARK tank, came to rest level with about 2ft. of freeboard above the water level. The banks sloped rather steeply, which gave the two ramps firm ground to rest on. Having driven his ARK into the water the driver subaltern, and his mate, a sergeant, clambered out and made their way back to their troop. So successful had the launch been that the second ARK was not required. Great credit is due to this Sapper officer for the success of his task.

This crossing was a significant action in the Rimini battle and was recognised by the following message ordered to be read out to all troops who took part in the battle, from the Prime Minister Winston Churchill and the Army Commander, Lieut. General Sir Oliver Leese.

> *To all Commanders, 4th British Division*
>
> The following messages have been received from the Prime Minister, the Army Commander, and the Corps Commander. I wish them to be read out to all ranks.
>
> All have fought extremely well, and again I am very proud of my Division.
>
> A Dudley Ward, Major General, Commander 4th British Division
>
> *The Prime Minister*
>
> The following extract from a message of congratulations received from the Prime Minister (Winston Churchill) is sent to you for publication in any form you may wish. "Many congratulations upon the storming of the Coriano ridge and passage of the Marano. I can see that this has been a grand feat of arms upon the part of all troops involved."
>
> *The Army Commander*
>
> Personal to Major General Ward. "You have won a great victory. By the bitterest fighting since El Alamein and Cassino you have beaten eleven German Divisions and broken through into the Po valley. The greater part of the German Armies in Italy were massed against us and they have been terribly mauled. I congratulate and thank you all."

*The Corps Commander*

Personal for GOC from Commander 1 Canadian Corps. "On conclusion of this phase of the operations I wish to congratulate you and your Division on the gallant and skilful way you have fought and to thank you all. By your capture of successive spurs you secured the left flank and in the end we were able all together to break out into the Lombardy Plain which has been the aim of the Allies in Italy for so long. This is a great success and all ranks of the Canadian Corps are proud and happy to have had with us at this time the fine fighting soldiers of 4th British Division."

Wednesday 20 September saw everyone on the move. Rumour had it that the 1/6 Surreys of 10 Brigade had reached the River Merecchia, the key to the Lombardy plain. But still the rains came. My diary notes read "torrential rain all day. Road and tracks are deep in mud." Next day John Notley and I watched the crossing of the Marecchia ford from the Fortunato ridge and we looked across the river and beyond into the great plain. The Marecchia is a wide shallow river which flows out into the sea at Rimini. At this time of the year it is easily fordable. On the right was Rimini, a sprawling white city, and beyond was the Adriatic sea. On the left the mountains rise quickly to the tiny state of San Marino. We had come a long way.

On Sunday 24 September, Malcolm with 3 Section built a small Bailey bridge on one of the approaches to the Marecchia and went on to build an improvised timber bridge at the main ford to make it a bit easier for wheeled vehicles. The rest of the Company was fully employed on repairing roads and tracks. What we needed was a fleet of tipper lorries to bring in rubble to fill in craters and make passing places. Curiously enough there were no mines. Perhaps the Germans had been pushed back faster than they expected – or perhaps they had used up all supplies on the Gothic Line way back on the Foglia between Urbino and Pesaro, where they had certainly meant to hold us.

On Monday 25 September, we handed over all our commitments to 225 Field Company and were told we could have a few days' rest to sort ourselves out and clean up generally.

The Company now moved through Rimini and a little way along route 9, which is the Rimini – Bologna highway, dead straight for miles to Cesena. We found a large farm with room in the farmyard for all our vehicles to park. Here we were able to wash and most of the men were able to get into the buildings and dry their clothes. But still the rains came. On Tuesday 26 September, we heard that the torrential rains had washed out Malcolm's Bailey and timber bridge on the Marecchia as the river rose rapidly. Fortunately, by now all traffic could use the main roads up to and through Rimini.

It appeared that, having put up a very determined fight first on the Gothic Line, then at Coriano, and finally at Rimini, the Germans on the right had now withdrawn right back, possibly as far as Ravenna and the River Po itself. The main battle now shifted further west around Cesena and Forli.

As often happens, the battle ended quickly and the war moved on. There followed a curious period of rest and tranquillity after the strain of the last few weeks. 4th Division settled down in Rimini and the Company moved again, on 30 September, into German barrack huts on the outskirts of Rimini. They were pretty filthy, but after we had given them a thorough scrubbing and cleaning they sufficed very well, and under the sharp eye of CSM Tutton the Company gradually smartened up. The men were allowed into Rimini; not that there was much for them; but there were a few cafés and bars, for it was quite a big town.

The Division requisitioned a beautiful luxury hotel on the sea front at Riccione, a suburb south of Rimini, as an officers' rest camp and we were allowed to send two officers at a time to stay a night or two in the comfort of a first-class hotel. So on 30 September, I took forty-eight hours' leave to stay in this hotel. On the morning of 1 October, the sun was shining and I went for a long walk along the beautiful golden sands of Riccione beach with not a single other soul in sight. It was wonderful. That evening Ben Chubb, John Notley and Malcolm Drummond came to dine, and we had a superb dinner together. Next day I returned and they moved in for two days of pure luxury. But it had started raining again. What a season! All the locals told us it was quite exceptional, for generally September is a good month in Italy.

A cutting from the DAILY MAIL reads as follows:

5th, 8th Armies in Race with Weather
Nazis' Breather
from EDWIN TETLOW
Daily Mail Special Correspondent

> Italian Front, Sunday
>
> It now looks as if the Allied armies here are going to have a close race with the weather in their bid to drive through the plains of Lombardy to the Alps.
>
> Heavy rains are at present bogging down men and machines, robbing the Eighth Army of the early fruits of its triumph in surmounting its last Apennine peak and the Fifth Army of its victory over the enemy on the Gothic Line.
>
> The weather has given Kesselring an unexpected breather. The odds lately have been all against the attacker in conditions where tracks and roads are layered with mud, and even tiny streams are swollen torrents.
>
> We shall soon know whether the present storms herald the end of the good campaigning weather.
>
> Decisive Days
>
> I am told that winter in Lombardy is a period of dark fogs, floods, and slime – no time for mobile warfare.

How right he was!

Next day on Monday 2 October, the CRE, Lieut. Colonel John Nelson, came to have lunch with us and told me that I would shortly be posted back to the UK as an Instructor at the School of Military Engineering. This came as rather a blow: I had commanded 59 Company for more than two years and I was deeply attached to it – but all good things must come to an end one day, and I had to accept his ruling with some gratitude and good grace.

With hind-sight I could see that I was getting very tired. I remember waking up with fear if I heard a motor cycle at night, wondering what new escapade I would have to organise – a sure sign of getting stale. We had in fact all been very short of sleep for a long time. Changes were to take place. First RM Hamilton returned to take over as second in command again. This was hailed with great rejoicing, especially as John Heath, who was second in command, was posted away with promotion. As Ham knew the Company well, it would help the new CO taking over from me.

My diary notes that on Wednesday 4 October read: Miss Patricia Burke put on an excellent ENSA show in our large mess hut. We had not had such a show since Bougie, nearly twelve months ago. On Thursday my posting home to the U.K. arrived. Friday I spent all day saying my farewells to many friends in the Division. Major General Dudley Ward was generous in his thanks and wished me good luck.

That evening we had a splendid, if somewhat drunken, party in the Mess. On Saturday, Major A. J. Pittam arrived to take over the Company and on Sunday 8 October I left 59 Field Company, after 2 years and 10 months, with driver Sullivan to make our way south to Naples where I was due to embark for the U.K.

It was a holiday for Sullivan, and I was in no great hurry to leave Italy, to which I had become very attached. My main regret that morning was that I could not take my batman Rodgers also for a little holiday break. It would have done him good, and he would have been company for Sullivan on his return drive; but obviously Major Pittam wanted him as his batman.

The first day, we retraced our drive back to Foligno where I planned to stay the night with Colonel Pat Foley, now Chief Engineer of a District. It was fascinating to see how many of our bridges were still taking traffic. Some were being replaced by more permanent steel girder bridges to release Bailey equipment. But the majority were still in place, including Pergola viaduct. This gave us a lot of pleasure.

I had a great gossip with Pat Foley and a most comfortable night in his requisitioned town house. Next day, a glorious sunny day, we drove straight to Rome through Spoleto and Terni, arriving in time for a pleasant lunch in a typically Italian restaurant. Rome was now a thriving city. All the shops were open and the streets crammed with traffic and pedestrians. All seemed very happy, the war was forgotten.

We drove on to Naples by the Appian way, the coast road, for I wanted to get there in time to get a billet for the night. We booked in to No.3 Transit Camp and then went out to have a good dinner. Next day, Wednesday 11 October, Sullivan drove me to the docks to find the *S.S. Monarch of Bermuda,* a cruise ship turned troop carrier. There we said goodbye and off he drove in our Jeep back to Rimini. I spent the day buying a few presents and having a last look at Italy as seen in a busy bustling Neapolitan crowd.

Next day I embarked and we sailed on Friday 13 October. A beautiful sunny day, just like the day we arrived in Naples way back in February. The voyage was totally without incident. I shared a cabin with seven other officers. Once more I was a nobody which, after a long period of authority, is no bad thing – although very frustrating at the time. Out in the Atlantic it was grey, cold, and rough. I was sea-sick.

On Monday 23 October we entered the Mersey and tied up at Princes Pier in Liverpool. It was cold and grey and Liverpool looked incredibly drab after Naples. However it was very good to be back in England and it was good to be on dry land again. Perhaps it was a good thing that my homecoming should have been so depressingly mundane. It does one good from time to time to be cut down to size. After all, the past eighteen months had been an exciting and stimulating safari, and it was time to come back to a different reality.

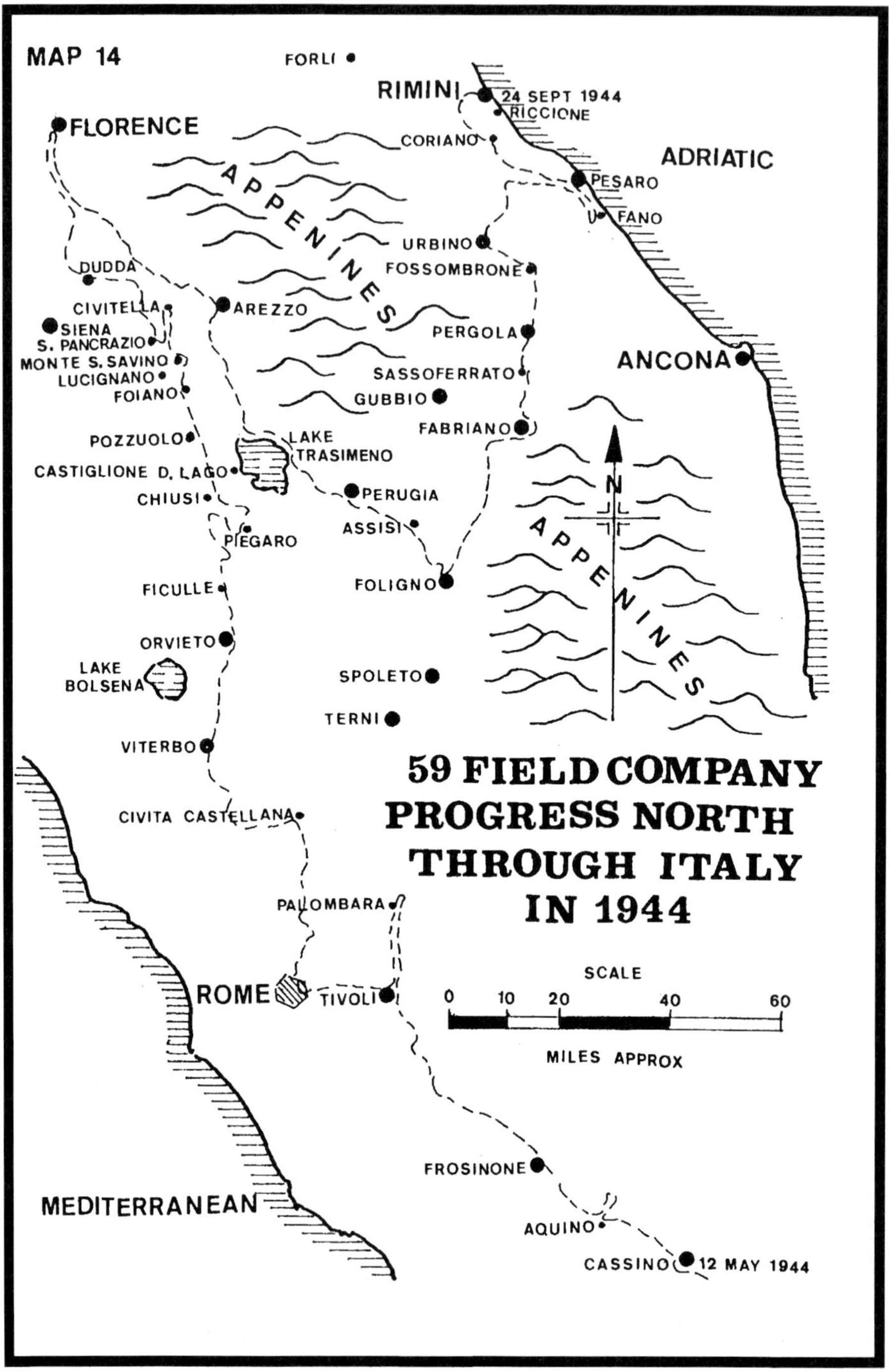
MAP 14
FORLI
RIMINI
24 SEPT 1944
RICCIONE
FLORENCE
CORIANO
ADRIATIC
APPENINES
PESARO
FANO
URBINO
DUDDA
FOSSOMBRONE
CIVITELLA
AREZZO
SIENA
S. PANCRAZIO
PERGOLA
MONTE S. SAVINO
ANCONA
LUCIGNANO
SASSOFERRATO
FOIANO
GUBBIO
FABRIANO
POZZUOLO
LAKE TRASIMENO
CASTIGLIONE D. LAGO
CHIUSI
PERUGIA
N
ASSISI
PIEGARO
APPENINES
FOLIGNO
FICULLE
ORVIETO
LAKE BOLSENA
SPOLETO
TERNI
VITERBO
59 FIELD COMPANY PROGRESS NORTH THROUGH ITALY IN 1944
CIVITA CASTELLANA
PALOMBARA
SCALE
ROME
TIVOLI
0 10 20 40 60
MILES APPROX
FROSINONE
MEDITERRANEAN
AQUINO
CASSINO
12 MAY 1944

# Epilogue

The weather and the terrain now determined the course of the war in Italy. On the 4th Division front, having come through the Rimini gap between the mountains and the sea and spread out into the flat Lombardy plain to nearby Forli, the Division was virtually brought to a standstill by continuous rain and the stickiest of mud. The Germans withdrew to Ravenna and later north of the river Po and thus the battle in this sector came to a halt.

The Lombardy plain and the delta of the River Po is completely flat in all directions, dissected by a network of deep dykes with high flood banks. The few roads are on high embankments. At this time of year, November, when the dykes are brim full of water and the land sodden with rain, the Germans had no need to defend such terrain – the conditions did it for them. The effective battle now moved further west to the area of Faenza and Bologna, and was being fought by X Corps.

Consequently, 4th Division found itself out of a job and was moved to Greece in November on what amounted to a peace-keeping mission. The Division, including 59 Company and all its divisional units, was established outside Athens with the aim of preventing civil war from breaking out between the Communists and the established Royalists.

It was an interesting role, but in no way up to the excitement and fulfilment of fighting the Germans towards their ultimate defeat. The Division with all its units, including 59 Company, remained in Greece doing an excellent and difficult job until the war in Europe ended in May of the following year.

In retrospect the nineteen months from its arrival in Tunisia in April 1943 to its bogging down in the mud of the Lombardy plain in October 1944 represented the effective fighting achievement of the Division, including 59 Field Company, in World War II. That may perhaps be taken as a rather simplistic statement, but on consideration cannot be far wrong. On a closer look at 59 Company's record, it can truthfully be said that the battle of Cassino was its finest hour.

This also applied equally to the other two Sapper Companies – 7 Company, a regular unit, and 225 Company, a territorial unit. Both had had their full share of adventures and both had served with equal distinction. Both contributed equally to the ultimate success of the battle at Cassino.

This was officially recognised in the honours awarded after this battle, which were one DSO to John Nelson as CRE, and six Military Crosses, two to each of the three Field Companies. These were given to the Company Commander and the particular officer in each Company who was most involved on "Amazon" bridge. In 59 Company this officer was of course Peter Boston.

The spirit of 59 Company lives on. The present unit is "59 Independent Commando Squadron Royal Engineers", a very fitting successor to the 59 Field Company of this book, and it gave me enormous pleasure to read of their magnificent work during the Falklands Campaign. Long live the "Fighting Fifty Ninth".

Meanwhile, the Chief Engineer of 6th Armoured Division – Brigadier Basil Davy – had been posted back to the U.K. to take up the appointment of Commander of the Royal Engineers' "Officer Cadet Training Unit" (OCTU), at Newark in Nottinghamshire. On arrival at the OCTU he found that many of the instructors had had very little useful battle experience. He determined to correct this state of affairs by collecting as many Sapper officers as possible who had either served with him or had served in North Africa or Italy.

Thus it came about that I found myself posted as Senior Bridging Instructor at the OCTU, with Mike Low of 7 Company, who had been wounded at Cassino, posted as Senior Field Work Instructor. I suppose this was not really surprising, since 59 Company had built a total of thirty Bailey Bridges in the last nineteen months. We were shortly joined by Ben Chubb, Brian Roberts, and others, all of whom had had plenty of experience of Sapper work in battle. We quickly formed a closely knit team and this, together with our combined recent experience, enabled us to give realistic training to the young cadets. We all had a great deal of fun.

Basil Davy was a very fine Commander and in no time at all created an enthusiastic and hard-working organisation. But he was too experienced a Sapper officer to be out of the battle for long and, unfortunately for us, he was soon posted away as Chief Engineer of an Army Corps in north-west Europe.

Finally, my story must end on V.E. Day (8th May 1945). It was a day of national rejoicing. Church bells rang throughout the land, street lights were turned on again and bonfires burned the length and breadth of Britain. How could we best celebrate at the RE OCTU at Newark? I decided that we would have a huge bonfire in the middle of the Parade Ground of all the black-out shutters of the Camp. Word quickly spread around and after dark our huge bonfire blazed away with all the staff and cadets dancing around it. A splendid and fitting end to my part in the War.

Next day I was summoned before the Commanding Officer to receive a very severe reprimand for having "wilfully destroyed valuable War Department Property" in the shape of black-out shutters, and for having ruined the tarmac surface of the Parade Ground. I very nearly had to pay for it all!

# Appendix I

## OPERATION LILAC BLOSSOM *(Flieder Blüte)*

*Extracts from Division Hermann Goering Operation Order, 575/43*

*The Division Hermann Goering* will destroy enemy forces South-east of Medjez-El-Bab, overcome enemy artillery in area Hir Zarzah (about 4 miles S.E. Medjez) thereby causing the enemy forces on the right front to be drawn onto this front and pinned down.

At the same time the Division will again during the night attack the high ground south west ("Banana Ridge" (?)) including Ragoubet El Hachene and the heights in area Dj el Mourhra to the road running along the western end of this feature.

*Own Troops*

(a) Group Audorff with one Grenadier Battalion
one A.A.Tp and
1/3 Engineer Company

(b) Group Schirmer with Parachute Regiment Hermann Goering
1/II Battalions Tank Regiment 7
2/3rds 4 Company Recce Unit Hermann Goering (A.Tk)
No. 1 Company Engineer Battalion Hermann Goering.

*OBJECTIVES (INTENTION)*

(a) Group Audorff will gain possession of the high ground southwest of 6534 including Ragoubet El Hechene, will hold this on a general north-westerly line blocking the road Medjez-El-Bab to Goubellat against enemy tanks. Group Audorff will be prepared to defend a line east of 60 Grid and will attack on a general line 6835 – 6532.

(b) Group Schirmer will overcome enemy artillery west of the line 6230-6227, destroy the enemy on the high ground 6529, and in conjunction with Group Audorff defend the general line 5933 – 5726, and the high ground north-east of 5924.

For this operation the group will be split into two sub-groups:-

*Sub-Group North,* consisting of one Parachute Battalion
11/Battalion Tank Regiment 7
one half of No.1 Company Engineer
Battalion Hermann Goering
will attack from its position east of the line 7131-7128, through 6730-6331.
*Sub-Group South,* consisting of one Parachute Battalion
1/Battalion Tank Regiment 7
one half of No.1 Company Engineering
Company Hermann Goering
will attack from its positions east of the line 7224-7120, through Goubellat – 5826

Group Schirmer will attach particular importance to its communications with Group Audorff in order to support the latter in the event of the loss of the high ground southwest of Tunis Road (Banana Ridge).

In addition it must be prepared to meet any threat from the Lalla Manna (3 miles northeast of Goubellat).

*BOUNDARIES*

Between Group Audorff and Group Schirmer (Including Audorff) main road Tunis – Medjez.

*ZERO FOR VARIOUS GROUPS*

D – 1 2300 hours

D in all probability 21/4/43

Actual D Day will be made known through G (Operations) at Division (Major-General Schmid) and confirmed to the Commanders of Groups as well as their Adjutants.

(translated by R. Hutchinson, 59 Field Company R.E.)

(refer to Map 2 and 3 on pages 28 and 40.)

# Appendix II

## *OPERATION "HONKER"*

Being the code name for the Allied Army's Assault on the German "Gustav Line"

*PERSONAL MESSAGE FROM THE ARMY COMMANDER*

"Great events lie ahead of us. All round Hitler's Germany, the Allies are closing in: on the East, the victorious Russians drive on – in the West, the British and American Armies are massed to invade.

- Now in the South, the Eighth and Fifth Armies are about to strike. Side by side with our French and American Allies we will break through the enemy's winter line and start our great advance Northwards. Our plan is worked out in every detail – we attack in great strength, with large numbers of tanks and guns, supported by a powerful American Air Force and our own Desert Air Force.

The peoples of the United Nations will be watching the Eighth Army. Let us live up to our great traditions and give them news of fresh achievements – great news such as they expect from this Army.

We welcome gladly to our ranks those Divisions whose first fight this is with the Eighth Army. We send a special message to our Polish Corps, now battling beside us to regain its beloved country.

I say to you all – Into action, with the light of battle in your eyes. Let every man do his duty throughout the fight, and the day is ours!

Good Luck and Good Speed to each one of you!"

OLIVER LEESE (Lieut. General)

ITALY — MAY, 1944

# Appendix III

## Bailey Bridges built by 59 Field Company, 1944

| No. | Location | Date | Type | Notes |
|---|---|---|---|---|
| 1 | Cassino "Amazon" | 12 May | 80 D/S | Built by Div RE 12 hours |
| 2 | Cassino "Blackwater" | 14 May | 80 D/S | Late evening, 2½ hours |
| 3 | Palombara | 9 June | 70 D/S | Daylight, no interference |
| 4 | Palombara | 9 June | 110 S/S | Bridge supported centrally |
| 5 | San Pancrazio | 6 July | 60 D/S | Built under occasional shellfire |
| 6 | San Pancrazio | 6 July | 40 S/S | Built at dusk in silence |
| 7 | Monte S. Savino | 7 July | 40 S/S | Replaced culvert washed out by storm |
| 8 | Monte Altuzzo | 9 July | 40 S/S | Pitch dark and in silence |
| 9 | Civitella | 16 July | 90 D/S | Over railway in daylight |
| 10 | Civitella | 16 July | 70 D/S | Built in a hurry, finished midnight |
| 11 | Capponale | 18 July | 50 D/S | By daylight, specifically for tanks |
| 12 | Capponale | 18 July | 30 D/S | Built on road surface over a collapse |
| 13 | Capponale | 18 July | 20 S/S | As above but in enemy view |
| 14 | Levane | 18 July | 60 D/S | At night to gain surprise |
| 15 | Dudda | 30 July | 60 D/S | Difficult site up hill road |
| 16 | Ponte | 31 July | 60 D/S | Difficult site on a bend |
| 17 | Strada | 1 August | 20 S/S | Over deep gap by night |
| 18 | Strada | 3 August | 80 D/S | Started 0200, finished 0800 |
| 19 | Sassoferrato | 24 Aug | 130 D/D | Longest yet built within 12 hrs |
| 20 | Pergola bypass | 26/28 Aug | 240 | Four separate spans, three days |
| 21 | Pergola | 25 Aug | 50 D/S | Built to reach far side of above |
| 22 | Sassoferrato | 26 Aug | 70 D/S | For down route through town |
| 23 | Pergola-Cagli | 27 Aug | 90 T/S | Difficult site, narrow embankment |
| 24 | Fossombrone | 31 Aug | 80 D/S | Easy site on Nat. Route 3 |
| 25 | Fossombrone | 31 Aug | 80 D/S | Built on a bend, slightly awkward |
| 26 | Coriano | 14 Sept | 40 S/S | Started pm, shelled, completed next day |
| 27 | Marecchia | 24 Sept | *30 S/S* | Built to ease Marecchia ford |
| | | | *total length: 1870 feet run* | |

Type of construction key:
S/S – single girder, single storey. D/S – double girder, single storey.
T/S – triple girder, single storey. D/D – double girder, double storey.

# Appendix IV

*EIGHTH ARMY NEWS* (shortly after the Battle of Cassino)

EIGHTH ARMY NEWS
AMAZON BRIDGE EPIC
THE SAPPERS BUILT IT UNDER WITHERING ENEMY FIRE
by Fred Redman
Special to "Eighth Army News"

This is the story of Amazon, the first bridge to be thrown across the Rapido by a British division fighting on the right flank of Eighth Army when the big attack went in.

The engineers who built it worked under withering fire, and with sheer guts got it across. Many men said "Thank goodness for the Sappers."

Amazon was one of several bridges planned to transport tanks and other vital equipment.

SNIPERS RAKED CHOSEN SITES

As the attack went in, shelling and mortaring made a hell of the river bank and snipers raked the sites chosen for the bridges.

But a bridge was essential for the tanks, and it was decided to build the Amazon at all costs. It was arranged that three companies should share the work, relieving each other as casualties in each became heavy.

In fact, men of all the companies engaged stuck grimly to their posts all night.

Work began on the evening of D plus one, and the first tank rolled across at five o'clock next morning.

Shellfire rocked and chipped the growing bridge and one sniper in particular took heavy toll of the men who swarmed over it.

There is a touch of grim humour in many of the tales now told about the Sappers and their job. One bulldozer driver watched bullets shower on his machine till they began to rip into the engine.

PUNCTURED SEAT

Setting the throttle, he got down and walked in front of the lumbering bulldozer - just as the seat he had left was neatly punctured.

# Appendix V

*DAIMLER "DINGO" SCOUT CAR*

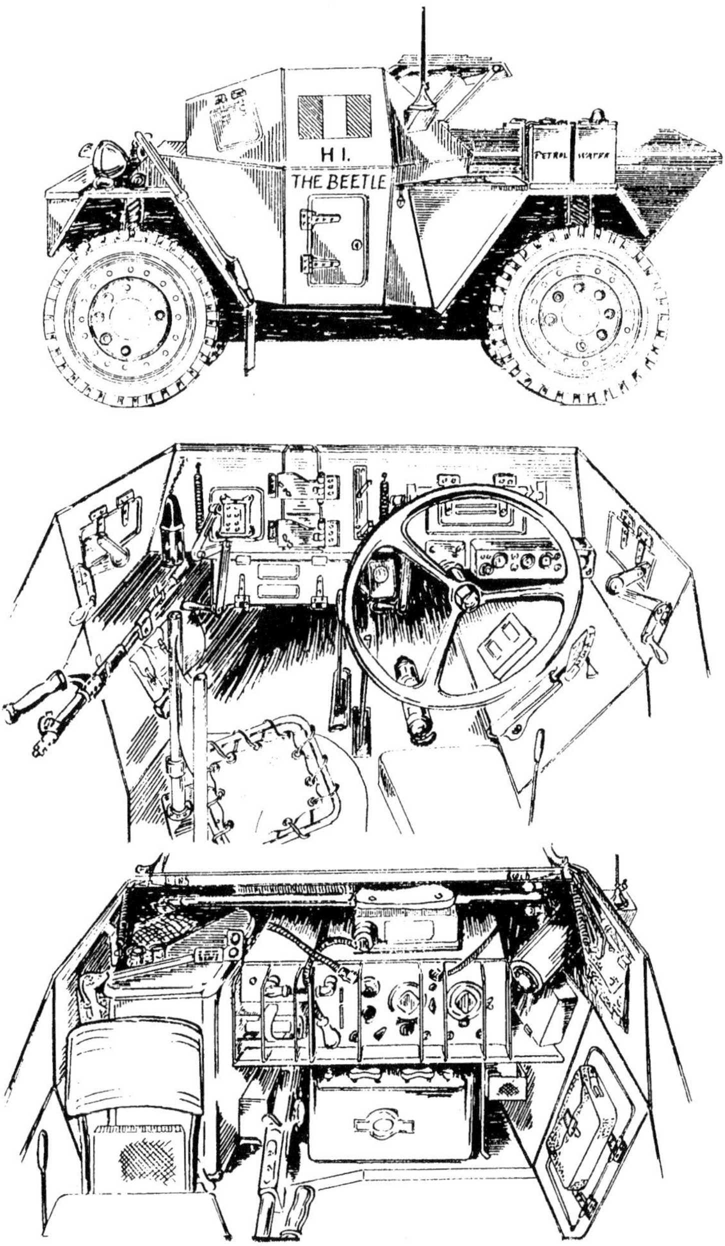

A FD COY SECTION IS ORGANIZED INTO
4 SUB-SECTIONS EACH OF 1 NCO & 11 SAPPERS.
GIVING 48 SAPPERS PER SECTION
AS AVAILABLE FOR WORK.